P9-EML-270

ALA Rules
for Filing Catalog Cards

A LA Rules for Filing Catalog Cards

Prepared by the A LA Editorial Committee's Subcommittee
on the A LA Rules for Filing Catalog Cards

Pauline A. Seely
Chairman and Editor

Second Edition

AMERICAN LIBRARY ASSOCIATION
Chicago

International Standard Book Number 0-8389-0002-X (1968)

Library of Congress Catalog Card Number 68-21019

Copyright © 1968 by the American Library Association

All rights reserved. No part of this publication
may be reproduced in any form without permission
in writing from the publisher, except by a reviewer
who may quote brief passages in a review.

Printed in the United States of America

Third Printing, August 1970

Preface

There have been many developments since the publication of the *A. L. A. Rules for Filing Catalog Cards* in 1942 that underscore the need for a new edition. There are new types of entries and new types of materials for which the earlier edition provides little or no guidance. Also, there has been a major restudy of rules for author and title entry, carried out by the Catalog Code Revision Committee of the American Library Association, which has culminated in a new edition of the *A. L. A. Cataloging Rules for Author and Title Entries.*[1] So that the publication of a new edition of the filing rules might be correlated with the new cataloging rules, in 1962 a Subcommittee on the A L A Rules for Filing Catalog Cards was established by the A L A Editorial Committee.

The Subcommittee has gathered information on current filing practices and on problem areas in filing through two widely distributed questionnaires, a large collection of filing rules from libraries of all types and sizes, a study of the literature, and personal contacts. Just as in the comparative study made for the 1942 edition, a wide diversity in practice was found. The 1942 edition included many of the variants found to be in use (60 percent of the rules gave alternatives), and thus it has served as a summary of various acceptable methods of arrangement. Because of the difficulties encountered in using that edition, and the many pleas for simpler rules that were received, it was decided that the new edition should be a consistent code of rules derived from one basic principle, with as few exceptions as possible. Those desiring to consider other arrangements than the one presented herein will find the 1942 *A. L. A. Rules for Filing Catalog Cards* useful, also the other filing codes and items about filing that are listed in the Bibliography (p. 240–47).

The basic order recommended in this edition is the straight alphabetical, disregarding punctuation, with just a few exceptions, the major one being that personal surname entries are always arranged before other entries beginning with the same word or combination of words. This code combines for the first

---

1. *Anglo-American Cataloging Rules.* Chicago, American Library Association, 1967.

time all of the rules and suggestions for single-alphabet arrangements that appeared in the 1942 edition (except the interfiling of personal names), and shows the results of this principle when applied consistently throughout all the rules. Admittedly, the results are not always entirely satisfactory, but on the whole the advantages seem to outweigh the disadvantages. Some of the drawbacks could be easily overcome by simple changes in heading forms, two of the most apparent being the addition of state or country designation after *all* city names and the use of parenthetical terms following *all* headings of the same word or words having different meanings, if used with any of them. From the filer's point of view, the simpler arrangements of the straight alphabetical order should result in more accurately filed catalogs; from the user's point of view, the inflexible order of the alphabet presents a uniform order that can be easily understood. An attempt was made to develop an alternative code of rules based on a consistent regard for punctuation, but that method also proved to be not entirely satisfactory, because of lack of consistency in punctuation.

The filing arrangements in this edition are presented as the direct result of the form in which headings and entries are commonly made, based on standard cataloging rules and practice, without resorting to mental insertions, deletions, or transpositions. The close correlation between filing order and cataloging rules is constantly emphasized. It is hoped that this feature will focus attention on the importance of consideration of filing in the formulation of headings, both author and subject, with the goal of producing fewer situations of "file as if." Present study of the use of machines for filing seems to point to the adoption of headings in a form more amenable to filing.

There are many instances where the rules in the new cataloging code, *Anglo-American Cataloging Rules*, are more effective from the filing viewpoint than the old rules, because either the resulting order of entries is better, or the present order is achieved more easily and directly. The Subcommittee on the A L A Rules for Filing Catalog Cards had the privilege of working with the Catalog Code Revision Committee with the mutual purpose of correlating author and title entries with filing order. Changes in the cataloging rules that have an effect on arrangement of entries are noted throughout the filing rules, and where pertinent, suggestions are given for methods of incorporating new-form with old-form headings in the same catalog. It should be noted that the filing system recommended in these rules will minimize the effects of the changes and so facilitate adoption of the new forms of headings.

These filing rules are basically for a dictionary card catalog, but are also generally applicable to divided catalogs, book catalogs, indexes, etc. Another limitation in the rules is that they are primarily for manual filing. The use of automated methods of filing is still in the experimental stage with many problems yet to be solved. The very difficulty of programming existing filing rules has led to much theoretical reconsideration of the rules themselves. It may well be that the development of machine methods of filing will result in changes both in the form of entries and in their arrangement, in the not too distant future.

The material contained in this book constitutes a full and detailed code, including much specialized and foreign material, as well as philosophical and descriptive notes pertaining to filing principles, correlation with cataloging rules, etc. An abridged edition is also being published, which consists of the same basic rules as the full version, but with most of the specialized and explanatory material omitted.

The Subcommittee wishes to thank all of the libraries that answered its questionnaires and so generously made copies of their filing rules available, also the many librarians who responded to questions and offered opinions, suggestions, etc.

Subcommittee on the

A L A Rules for Filing Catalog Cards (of the A L A Editorial Committee)

VIRGINIA DREWRY   ORCENA MAHONEY PETERSON
DORALYN J. HICKEY   CLARIBEL SOMMERVILLE PROUDFIT
FRANCES R. LUBOVITZ   CATHARINE WHITEHORN
PAULINE A. SEELY, *Chairman*

Contents

PART I

Alphabetical arrangement

PART II

Order of entries

Explanatory notes on the text

Most of the examples are authentic entries that have been found in library catalogs or national bibliographies, the primary source being the Library of Congress printed catalogs.

Headings are usually given in Library of Congress cataloging form. Some are in the new form that will result from application of the 1967 *Anglo-American Cataloging Rules*. The new forms were used when it was known that they would be different from the old, and especially when the variation would affect the filing. Some old forms are purposely included because undoubtedly old forms will remain in catalogs for many years to come.

The headings in the examples are not always complete when completeness is not essential to illustrate the rule. For instance, dates are not usually included with names, forenames are not always given after surnames, nor is *see* added after all headings that are references, unless those elements are needed to illustrate the rule or to clarify the examples.

Subject headings are indicated by full capitals. Italics are not used for subheadings, etc. as they are in the *Anglo-American Cataloging Rules* and on Library of Congress cards. Such typography would have no effect on the filing.

Basic principle and basic order

BASIC PRINCIPLE

Filing should be straightforward, item by item through the entry, not disregarding or transposing any of the elements, nor mentally inserting designations. In the following rules there are only a few situations where this principle is not applied; these are usually due to the structure of the heading.

BASIC ORDER

1) The basic order is alphabetical, word by word, except in certain areas where a numerical or chronological arrangement is preferable.

2) When the same word, or combination of words, is used as the heading of different kinds of entry, the entries are arranged alphabetically word by word, disregarding kind of entry, form of heading, and punctuation, except that personal surname entries are arranged before other entries beginning with the same word or combination of words.

PART I

Alphabetical arrangement (Rules 1-18)

This part covers the rules for determining the alphabetical position of, or point of access for, all types of headings.

BASIC RULES (RULES 1–4)

1. Basic alphabeting rule

A. Alphabet. Arrange all entries, both English and foreign, alphabetically according to the order of the English alphabet; e. g., interfile ñ with n, instead of using the Spanish arrangement, which places ñ after n.[2]

If entries not written in the Roman alphabet are included in the same catalog with entries in the Roman alphabet, arrange them by their romanized titles. On Library of Congress cards this information is given in a note in the lower right corner of the card.[3]

For treatment of modified foreign letters and special letters, see Rule 2. For non-alphabetical characters, see Rule 8, Signs and symbols, and Rule 9, Numerals.

B. Word by word. Arrange word by word, alphabeting letter by letter within the word. Begin with the first word on the first line, then go to the next word, etc. Apply the principle of "nothing before something," considering the space between words as "nothing." Thus, a single letter or shorter word pre-

---

2. In a catalog which is all or predominantly in a language that has an alphabetic order different from English, arrangement may be according to the order of the alphabet of that language.

3. For usage of the terms "Title romanized" and "Title transliterated," see Glossary (under "Romanized title"), p. 238.

2

cedes a longer word beginning with the same letter or letters. When two or more headings begin with the same word, arrange next by the first different word.

In general, every word in the entry is regarded, including articles, prepositions, and conjunctions. Two major exceptions are initial articles (see Rule 4A) and articles at the beginning of certain proper names (see Rules 14 and 15). Minor exceptions are noted in the rules covering the particular cases.

Example:

> I met a man
> Im Wandel der Jahre
> Image books
> Image of America
> Images of America
> Imaginary conversations
> Imagism and the imagists
> In an unknown land
> In the days of giants
> Inca

C. Dictionary catalog. In a dictionary catalog, interfile all types of entries (author, title, subject, series, etc.) and their related references, in one general alphabet.

2. Modified and special letters

A. General rules

1. Disregard the modification of all letters.[4] This includes umlauts, accents, diereses and other diacritical marks in foreign languages, and dots, lines, etc. above or below letters in romanization. For example, arrange ä, á, å, ê, ī, ö, ő, ø, ü, as a, e, i, o, u; ç, ć, č, ḥ, ł, ñ, š, ż, as c, h, l, n, s, z.[5]

2. **References.** In the case of headings with an umlaut in the first syllable, general cross references should be made from, and to, the form spelled with an "e." Arrange these references before entries under the name. If desired, a direct reference, including an explanatory note, may also be made for names with an umlaut in the first syllable, e. g.,

> Mueller, Peter, 1870–1930, *see* Müller, Peter, 1870–1930 (filed as if spelled Muller)

---

4. For the alphabets and diacritical marks used in foreign languages, see U. S. Government Printing Office. *Manual of Foreign Languages.* 4th ed., rev. and enl. New York, Central Book Co., 1952.

5. In a catalog which is all or predominantly in a language in which modified letters have a special interpretation, arrangement may be according to the usage of that language.

Examples for 2A1–2:

Baat, Marinus
Bååth, Albert
Baath, Rolf

Muel, Léon
Muellen, *see also* the spelling Mullen (or Müllen, filed as Mullen)
Muellen, Abraham
Muellenbach, Ernst
Mueller, *see also* the spelling Muller (or Müller, filed as Muller)
Mueller, Alfred Don
Mueller, Peter, 1870–1930, *see* Müller, Peter, 1870–1930 (filed as if spelled Muller)
Muenscher, Joseph
La muerta de Nerón
Mullen (or Müllen) *see also* the spelling Muellen
Mullen, Allen
Müllen, Gustav
Mullen, Pat
Müllendorff, Ernst
Muller (or Müller) *see also* the spelling Mueller
Müller, Adam
Muller, Arnold
Müller, Peter, 1870–1930
Münch, Amalie

Rolston, Brown
Rølvaag, Ole Edvart
Rolyat, Jane

3. When names are identical except for a modified letter, arrangement is by date or designation, according to the provisions of Rule 20, Surname entries— General rules. Care should be taken in cataloging to see that, if possible, such distinguishing additions are provided. If neither dates nor designations are available, the names are interfiled alphabetically by titles, disregarding the modified letter.

Examples:

Muller, Richard Arthur

Müller, Robert
Kiesewetter, Raphael Georg
History of the modern music of western Europe.

Muller, Robert
Le rattachement économique de la Sarre.
Müller, Robert, musician

Müller, Robert, of Mannheim
Müller, Robert, 1897–1952
Muller, Robert, 1920–
Muller, Robert, 1925–
Muller, Samuel

B. Ligatures. Arrange ligatures in words as separate letters. For ligatures in initials see Rule 5J.

Examples:

Iuga, Georg Eugen
I͡Uldashev, Khalil
Iulo, William
I͡Umin, Nafanail Aleksandrovich
Iung, Nicolas

Itschner, Emerson C
It͡sikzon, M   R
Ittelson, William H

Aetius, of Amida
Ætna Casualty & Surety Company, Hartford
Aetna Explosives Co., inc.
Ætna Life Insurance Company, Hartford, Conn.
Afán de Ribera, Antonio Joaquín

C. Special letters

1. Anglo-Saxon. See also 2C6 Icelandic and Anglo-Saxon, below.

ᵹ *File as* g

2. Dutch. File ij and ÿ as written.

Example:

Bruges
Bruijn, Hendrik de
Bruijn, Jeanne de, *see* Bruyn, Jeanne de
Bruijn, L. A. de
Brussels
Bruyn, Hendrik de, *see* Bruijn, Hendrik de
Bruyn, Jeanne de
Bruÿn, Kathleen
Bruyn, Willem Karel Hendrik Feuilletau de

3. German

ß *File as* ss

5

4. Gothic

u (for v)	*File as* v
v (for u)	*File as* u
vv (for w)	*File as* w

Examples:

Evangelia apocrypha
Euangelia gothice & Anglo-Saxonice
Evans,

The queen's minister
The qveen's mvsevm
The queen's necklace

Wonderful wings
VVonderful yeare
Wonders of nature

Note. A change in the form of these letters on most catalog cards came in 1949 when *Rules for Descriptive Cataloging*[6] stipulated that typographic peculiarities such as these be disregarded in transcription of the title page for works of the nineteenth and twentieth centuries.

5. Greek. Greek words are romanized but Greek letters used in the names of societies or in technical subjects are filed as though spelled out in Roman letters.

Examples:

Phi Beta Kappa
ΦBK annals   ɪPhi Beta Kappaɪ
Phi Beta Kappa Foundation

Dictionary of phrases
Dictionary of π-electron calculations   ɪπ = piɪ
Dictionary of platitudes

6. Icelandic and Anglo-Saxon

Ð Đ ð	*File as* d
þ þ (Thorn)	*File as* th

Example:

Thord Firetooth
þórðar saga Hreðu   ɪThordarɪ
Thórdarson, Björn

---

6. U. S. Library of Congress. Descriptive Cataloging Division. *Rules for Descriptive Cataloging in the Library of Congress.* Washington, 1949. Rule 3:5.

þórðarson, Matthías   ₍Thordarson₎
Thordeman, Bengt Johan Nerén

7. Latin. Arrange the Latin i and j as distinct letters, even though entries may be separated because they begin with the same word spelled in two ways, e. g., Jus and Ius. Cross references should be made from one to the other and filed before entries under the word.

Examples:
Iung, Théodore
Ius (as first word of title) *see also* Latin titles beginning with "Jus"
Ius musicae liturgicae
Ius talionis
ĪŪvachev, Ivan Pavlovich

Jury system
Jus (as first word of title) *see also* Latin titles beginning with "Ius"
Jus feudale
Jus romanum
Jusselain, Armand

Arrange the typographical characters and abbreviations used in Latin incunabula as if written in full.[7]

8. Turkish. Arrange the undotted ı in Turkish as "I."

D. Marks

1. General rule. Disregard marks preceding, following, or around letters, for example, aspirates and primes (in Arabic, Chinese, Hebrew, Russian, etc.), dots, parentheses. For hyphens see Rule 11, Words written in different ways; Rule 13, Compound proper names; Rule 15, Oriental names; Rule 16, American Indian names.

Examples:	*File as:*	
ʻAẓīm, ʻAbd al-ʻAẓīm	Azim, Abd al-Azim	
Saʻīdah Maẓhar	Saidah Mazhar	
ʻAbd al-Raʼūf Nawshihrawī	Abd al-Rauf Nawshihrawi	
Chʻen	Chen	
Gurʼeli, Yaʻakov	Gureli, Yaakov	
Ulʼīanov, Georgiĭ Vasilʼevich	Ulianov, Georgii Vasilevich	
Podʺemy	Podemy	
Col•leccio	Colleccio	₍Catalan₎
Ko•sè•d Sàthiăn	Kosed Sathian	₍Thai₎
O:ba	Oba	₍Burmese₎
Wǫrasin, Čhak(r)	Worasin, Chakr	₍Thai₎

---

7. For a list of typographical characters and abbreviations most commonly used in 15th and 16th century books, see U. S. Government Printing Office. *Manual of Foreign Languages.* 4th ed., rev. and enl.   New York, Central Book Co., 1952. p. 165.

7

2. Indonesian "2." A "2" following an Indonesian word, written either superior or on the same line, means that the word is plural, the same as when the word is written twice. File it as if the word were repeated.

Examples:

Dasar dan halvan negara Republik Indonesia
Dasar^2 anthropologi Indonesia   [= Dasar dasar]
Dasar-dasar ekonomi Islam
Dasar falsafah adat Minangkabau

Dokumen dari "Malaysia"
Dokumen2 bersedjarah dalam revolusi Indonesia [= Dokumen dokumen]
Dokumen-dokumen Konperensi Medja Bundar
Dokument

3. Punctuation marks

Disregard punctuation marks that are part of a title or corporate name. This includes such marks as comma, colon, interrogation and exclamation points, apostrophe, parentheses, brackets, the dash, quotation marks, and virgule, also ellipses such as three dots, etc. Punctuation marks preceding subtitles in title main entries are an exception to this rule (see Rule 33C).

For inverted titles, see Rule 33E; for apostrophes, see Rule 7. For punctuation in relation to order of entries under the same word, see Rule 19 and the specific rules for name entries, author and subject arrangement, etc.

Examples:

Life
Life—a bowl of rice
"Life after death"
Life:—its perils and salvation
Life, its true genesis
Life of . . . Frances Schlatter
Life! physical and spiritual

Que dira le monde?
¿Qué es España?
¡Qué mal huele Barcelona!
Que veut le Japon?

American Association for Health and Physical Education
American Association for Health, Physical Education, and Recreation
American Association for International Conciliation

Note. Parentheses, brackets, or angle brackets ($<$ $>$) are sometimes added in pencil by the cataloger to indicate that the enclosed portion of the entry is to be disregarded in filing. The filer must recognize the local meaning of the marks and file accordingly. Examples may be found in Rules 26B6 and 33D3.

4. Articles

A. Initial articles

1. General rule. Disregard an initial article in the nominative case in all languages and file by the word following it. This applies to all types of entries with two exceptions: certain proper names beginning with articles (see Rule 14, Proper names with a prefix, and Rule 15A1, Oriental names) and certain nickname references (see Rule 17). It applies also to the arrangement of titles under author entries.

In English the articles are "A," "An," and "The." For a comprehensive list of initial articles to be disregarded in filing, see Appendix. See also U. S. Government Printing Office. *Manual of Foreign Languages.*[8]

For "de" and "ye" used as initial articles see Rule 12A.

Foreign elided initial articles (e. g., L', 'n, 't, etc.) are disregarded the same as those written in full. The Dutch "'k" for Ik (pronoun in the first person singular), and "'s" (see 4A2 below) are also disregarded when occurring as the initial letters of a title.

2. Foreign article compounded or declined. In foreign languages, do not disregard initial articles compounded with a preposition (e. g., the French "des," "du") and those in a declined form (e. g., the German "dem," "den," "des"). One exception to this is the Dutch "'s," which is disregarded when it occurs as an initial article, even though it is a contraction of "des," the genitive singular (masculine and neuter) of the definite article.

3. Article vs. numeral "one." In many languages the form of the indefinite article is the same as that of the cardinal numeral "one" (e. g., the French "un" or "une," the German "ein" or "eine," etc.). Care must be taken to distinguish between them because an initial numeral, whether used as a noun or an adjective, must be regarded in filing in all languages. When it is not certain from the context whether an adjective-modifier is an indefinite article or a numeral, assume it to be an article and disregard it. In the list of initial articles to be disregarded (see Appendix), those indefinite articles that are the same as the cardinal numeral "one" are indicated by an asterisk.

4. *Caution:* Thought must be given to any short initial word, especially in foreign languages, where the same word may serve not only as an article but also as some other part of speech. A word may also be an article in one language but an entirely different part of speech in another language. Following are a few examples:

---

8. Op. cit.

A—in English "A" is an article and is disregarded as an initial article when it means the same as "An." "A" may also be used as a letter of the alphabet, as in the title "A apple pie" see Rule 5, Initials), or as a prefix, as in the title "A-boating we will go" (see Rule 12A, Dialect, colloquial, humorous forms), in both of which cases it is regarded in filing.

in Hungarian, Portuguese and Yiddish, "A" is an article and so is disregarded when it is an initial article.

in some of the romance languages, "A" is a preposition, in which case it is regarded.

De—in Dutch and the Scandinavian languages, "De" is an article and so is disregarded when it is an initial article.

in Latin and the romance languages, "De" is a preposition and must be regarded.

El—in Spanish titles beginning "el que, la cual," etc., the apparent article must be regarded since it has become a different part of speech.

Distinguish between initial articles in proper names and initial articles in other types of entry. In most proper names the articles are to be regarded.

5. References. An explanatory reference may be made under articles, including those in English, that are to be disregarded, as:

> The
>
>   Entries beginning with the above article are filed under the word following the article.

If the article is also used as a prefix in a proper name, a combined note card may be made (see Rule 14A2).

Examples for 4A1–5:

> A apple pie
> L'A. C. N. A. per l'addestramento professionale delle maestranze
> A travers la France
> Apache
> An April after
> Az apró gentry és a nép
> Aquarium
> L'art des jardins
> Artists
> Charles
> The Club, London
> De dansk-ostindiske koloniers historie
> De, Harinath

De re poetica
De toute son âme
Deacon, Arthur Bernard
Dem Pol entgegen
Eine von zu Vielen   ⌈Eine = One⌉
El goes South
El que vendrá
El y yo
Ela, Arthur John
L'enfant
Español, Raquel
El español comercial
's Gravenhaagse courant
Un homme à la mer
L'homme qui rit
't Is Guusjen
De jonge dokter
Eine kleine Gefälligkeit
Das kleine Heldenbuch
Le   ⌈explanatory reference⌉
Levens, Henry C.
's Levens gang   ⌈title⌉
Levensgang   ⌈title⌉
Levenshon, Lotta
Man and boy
The man of his time
Man of mark
A man of the age
Man of the world
Les misérables
La plume de ma tante
The   ⌈explanatory reference⌉
Tisa
ha-Tisah la-ma'adim
Tisato, Renato
Triumph
El Triunfo de la Cruz (Ship)
Une des terres inconnues   ⌈Une = One⌉
Unemployed
Weest bereid!
'k Weet niet wat hij zegt
Weetman, Leslie Maurice
West, William
THE WEST
West African botany

Hemingway, Ernest
　　Men without women
　　A moveable feast
　　The old man and the sea
　　Short stories

6. Special usages

a. If a foreign initial article has been used with an English title, obviously for effect, file under the article, as a separate word.

Examples:

Les, Edwin Paul
Les girls
Lesar, Hubert

Ekwall, Eilert
El Tommy
Ela, Arthur John

b. But in a foreign title with an adopted English word following the article, disregard the article.

Example:

Bridge player's dictionary
Le bridge, sport d'equipe
Bridge to brotherhood

B. Articles within the entry. All articles occurring within a title or a heading are to be regarded, except those that actually are initial articles in an inverted position or at the beginning of a subdivision.

Examples:

Work for a man
Work for Julia
Work for the beginner

Stassen, Harold Edward
STATE, THE
STATE AND CHURCH

LONDON—CHURCHES
London.　The Club, *see* The Club, London
London.　Corporation

AGRICULTURE—U. S.
AGRICULTURE—THE WEST
AGRICULTURE—WYOMING

Further examples of the exception are inverted articles in place name references (see Rule 14F), the Arabic "al-" and the Hebrew "ha-" at the beginning of a subheading (see Rule 15A5), articles at the beginning of the name of a part of a work in a uniform title (see Rule 27C1, Organized author arrangement, and Rule 37B5 and 6, Music), and inverted titles (see Rule 33E).

ABBREVIATED FORMS (RULES 5–9)

Introductory notes. An abbreviation is a word or phrase shortened by any method.

This section covers the filing rules for the various types of abbreviation—initials, standard abbreviations, elisions, contractions, signs and symbols, and numerals; also possessives, because of their similarity to elisions and contractions. The basic principle for arrangement of the items in this group is how they are spoken. With a very few exceptions, pronunciation takes precedence over typography. When the same heading may be written in different typographical forms (as NATO and Nato, Rh factor and RH FACTOR), or for any reason of pronunciation or form of heading the filing position is uncertain, references should be used to explain the situation. In certain cases a numerical order may be preferred to an alphabetical.

5. Initials

Preliminary note. Included in this rule are:
1) Single letters—a letter of the alphabet, as A, B.
2) One-letter words—as I, O, A (French, etc.), Y (Spanish).
3) Initials, initialisms—a form of abbreviation for personal or corporate names, consisting of the first letters or syllables of the words forming those names. They may be a single letter or a group of letters, as A.; A. E.; A. L. A. Also, abbreviations of common terms and phrases when they are by custom spoken as individual letters, as I. O. U.; IQ. But for abbreviations in science, etc. (e. g., pH, Rh) see Rule 6F. For initialisms that form words, see 5K, Acronyms, below.

For initials standing for geographical names, see Rule 6B.

For initials combined with signs, see Rule 8B.

For letters that are abbreviations of common words and commonly spoken as the full word, e. g., M. (Monsieur), K. (Königlich), see Rule 6.

For forename initials in inverted name entries, see Rule 20.

A. Arrange initials, single or in combination, as one-letter words, before longer words beginning with the same initial letter, wherever they occur in an entry. Interfile entries consisting of initials plus words with entries consist-

13

ing of initials only. Note that this may result in initials with the same meaning being separated from each other (see U. N. in Examples for 5A-E below).

B. Disregard variations in spacing and punctuation and arrange in one straight alphabetical file. For example, initials written A B C; ABC; A. B. C.; A., B. C.; A.-B., C., etc., all file as if written A B C. For combinations of upper and lower case letters see 5H below and 6F.

C. Disregard umlauts and other modifications of letters, according to Rule 2. For ligatures, see 5J below.

D. Arrange initials standing for names of organizations as initials, not as abbreviations, i. e., not as if spelled in full. File a title or other entry beginning with the initials of an organization after a reference from those initials to a full name. For initialisms that form a word, see 5K, Acronyms, below.

E. Arrange inverted initials standing for authors' names alphabetically with other initials, disregarding the inversion and the punctuation. Disregard a title of address or honor preceding forename initials. If the first and last initials are the same, only those in direct order need be used (e. g., A. A., omitting A., A.).

Arrange compound inverted initials (e. g., A. F., V. A.) alphabetically letter by letter with other initials.

If an initial is preceded by a prefix (e. g., De O., A.), treat the prefix and initial as one word, according to the rule for Proper names with a prefix (14).

Examples for 5A–E:

A.
A. A.
A. A. A., *see* . . .
AAAA
AAA Foundation for Traffic Safety
AAAS Conference on Science Teaching . . .
AACE
A., A. J. G.
AAUN news
"A" and "B" mandates
A., André C. H., *see* . . .
A apple pie
A. B.
ABA
The ABC about collecting
A B C and X Y Z
ABCD; archives, bibliothèques . . .   [title entry]
A. B. C., Madrid   [author entry]
A. B. C. programs
The ABC world airways guide
À bas les masques

AC
A chacun sa chance
The A Company
A. F. N.
A. F., V. A.
A., J.
A. L. A.
A.-L., R. A.
A. M.
AVPR
A., Mrs. V. R.
AVRG
A was an archer
A. y S., R. de
The A. Z. A. leader
Aa, Pieter van der
Aabel, Marie

Denzler, Hans Rudolf
De O., A.
Deo, Bettino de
Deo Prakash Patanjal
Deoband, India

I (For examples of I see p. 85–86)

ODC
ÖDV
OEA
Oakland

UHF television
U Le Lah
U. N.
    see United Nations
    Titles and other entries beginning with these initials are filed fol-
  lowing this card.
U. N. diary
U. N. E. C. A.   [reference]
UN headquarters
U. N. I. C. E. F.   [reference]
U. N. R. R. A.   [reference]
The UN record
"U No" letters
U. S. O.
U. T. M.
U-2 INCIDENT, 1960   [U-TWO]

UZTM
Uarov, M. I.
(For additional examples of U see p. 25–26 and 86–87)

My brother, A. E. Housman
My brother, Adlai

F. Different entries under same initials—Subarrangement. Subarrange entries consisting of the same initials alphabetically by titles, according to the regular rules for order of entries. A *see* reference from initials is filed before actual entries under the same initials.

Examples:

    "A."   ɾadded entryɹ
Love-in-memory, an elegy by "A."

A.
    Peregrinacion de Luz del Dia
    see Alberdi, Juan Bautista

    A., tr.
Monk, Maria
    Vienvolyno slaptybēs.

A. B.
    An answer to a minister of the Church of England
    see Cartwright, Thomas, Bp. of Chester

    A. B.   ɾadded entryɹ
Baggage & boots; or Smith's first peep at America.

    A. B., ed.
England's Helicon.

    A., B., ed.
Spencer, Herbert
    Philosophy of style.

A   , B.
    Up and down the Rhine for £ 51. By B. A.

ABA, *see* American Bankers Association
ABA. v. 1–   ɾserial titleɹ

AP, *see* Associated Press
A., P.
    Three curious pieces.

A. S. P., *see* Warsaw.   Akademia Sztuk Pięknych
A. S. P.
    The home circle
    see Paschall, Ann S

M'
> Celtic names beginning with M' are filed as if spelled "Mac," e. g., M'Laren is filed as Maclaren.
>
> African names beginning with M' are filed as one word as spelled, e. g., M'bala is filed as Mbala.

M.
> For entries beginning with the above abbreviation, see the word "Monsieur."

M., *see* Manners, Robert Rutland

> M.

The Dayspring of youth, by M.

M.
> Letters from three continents
> *see* Ward, Mathew Flournoy

> "M."

Thence and hence.

M., A. D.

G. References to more than one heading. When there are references from the same initials to more than one heading, arrange them alphabetically by the headings referred to. It is recommended, however, that all such headings be combined in one reference (to avoid the danger of some of them being missed). They may be combined even though the initials representing them may be typographically different (e. g., some with periods, some without), or they include both personal and corporate names.

Examples:

AMA
> *see* American Management Association
> American Marketing Association
> American Medical Association
> American Municipal Association

A. A.
> *see* Alcoholics Anonymous
> Automobile Association
> Ayres, Anne
> Willis, Anthony Armstrong

H. Mixed initialisms. In a mixed initialism, i. e., one composed of upper and lower case letters (as A. I. Ch. E.), treat the capital and lower case letter combination as a unit (i. e., as a word) and file it after the same first letter used as a single letter. This applies also in the case of a plural formed with an apostrophe (as ABC's). However, single letters that happen to be written in

17

lower case (as Abc) are treated as single letters, not as a word. For initialisms of Hebrew authors written in upper and lower case (e. g., RaSHI) see Rule 15A9.

Examples:
AICPA injunction case
A. I. Ch. E. journal
A. I. D.
ASTIA
A Sc W journal
A. Schilling and Company
ASuKh
ATB

ABC simplified shorthand in ten days
The ABC world airways guide
AB commercial directory of the Philippines
ABC's of painting
Abc's of transistors
À bas les masques

KVA
Kaa, Herman van der
Kaz, T͡Sili͡a Moiseevna
KazMZ
Kaza ve vilâyet idaresi
Kgama, Ruth Williams
KhDU
Kh., E.
KhĖM
KhIIT
Kh., M.
Kh., P.
KhSZ
KhabIIZhT
Khabachev, S. V.

I. Virgules. Initials separated by a virgule are treated as separate letters, whether lower case or capital.

Example:
ASFEC
A/s Fisker & Nielsen
ASHRAE
ASM
A/S Norsk frø

A/s Otto Treiders handelsskole, Oslo
ASPA

J. Ligatures. Treat ligatures in initials the same as a mixed initialism (see
5H above), e. g., I͡U as if written Iu.

Examples:

Itzling, Austria
I͡U. E.
I͡U, G   G
I͡U., I.
Iu kiao li, *see* . . .
I͡U, T͡Szun-ĭao
I͡Uan', T͡Sĭŭi, *see* . . .
Iubilaria friburgensia

Trzyna, Edward
T͡SDKZh
T͡SNIISK
Tsacas, Léonidas
T͡Sagolov, Nikolaĭ Aleksandrovich
Ts'ai, Ch'iao

K. Acronyms

Preliminary note. An acronym is a brief form of a corporate name or term
made up of a group of letters that are commonly written and/or spoken as a
word. It may consist of the initial letters, or syllables, or a combination of
initial letters and syllables, of the full name or term. Examples: NATO, EURATOM,
SACLANT, FORTRAN.

1. Arrange acronyms as words, unless written in all capitals with a space
or period between the letters.

This rule is not precise because it is not always known whether the initials
are commonly written or spoken as a word. If it is uncertain, treat them as
initials.

Acronyms may appear in several different typographical forms.[9] In some of
these the filing position is determined conclusively by the typographical form,
in others it is not. These are as follows:

1) Capital and lower case letters (e. g., Unesco)
   File as a word.

---

9. Most cross references and explanatory notes under acronyms have been made with
the letters in all capitals with no spaces between them (e. g., UNESCO). The new forms in
Anglo-American Cataloging Rules (122C, p. 182–83) show capitals with periods between
the letters for the one to be filed as initials (e.g., N. A. T. O.), and capital and lower case
letters for the one to be filed as a word (e. g., Nato). These forms will facilitate filing in the
desired positions.

2) All capitals with a space or period between the letters (e. g., U N E S C O; U. N. E. S. C. O.)

File as initials.

3) All capitals with no space between the letters (e. g., UNESCO)

a) At the beginning of a title and other entries

File as a word.

b) As a subject

File as a word.

c) As a cross reference or explanatory note

May be filed either as a word or as initials. If there are two entries in the same form, one to be filed as initials and one as a word, notes may be added to the cards as a guide to the filers: (File as initials), (File as a word).

2. References. When the entry is established under the full name and its initialism is considered to be a word, it is desirable that the catalog contain an approach to the full name from its acronym both as initials and as a word. Therefore, in general, two explanatory references should be made from each acronym not used as entry; one to file as initials, the other as a word.[9]

Example for 5K1–2:

AFSCME

A. G. A. P. E.

A. G. A. R. D.   ₁Information card₁   ₁also if written AGARD₁

Initials of North Atlantic Treaty Organization.   Advisory Group for Aeronautical Research and Development. Publications by and about this body are entered under its name written in full.

When these initials occur in the form of an acronym at the beginning of titles and other entries they are treated as constituting a word.

AGC Contracts Conference

Agard, Frederick Browning

Agard   ₁Information card₁   ₁also if written AGARD₁

Initials of North Atlantic Treaty Organization.   Advisory Group for Aeronautical Research and Development. Publications by and about this body are entered under its name written in full.

When these initials occur in the form of an acronym at the beginning of titles and other entries they are treated as constituting a word.

AGARD Aeromedical Panel

AGARD Conference on Refractory Metals, Oslo, 1963

AGARD-NATO Specialists' Meeting, Sint-Genesius-Rode, Belgium, 1962

AGARD-Tagung über "High Temperature Aspects of Hypersonic Flow," Brussels, 1962

---

9. See footnote, p. 19.

AGARDograph
Agardy, Franklin Joseph

3. Acronym used as heading. When an acronym standing for the name of a body is used as an actual heading for that body (according to *Anglo-American Cataloging Rules* 62A1–2), it is written and filed as a word, e. g., Unesco, Euratom. In catalogs where subject headings are typed in all capitals, the subject forms UNESCO, EURATOM are also filed as words. There should also be a reference, with an explanatory note, from the acronym as initials.

Example:

U. D. F.
U. N. E. S. C. O., *see* Unesco (filed as a word)
U. R. S. S.
Unemployment
Unesco   [author entry]
UNESCO   [subject entry]
UNESCO bibliographical handbooks
UNESCO bulletin for libraries
Unesco.   Dept. of Mass Communications
Unesco fellowship handbook
Unesco.   Middle East Science Cooperation Office
Ungar, Frederick

4. Other acronyms that are used as entry are filed as words, whether written with capital and lower case letters or in all capitals with no space between the letters.

Example:

F. O. B. Detroit
F. O. R. T. R. A. N., *see* FORTRAN (COMPUTER PROGRAM LAN-
      GUAGE) (FORTRAN filed as a word)
F. P. A.

Forton, Jean
FORTRAN (COMPUTER PROGRAM LANGUAGE)
Fortress

6. Abbreviations

Preliminary note. This rule covers standard abbreviations that are conventional short forms of words, usually with a period and without apostrophes, that are naturally spoken as the full words for which they stand. Such abbreviations are commonly made by the omission of letters from one or more parts of the word (as "Dr." for "Doctor"), but sometimes show substitution in the part or parts retained (as "oz." for "ounce," "Xmas" for "Christmas"). This rule also includes initials and other abbreviations for geographical names.

For other types of abbreviations see Rule 7, Elisions, possessives, etc., Rule 5, Initials, and Rule 8, Signs and symbols.

For proper names beginning with the abbreviation M' or Mc, see Rule 14B.

A. General rule

1. Arrange abbreviations as if spelled in full in the language of the entry, except "Mrs.," which is better filed as written (because of lack of standardization in the pronunciation and spelling of the spoken word, and because the meaning "Mistress" is obsolete[10]). If the meaning of an abbreviation is uncertain, file it as written.

2. References. An explanatory reference from the abbreviation to the full form should be made whenever necessary, as:

Mr.
> Entries beginning with the above abbreviation are filed as if spelled "Mister."

No.
> Entries beginning with the above abbreviation standing for Number (or a variant in a foreign language, as Numéro in French) are filed as if spelled "Number" (or "Numéro," etc.)

These abbreviated forms are filed according to the spelling of the abbreviation. For position of "M." see Examples, p. 17.

3. List. Following is a list of the more commonly encountered abbreviations and their corresponding full forms to be used in filing:

&c.	Et cetera
Abp.	Archbishop
Bp.	Bishop
Capt.	Captain
Cie.	Compagnie
Co.	Company, County
c/o	Care of
Col.	Colonel
Cpl.	Corporal
Dr.	Doctor (Docteur, Doktor)
Esq.	Esquire
Etc.	Et cetera, but when used as a title more commonly filed as written
F.	Fahrenheit
Hnos.	Hermanos
Hon.	Honorable
Lt.	Lieutenant
M.	Monsieur
Mlle.	Mademoiselle

---

10. *Webster's Third New International Dictionary.* 1961.

MM.	Messieurs
Mme.	Madame
Mr.	Mister
Mrs.	Mrs.
Ms., MS.	Manuscript
Mss., MSS.	Manuscripts
Mt.	Mount, Mountain
N.	North
N.W.	Northwest
No.	North, Number (Numéro)
Prof.	Professor (Professeur)
Rev.	Reverend
S.	Saint (see St.), South
So.	South
Sra.	Señora
Srta.	Señorita
St.	Saint (Some of the forms of Saint in the more common languages are Sá, San, Sanctus, Sankt, Sant, Sant', Santa, Santi, Santo, São, Sint); Street
Ste.	Sainte
v., vs.	Versus
Xmas	Christmas

Examples for 6A:

The Christmas story in art
The Xmas trio
Christmas wanderings

Doctor at sea
Dr. Christian's office
Doctor come quickly
Doktor Brents Wandlung
Dr. Mabuse der Spieler   [Doktor]
Doktor Mamlocks Ausweg

. . . et ce fut la guerre
Et cetera[11]
Et in Arcadia ego
The Eta cook book
Etc.   [title]
Etca,
Etcetera[11]
Etch proofs

---

11. If both "Et cetera" and "Etcetera" appear in the catalog, interfile them as one word (Etcetera) with explanatory notes and references, according to Rule 11B1.

23

Mis' Stone and other Vermont monologues   ɪfiled as spelledɪ
The misadventures of a tropical medico
MISSIONS
Missis Flinders   ɪfiled as spelledɪ
Mississippi
Mistakes
Mister Abbott
Mr. Adam
Mister Barney Ford
Mr. Fixit
Mr. Zip and the U. S. mail
Misterio
Mistress, *see also* entries beginning with "Mrs.," filed under that spelling
Mistress Anne
The mistress art
Mists and monsoons
Monsieur et Madame Curie
M. & Mme. Lhomme   ɪMonsieur et Madameɪ
Monsieur et Madame Moloch
Mr.
        Entries beginning with the above abbreviation are filed as if spelled
    "Mister."
Mrs., *see also* entries beginning with "Mistress"
Mrs. Abraham Lincoln
Mrs. Miniver
Mrs. Wiggs of the cabbage patch
M'sieu Gustave   ɪfiled as spelledɪ
Much

S., St., Ste. (For examples of Saint see p. 67–68 and 104)

B. Abbreviations of geographical names. Arrange initials and other abbreviations for geographical names in author and subject headings as if written
in full, whether at the beginning or the end of the heading. Follow the same
rule when they occur in titles and other entries if the full name of the place
for which they stand is commonly known.

Examples:
    Concord in jeopardy
    Concord, Mass.
    Concord, N. H.
    Concord saunterer
    Concord, Vt.
    Concord, Va.

    The great Brink's holdup

Gt. Brit.   Office of Commonwealth Relations
Gt. Brit. on trial
Great Britain or little England?
Gt. Brit.   Parliament
The great buccaneer

New York Institute of Photography
N. Y. is all ours!
New York is like this

U. R. S. I.
The U. R. S. S. and the capitalist countries
U. S.
      Entries beginning with the above abbreviation standing for United
States are filed as if spelled "United States."
U. S. A., *see also* entries beginning with United States of America
U. S. A.   ⌈title⌉
U. S. A. and its economic future
Die U. S. A. im deutschen Schulbuch
U. S. A., the permanent revolution
USBE
USDA
U. S. Grant, young horseman
U. S. I. A.
U. S. S. Middletown
U. S. S. R.
      For official government agencies see headings beginning with Rus-
sia (U. S. S. R.)
      For subject entries see RUSSIA.
      Titles and other entries beginning with these initials are filed fol-
lowing this card.
The U. S. S. R. and eastern Europe
U. S. S. Seawolf
U. T. D.
Uarov, M. I.

United States
U. S. and Chilean Claims Commission
U. S.   Bureau of . . .
United States calendar
U. S. camera
U. S.—FOREIGN OPINION
United States foreign policy   ⌈title by Johnson⌉
U. S. foreign policy   ⌈title by Lippmann⌉
United States foreign policy   ⌈title by Pratt⌉
U. S. foreign policy and international organizations

U. S.—FOREIGN POPULATION
United States IGY bibliography
U. S. iana, 1650–1950
U. S. -iana (1700–1950)
U. S.   Immigration and Naturalization Service
U. S.   Naval Academy, Annapolis[12]
United States Naval Academy Foreign Affairs Conference, Annapolis, 2d,
     1962
United States Naval Institute, Annapolis
U. S.—OCCUPATIONS
United States of America, *see also* entries beginning U. S. A.
The United States of America   ɪtitleɪ
United States of America, plaintiff, against Henry S. Morgan . . .   ɪtitleɪ
United States of Europe
United States park ranger   ɪtitle by Arco Pub. Co., 1st ed.ɪ
U. S. park ranger   ɪsame, 2d and 3d ed.ɪ
U. S.   Patent Office

C. Arrange initials and abbreviations of forenames in titles, corporate entries, etc., as they are written, not as if spelled in full (since the correct full
name is not always known).

Examples:

Charles W. Morgan (Ship)
Charles Warrington Earle   ɪtitle main entryɪ
Charykova, T. N.
Chas, Jean
Chas. D. Barney & Co.
Chas de Chruz, Israel
Chase, Agnes

Ecumenism and Vatican II
Ed è subito sera
Ed. J. Burrow & Co., ltd.
Ed Wynn's son
Edda
Edvard Grieg, boy of the Northland
Edw. Malley Company
Edwall, Gustavo
Edward, David R.

D. Abbreviations used in designations with personal name headings and at
the end of corporate names may usually be disregarded, but when necessary

---

12. The form of this heading according to the *Anglo-American Cataloging Rules* will be
United States Naval Academy. The two forms will file in the same position.

to distinguish between names that would otherwise be identical, they are filed as if spelled in full.

Example:

Thomas Aquinas, Saint
Thomas, Apb. of Syria   [archbishop]
Thomas av Strängnäs

E. Abbreviated adjectives denoting royal privilege

Note. In the names of foreign learned academies, societies, etc., initial adjectives denoting royal privilege, whether written in full or abbreviated, e. g., K. (Königlich, Kongelige, Kungliga, etc.), K. K. (Kaiserlich-Königlich), I. (Imperiale), R. (Real, Reale, Regia), etc., are now omitted from the heading in any European language except English, unless the omission would reduce the name to a common word or phrase.

In older headings that begin with such an abbreviation disregard the initial letter and arrange by the word following. However, a reference from the name beginning with the initial is to be filed under the initial, unless it is an old-style reference referring to the entry under place (see "K. K. Hof- . . ." example). When the heading or reference begins with the full word, file by that word.

This rule to disregard the abbreviation in old-style headings applies also when entry is under place, as in the "Austria. K. K. Hof- und Staatsdruckerei" example.

Example:

Academia de Bellas Artes de San Jorge
R. Accademia filarmonica, Bologna
Accademia peloritana
K. K. Akademie der bildenden Künste, Vienna
Akademie der Künste, Berlin
Austria. Haupt-münzamt in Wien
Austria. K. K. Hof- und Staatsdruckerei
Austria. Hydrographisches Zentralbüro
Hoepli, Ulrico
K. K. Hof- und Staatsdruckerei, Austria, *see* Austria. K. K. Hof- und
    Staatsdruckerei (filed as Austria. Hof- und Staatsdruckerei)
                                                         [old-style reference]
Hoffer, Andreas
K. Akademie der Künste, Berlin, *see* Akademie der Künste, Berlin
K. K. Geographische Gesellschaft in Wien, *see* Geographische Gesellschaft
    in Wien
Katherine
Det Kongelige Bibliotek
Koninklijk Instituut voor de Tropen, *see* Instituut voor de Tropen
Kungliga Automobil Klubben

Quito
R. Accademia peloritana, *see* Accademia peloritana
Real Academia de Bellas Artes de San Jorge, *see* Academia de Bellas Artes
    de San Jorge
Regia Accademia peloritana, *see* Accademia peloritana
Royal Aeronautical Society

If such abbreviations occur, however, in a title they are arranged as if written in full. In the future the word for which the abbreviation stands will be supplied in a title, e. g.,

    R. ⌐i. e. Regia⌐ Galleria di Firenze illustrata

F. Abbreviations and symbols in science. Arrange conventional abbreviations and symbols in science, medicine, etc. customarily written with upper and lower case letters and without periods, as words as written, even though spoken as separate letters.[13] When the entry might be looked for among the initials, a reference should be made, with an explanatory note, to file under the letters as initials.

Examples:

Mo, Ragnvald
Mo   ⌐symbol for Molybdenum⌐
Moabite stone

P., H., *see* . . .
pH, *see* pH filed as a word.
P. H. Brans' vade-mecum

Pfuhl, Ernest
pH and electro titrations
Phaedrus

R. F. D.
RH FACTOR, *see* RH FACTOR (RH filed as a word)
R., H. T.

Reznikoff, Charles
RH FACTOR
Rh-Hr blood
Rhamy, B   S

Rwanda
℞ *see* ℞ (filed as the letter R)   ⌐see Rule 12A⌐
Rx in therapeutics
Ryall, Richard John Hawkes

---

13. Chemical elements are not strictly symbols but rather abbreviations. (U. S. Government Printing Office. *Style manual.* 1945. p. 108)

G. Subject subdivision abbreviations. If subject subdivisions are abbreviated in subject headings as they commonly are in the tracing, arrange them as if written in full.

Example:

U. S.—FOREIGN POPULATION
U. S.—FOR. REL.   ɪFOREIGN RELATIONSɪ
U. S. foreign trade policy

Following is the list of subject subdivisions as abbreviated by the Library of Congress:

Antiq.	Antiquities
Bibl.	Bibliography
Bio-bibl.	Bio-bibliography
Biog.	Biography
Bound.	Boundaries
Comm.	Commerce
Descr.	Description
Descr. & trav.	Description and travel
Dict. & encyc.	Dictionaries and encyclopedias
Direct. .	Directories
Disc. & explor.	Discovery & exploration
Econ. condit	Economic conditions
Emig. & immig.	Emigration and immigration
For. rel.	Foreign relations
Geneal.	Genealogy
Hist.	History
Hist. & crit.	History and criticism
Indus.	Industries
Manuf.	Manufactures
Period.	Periodicals
Pol. & govt.	Politics and government
Sanit. affairs	Sanitary affairs
Soc. condit.	Social conditions
Soc. life & cust.	Social life and customs
Stat.	Statistics

7. Elisions, possessives, etc.

Preliminary note. This rule covers separate words or word groups that are shortened by the omission of certain letters, with the omission shown by an apostrophe and the resulting word or combination of words spoken as written (elisions, contractions, dialect and colloquial forms that contain an apostrophe). These omissions include (1) letters in the interior of or at the beginning or end of a word (as "o'er" for "over," "cap'n" for "captain," "o'" for "of," "'n'" for "and," "'t" for "het" (Dutch); (2) letters at the beginning of or between two

29

words (as "'tis" for "it is," "they'll" for "they will"); and (3) the final vowel in foreign articles, prepositions and pronouns when the following word begins with a vowel (as "l'été" for "le été," "d'art" for "de art," "j'accuse" for "je accuse").

The rule also covers words in the possessive case when they contain an apostrophe (as "boy's," "boys'"), and plural and other grammatical forms.

For names with an elided prefix, see Rule 14, Proper names with a prefix, and Rule 13A, Compound proper names.

A. Arrange elisions, contractions, and possessives as written. Do not supply missing letters. Disregard the apostrophe and treat as one word any word or contraction of two words that contains an apostrophe, unless the apostrophe is followed by a space (but see exception for this in 7B below). Disregard all grammatical distinctions and interfile nouns, adjectives, plurals, possessives, elisions and contractions.

Exceptions:

1) Elided *initial* articles in foreign languages are disregarded (see Rule 4A1).
2) For 'k, 'n, 's, and 't in Dutch titles, see 7C below.

Examples:

The boy with wings
Boynton, Winifred Case
Boys and girls at school
Boys' and girls' book of indoor games
The boys' book of airships
Boy's book of body building
Boys will be boys
Boyse, Samuel

Cinquant' anni di vita italiana . . .
Cinquanta lire

Donovan, Timothy Paul
Dont, Jacob
Don't be afraid
Don'ts
Dony, Yvonne P   de

East o' the sun and west o' the moon
East of Eden
East of the sun and west of the moon

The taint in politics
'Tain't me, it's Democracy speakin'
'T aint right
Tainted contacts

Who is who in music
Whoa, Grandma!
Who'd be a doctor?
Whodunit?
Whom God hath joined
Who's who
Whose love was the greater?

Bibliothèque d'art
Bibliothèque de la Fondation Thiers
Bibliothèque de l'École des chartes
Bibliothèque de l'Usine
Bibliothèque d'histoire

SIKSIKA LANGUAGE
S'il avait su!
Sil-Vara, *see* . . .
Silage
S'ils connaissaient leur bonheur!
Silt
S'instruire en s'amusant
Sinus

B. If the same words appear in the catalog written both with an apostrophe and space between them and with an apostrophe and no space or as one word, interfile them all under the one-word form. File an explanatory reference under the two-word form, and an explanatory note preceding all entries under the one-word form. (cf. Rule 11B)

Example:

Cinquant' anni
> For entries beginning with the above words see the one-word form "Cinquantanni."

Cinquanta lire
Cinquantanni
> Here are filed all entries beginning with the words "Cinquantanni," "Cinquant'anni," and "Cinquant' anni."

Cinquantanni di palcoscènico
Cinquant' anni di vita italiana . . .
Cinquante

C. In Dutch titles, 'k, 'n, 's, and 't are filed as separate words.

Example:

In suspicion's shadow
In 't hartje de stad
In 't zicht der derde Vredesconferentie
In Tamal land

31

Likewise, 't within a compound name is filed as a separate word (for an example see Visser 't Hooft, p. 68). However, a name beginning with a prefix containing 't is filed as one word (see Van 't [or Van't] in Comprehensive list of prefixes in Rule 14A3).

For the use of these letters as initial articles see Rule 4A1; at the beginning of a place name, Rule 14E.

8. Signs and symbols

A. Signs without letters (used as author headings)

Note. According to the *Anglo-American Cataloging Rules* entries under non-alphabetical typographical devices that stand for authors' names are not to be made. Since non-alphabetic forms that have no pertinent verbal equivalents are difficult to file and have little value (there should always be an author-title and/or title entry for the item), it is recommended that all name entries consisting of signs without preceding or following letters be removed from the catalog. If such entries are retained, arrange them according to the following rule.

Arrange signs without letters, when used instead of the author's name, before the letter A. Disregard the signs altogether and such terms as "comp.," "ed.," "pseud.," "tr.," etc. following them and arrange in groups in the following order:

1) Signs alone: cross references without title. Subarrange alphabetically by the names referred to.
2) Signs alone: cross references with titles, and unit cards, interfiled. Alphabet the references by title, the unit cards by main entry.
3) Signs followed by titles of honor or address, descriptive words or phrases, forenames or forename initials. Subarrange alphabetically by the designation, name, or initials following the signs, disregarding an initial article.

Examples:

****, tr., *see* Pereira da Costa, Constantino
***, *see* Pereira dos Reis, Antonio
***, *see* Seton, William, esquire

   ***

As we will be, by ***.

???

   Doit-on pleurer sa femme
   see Dumoulin, Joseph

   ———?

East and West; the confessions of a princess, by ———?

***, ed. and tr.
Saint-Pardoux,   baron de
>Campanhas de Portugal em 1833 e 1834 . . . extrahida do francez ampliada por ***.

Ṗ

>Shakespeare a revelation
>*see* Lumley, Henry

***, L'abbé, *see* Michon, Jean Hippolyte
***, Adrien
>Les savanes
>*see* Rouquette, Adrien Emmanuel

>*******, countess of
Mixing in society . . . By the Right Hon. the Countess of *******.

———, James J., *see* Guthrie, James Joshua
A.
ABC of painting

B. Signs combined with letters

1. When a letter or syllable is followed or preceded by signs, disregard the signs and arrange by the letter or letters. Thus, letters with signs are interfiled with letters without signs, arranged according to the rule for Initials (Rule 5). When "x" is used as a sign following a letter, disregard it, the same as other signs.

Example:
>"A."
Love-in-memory, an elegy by "A."

A***
>Le passeport
>*see* Chavanges, Alphonse
A.
>Peregrinacion de Luz del Dia
>*see* Alberdi, Juan Bautista

>*——A——*, tr.
Delabarre, Christophe François
>A treatise on second dentition.

>A., tr.
Monk, Maria
>Vienvolyno slaptybēs.

>*A. . . . .
Vocabulaires guilof, mandiongue . . .

M., *see* Manners, Robert Rutland
M***
    Amusemens géographiques et historiques
    see Navarre, P.
M . . .
    Ancien résident de France . . .
    see Prévost, Antoine François
M., A. D., *see* Dominick, Maynard A.
M***, A. D. B., *see* Monier, A   D   B
M***, Alexandre, *see* Martineau, Alexandre
M*** D***, *see* Ancillon, Charles
M. D., *see* Dufour
M. D***
    Catalogue de livres
    see Deville
M. D . . .
    Catalogues des livres rares et précieux
    see Detune
M., Mr. D.
    Essai sur les préjués
    see Holbach, Paul Henri Thiry, baron d'
M. D.
    Esplicacion de la Table sinoptica de jurisprudencia
    see Delmonte y de las Cuevas, Manuel
M. D. Anderson Memorial Library, Houston, Tex.
M*** d'Ohsson, *see* Mouradgea d'Ohsson Ignatius
M***, Madame
    Madame Récamier
    see Mohl, Mary Elizabeth Clarke
M———, Mr.
    The shen's pigtail
    see Mason, Charles Welsh
M., S.
    'Black-letter' text
    see Morison, Stanley
M***, Sylvain
    Bibliothèque des amans
    see Maréchal, Pierre Sylvain

W. I. M., *see* Morse, William Inglis
W*********, J***, *see* Williamson, John
Wxxxxxxx, Jxxx, *see* Woodward, Josiah
W., J.
    A compendius view
    see Wright, James
W., J. B. N., *see* Wyatt, James Bosley Noel

2. If a letter is followed by signs and further letters of the name or word (e. g., B———v), disregard the signs and arrange letter by letter, interfiling with other initials. When there are two or more letters together, arrange them following the first of the consecutive letters as a single letter, e. g., B———de after B. D. H.

Examples:

B., D., *see* Bartolotti, Davide
B. D. H., *see* British Drug Houses, ltd.
B———de, ———
B. de M***, L.
B . . . . des E . . . . , J. F. A.
B., E.
BIBM
B. I. R.
B . . . ïi, V.
B., J.
B.-J., G.
B. J. S. P. C.
B . . . Jourdain, de
B., S.
B   s, F.
B. S. I.
B. Sémis, pseud.
BTG
B———t———n, Richard
B., Th., B. D.
B. V. L.
B———v, M
B. V. T. S.
B———vié, B.
B., Z. G.
B———z, G. H.
Ba, Amadou Hampaté

RKSM
The r———l fowls
RLKSM
RLM
The r— —l register
R., L. S.
The r———l stranger
R. M. A.
R. V. D.
Raab, Arthur E

35

3. Disregard such typographical devices as hyphens, asterisks, commas, and spaces between the letters or syllables of a complete word and arrange the word as a single word.

Examples:

> Equality by statute
> E-qual-ity education in North Carolina among Negroes
> Equality in America

> Return of Hercules, esq.
> The return of H*y*m*a*n K*a*p*l*a*n
> Return of Imray

> Humor and humanity
> H,u,m,o,r, do 1° ao 5°
> Humor in American song

> Archy does his part
> Archys life of Mehitabel. 1933
> archy s life of mehitabel. 1966
> Arciniegas, Germán

C. Signs in titles. Disregard signs, such as • • • or ——, at the beginning of or within titles and arrange by the word following the signs, except disregard an initial article. For words in titles in which some of the letters are represented by signs, see 8B2 above. For signs between the separate letters or syllables of a complete word, see 8B3 above.

Examples:

> And another thing
> —— and beat him when he sneezes
> And now good-bye
> • • • and now Miguel
> And so • • • accounting
> And so —— Victoria
> And they shall walk

> Civitas Dei
> ——ck., die schönsten Geschichten von Rudolf Geck
> Claassen, Cornelius Jansen

> More people
> "• • • a more perfect union"
> More pictures to grow up with

D. Ampersand. Arrange the ampersand (&) as "and," "et," "und," etc., according to the language in which it is used.

Examples:

Art and beauty
Art & commonsense
ART AND INDUSTRY

L'art et la beauté
L'art & la guerre
L'art et les artistes

Berlin und Bodensee
Berlin & seine Bauten
Berlin und seine Kunstschätze

The word "and" in various languages:

Danish	og
Dutch	en
French	et
German	und
Italian	e (but becomes "ed" before a word beginning with "e")
Latin	et
Norwegian	og
Portuguese	e
Rumanian	si
Spanish	y (but becomes "é" before a word beginning with "i" or "hi")
Swedish	och

The abbreviation "&c" is arranged as if written in full, i. e., "et cetera" (see Rule 6A3, and Examples p. 23).

> *Note.* On Library of Congress cards for foreign titles that contain an ampersand that affects the filing, the corresponding word is now being supplied for the ampersand, as provided for in *Anglo-American Cataloging Rules* 133E2, e. g.,

Automobilismo & ɪi. e. eɪ automobilismo industriale
File as: Automobilismo e automobilismo industriale

E. Signs and symbols spoken as words. Arrange signs and symbols that are ordinarily spoken as words as if they were written out, in the context of the title, in the language of the rest of the title.

Following is a list of the more commonly encountered signs and symbols with their corresponding words in English:

×	times *or* by
+	plus *or* and
—	minus
÷	divided by
=	equals
%	percent

$	dollar, dollars	(when accompanied by figures, read it following the figures)
£	pound, pounds	(when accompanied by figures, read it following the figures)
°	degrees	
+mas	Christmas	
§	paragraph	

Examples:	*File as:*
$2 \times 2 = 5$	Two times two equals five
3×3: Stairway to the sea	Three by three . . .
Vision + value series	Vision plus value series
% of gain	Percent of gain
$$$ and sense	Dollars and sense
$20 a week	Twenty dollars a week
£ 60 a second on defence	Sixty pounds a second on defence
90° in the shade	Ninety degrees in the shade
The +mas star for the poor	The Christmas star for the poor
Das in §1 des Gesetzes . . .	Das in Paragraph eins des Gesetzes . . .

Note. On Library of Congress cards for foreign titles that contain a sign or symbol that affects the filing, the corresponding word is now being supplied for the sign or symbol, as provided for in *Anglo-American Cataloging Rules* 133E2, e. g.,

Jugend + ⌊i. e. und⌋ Lektüre

File as: Jugend und Lektüre

9. Numerals

For numerals and dates that indicate a sequence see Rule 36.

A. General rule. Arrange numerals in the titles of books, corporate names, cross references, etc. as if spelled out in the language of the entry.[14] Spell

---

14. Because long series of entries beginning with numerals are apt to be confusing when arranged alphabetically, there have been some attempts to provide a numerical arrangement. In these plans numerals, whether they occur as words or as figures, are filed in terms of a base number which is interpreted as a word, followed when necessary by figures. Explanations and examples of this method may be found in Moakley's *Basic Filing Rules,* the rules of the Queens Borough Public Library and the Agricultural and Mechanical College of Texas Library, and the article in *Library Trends* by Osborn and Haskins describing the Harvard plan (for full references see Bibliography). The subcommittee studied all of these, and even experimented with a completely numerical file entirely separate from the main alphabetical catalog. So many problems were encountered that the idea of either a total or a partial numerical arrangement was abandoned. There seems to be no entirely satisfactory solution to the vexing problem of filing numerals. The alphabetical pattern of arrangement in a long file of numerals in English language entries could be made more apparent if the corresponding words were added in brackets after complex numerals, as is done for foreign languages (see 9B below).

numerals and dates as they are spoken, placing "and" before the last element in compound numbers in English, except in a decimal fraction where the "and" must be omitted. Examples follow 9A5 below.

   Note. This rule is not precise because numerals are not always spoken the same. The inclusion of "and" is recommended because it usually appears on title pages where numerals are written out and this form predominates in catalogs. There seems to be no uniform standard practice for "and"—most English grammars and handbooks specify its inclusion in written forms, while textbooks used in American public schools prescribe its omission in spoken forms.

   1. Basic table. The following table gives examples of basic numerals and their corresponding words in English for filing as numbers and as dates.

	Number	*Date*
100	One hundred	One hundred
101	One hundred and one	One hundred one
200	Two hundred	Two hundred
221	Two hundred and twenty-one	Two twenty-one
1000	One thousand	One thousand
⎰1001–	One thousand and one–	⎰One thousand one–
⎱1999	One thousand nine hundred and ninety-nine	⎱Nineteen ninety-nine
	except round thousands, e. g.	
⎰1100	Eleven hundred	⎰Eleven hundred
⎱1600	Sixteen hundred	⎱Sixteen hundred
2000	Two thousand	Two thousand
⎰2001–	Two thousand and one–	Two thousand one B.C.
⎱2999	Two thousand nine hundred and ninety-nine	
	except round thousands, e. g.	
2400	Twenty-four hundred	
10,000	Ten thousand	
15,210	Fifteen thousand, two hundred and ten	
100,000	One hundred thousand	
110908	One hundred and ten thousand, nine hundred and eight	
1,000,000	One million	
2,341,406	Two million, three hundred and forty-one thousand, four hundred and six	
100,000,000	One hundred million	
1,000,000,000	One billion	
.624	Six hundred twenty-four thousandths	
600.024	Six hundred and twenty-four thousandths	
6½	Six and a half	

2. Special usages. Examples of numerals used in special ways, as addresses, time of day, shortened dates.

Examples:	*File as:*
112 Elm Street	One twelve
1000 Chestnut St.	Ten hundred
5:30 to midnight	Five-thirty
'49 to '94	Forty-nine to ninety-four

3. Roman numerals. Roman numerals are treated the same as Arabic. Occasionally a Roman numeral that is written as a cardinal number would be spoken as an ordinal, and so filed as an ordinal. See 9A4 and 9C below.

4. Military units. Certain numerical designations of military units present problems when the heading is to be filed alphabetically (e. g., a cross reference). A Roman numeral in a United States unit is to be considered an ordinal. In British countries the numbers are usually written and spoken as cardinal numbers.

Examples:	*File as:*
IX Air Force Service Command	Ninth
112 Squadron (Gt. Brit. Royal Air Force)	One hundred and twelve

5. References. When a numeral is spelled out on a title page it is of course filed as written. If there are entries in the catalog under two different forms of the same number (whether both are spelled out or one is spelled out and the other is a numeral), cross references should be made from one spelling to the other. Arrange these references before entries under each spelling. When there is uncertainty as to the spoken form of a particular numeral, file it according to the general rule and make references from alternative forms.

Examples for 9A:

General examples:

One America
One half the people
One hundred, *see also* entries beginning with "Hundred"
100 American poems   ⌜one hundred⌝
115 homes for family living   ⌜one hundred and fifteen⌝
150 science experiments step-by-step   ⌜one hundred and fifty⌝
157th Regiment (U. S.   Infantry) *see* . . . ⌜one hundred and fifty-seventh⌝
150 techniques in art   ⌜one hundred and fifty⌝
101st Division (U. S.   Army) *see* . . .   ⌜one hundred and first⌝
One hundred and five sonnets
105 Squadron (Gt. Brit.   Royal Air Force) *see* . . . ⌜one hundred and five⌝

One hundred and one, *see also* entries beginning
    "One hundred one"
101 best games for teen-agers   ſone hundred and oneʼ
One hundred and one patchwork patterns
101 RANCH, OKLAHOMA   ſone hundred and oneʼ
One hundred & seventy Chinese poems
110 tested plans . . .   ſone hundred and tenʼ
110908   ſauthor entryʼ   ſone hundred and ten thousand,
                                        nine hundred and eightʼ
130 feet down   ſone hundred and thirtyʼ
130,000 kilowatt power station   ſone hundred and thirty thousandʼ
103 simple transistor projects   ſone hundred and threeʼ
112 Squadron (Gt. Brit. Royal Air Force)   ſone hundred and twelveʼ
    see . . .
125 simple home repairs   ſone hundred and twenty-fiveʼ
One hundred best books
100 most honorable Chinese recipes   ſone hundredʼ
One hundred one, *see also* entries beginning
    "One hundred and one"
One hundred one ways of cooking potatoes
100 soviet chess miniatures   ſone hundredʼ
100,000 years of daily life   ſone hundred thousandʼ
100 to dinner   ſone hundredʼ
One hundred years ago
One is only human
One million dead
1,000,000 delinquents   ſone millionʼ
One million islands for sale
101 ſOne-oh-oneʼ Ranch, *see* 101 Ranch (101 filed as
    One hundred and one)
110908 ſOne one oh nine oh eightʼ *see* 110908 (filed as
    One hundred and ten thousand nine hundred
    and eight)
One summer in Hawaii
One thousand, *see also* entries beginning with "Thousand"
ONE THOUSAND, A. D.
One thousand Americans
1050 jewelry designs   ſone thousand and fiftyʼ
1001 African violet questions   ſone thousand and oneʼ
One thousand and one night stands
1001 questions answered about trees
1010 tested ideas that move merchandise   ſone thousand and tenʼ
1,000 destroyed   ſone thousandʼ
1880th Aviation Battalion (U. S. Army.   ſone thousand eight hundred
    Corps of Engineers) *see* . . .   and eightiethʼ

1,999 belly laughs ⌈one thousand nine hundred and ninety-nine⌉
One thousand poems for children
112 Elm Street ⌈one twelve⌉
One's, two's, three's

Round thousands (also Fractions):
Twelve against the gods
12 against the law
12½ Plymouth Street ⌈twelve and a half⌉
Twelve and after
Twelve days of Christmas
1200 bottles priced ⌈twelve hundred⌉
1200 Chinese basic characters
12 lessons to better golf
Twelve men
12 million black voices
The twelve Olympians

Twenty-four hours
2400 business books ⌈twenty-four hundred⌉
Twenty-four hundred Tennessee pensioners
Twenty-four portraits

Roman numeral—Cardinal:
The twenty-four days before Christmas
XXIV elegies ⌈twenty-four⌉
Twenty four fables of Aesop

Roman numeral—Ordinal (also Corporate name):
Twentieth century checkers
20th century China ⌈twentieth⌉
Twentieth century church music
The XXth century citizen's atlas of the world ⌈twentieth⌉
The 20th Century Correspondence School, New York ⌈twentieth⌉
The twentieth century crusade
XX century cyclopaedia and atlas ⌈twentieth⌉
Twentieth century design

The Ninth Air Force Service Command in the European
    theatre of operations
IX Air Force Service Command (U. S. Army Air Forces) *see* . . . ⌈ninth⌉
The ninth hour
9th Regiment (U. S. Marine Corps) *see* . . . ⌈ninth⌉
The 9th sees France and England
The ninth wave

Dates:

Ten seconds from now
1066   ɩten sixty-sixɩ
1066 and all that
1066, the story of a year
Ten steps forward

Nineteen centuries of Christian song
1918, the last act   ɩnineteen eighteenɩ
Nineteen eighty-four
The 1950's come first   ɩnineteen fiftiesɩ
The 1956 Presidential campaign   ɩnineteen fifty-sixɩ
1950 world ski championships   ɩnineteen fiftyɩ
1940 E. W. Scripps cruise to the Gulf of California   ɩnineteen fortyɩ
1943 war job guide for women   ɩnineteen forty-threeɩ
1940–1942 ɩpoemɩ   ɩnineteen forty to nineteen forty-twoɩ
A 1914 single tax catechism   ɩnineteen fourteenɩ
Nineteen from Seventeen
1900 A.D.   ɩnineteen hundredɩ
Nineteen hundreds
Nineteen million elephants
1975 and the changes to come   ɩnineteen seventy-fiveɩ
Nineteen stories
The nineteen-thirties in America
1939 ɩtitleɩ   ɩnineteen thirty-nineɩ
1937 Australian test tour   ɩnineteen thirty-sevenɩ
1937–   in Europe   ɩnineteen thirty-seven inɩ
Nineteen to the dozen
The nineteenth century

Shortened date:

Forty miles a day on beans and hay
Forty-nine poems
'49, the gold seeker of the Sierras   ɩforty-nineɩ
'49 to '94

    Forty-niners
Hulbert, Archer Butler

    The '49ers   ɩforty-ninersɩ
Wells, Evelyn

    The forty-niners
White, Stewart Edward

Forty-ninth parallel survey
Forty odd

Time of day:

Five tales
5:30 to midnight   ₁five-thirty₁
The five thousand dictionary

Address:

Nine to five
920 O'Farrell Street   ₁nine twenty₁
The nine unknown

Special usage:

Double muscadine

    Double O seven
Snelling, O   F
    Double O seven.   James Bond; a report. ₁London₁ N. Spearman
    ₁1964₁

    007   ₁double O seven₁
Snelling, O   F
    007. James Bond; a report. ₁New York₁ New American Library
    ₁1964₁
Double or nothing

Numerals within entry:

Europe since 1815   ₁eighteen fifteen₁
Europe since 1870   ₁eighteen seventy₁
Europe since 1500   ₁fifteen hundred₁
Europe since Napoleon
Europe since 1918   ₁nineteen eighteen₁
Europe since 1914   ₁nineteen fourteen₁
Europe since 1789   ₁seventeen eighty-nine₁
Europe since the war

B. Foreign languages. Arrange numerals in foreign languages as if spelled out according to the usage of the particular language. When the corresponding word or words are supplied in the entry (see *Note*), disregard the introductory "i. e."

    Note. It is the cataloger's responsibility to supply the corresponding word when a title in a foreign language begins with a numeral or contains a numeral that affects the filing. For titles in the Latin alphabet the word is added in brackets after the numeral, e. g., 150 ₁i. e. Hundertfünfzig₁ kleine Gärten. For titles in other alphabets the word is substituted for the numeral in the "Title romanized" note.[15] This kind of information has

---

15. *Anglo-American Cataloging Rules* 133E2.

appeared on Library of Congress cards since 1948.[16] In the examples below, the corresponding words are given at the right margin rather than within the heading.

1. Basic table. The following table gives examples of basic numerals with some corresponding words in French and German for filing as numbers and as dates. For complete lists of numerals in various languages consult U. S. Government Printing Office. *Manual of Foreign Languages*[17] and recent foreign language grammars and dictionaries.

French

	Number	Date
100	Cent	
101	Cent un	Cent un
200	Deux cents	Deux cent
201	Deux cent un	Deux cent un
1000	Mille	Mil
⌠1001–	Mille un–	Mil un–
⌡1099	Mille quatre-vingt-dix-neuf	Mil quatre-vingt-dix-neuf
⌠1100–	Mille un cent–	Onze cent–
⌡1999	Mille neuf cent quatre-vingt-dix-neuf	Dix-neuf cent quatre-vingt-dix-neuf
2000	Deux mille	Deux mil
1,000,000	Million	
2e	Deuxième	

German

	Number	Date
100	Hundert	
101	Hunderteins [not Hundertundeins]	
200	Zweihundert	
201	Zweihunderteins	
221	Zweihunderteinundzwanzig	
1000	Tausend	
⌠1001–	Tausendeins–	
⌡1999	Tausendneunhundertneunundneunzig	Neunzehnhundertneunundneunzig
	except round thousands, e. g.	
1100	Elfhundert	
1200	Zwölfhundert	
2000	Zweitausend	
100,000	Hunderttausend	

16. U. S. Library of Congress. Processing Dept. *Cataloging Service.* Washington, D. C. Bulletin 16, April 1948, p. 2.
17. Op. cit.

One exception to the omission of "und" in German numerals is an ordinal in which the last element is "-erste"; in this case "und" must be included, e. g., Hundertunderste (101st).

Note. It should be noted that it is now the practice of the Library of Congress to write certain compound numerals as one word, e. g., achtzehnhundertsechs, not achtzehnhundert sechs (1806, German); dieciséis, not diez y seis (16, Spanish).

Examples:

Dix, Morgan
10 ans de politique sociale en Pologne   ɟdixɹ
Dix ans d'études historiques
1870. Armée de Metz   ɟdix huit cent soixante-dixɹ
Dix Lumber Company, North Cambridge, Mass.
1915; revue de guerre en deux actes   ɟdix neuf cent quinzeɹ
Le XIXe siècle   ɟdix-neuvièmeɹ
1789   ɟdix sept cent quatre vingt neufɹ
XVIIe & XVIIIe siècles   ɟdix-septièmeɹ
Dix vues de Lisbonne

Acht Lehr- und Wanderjahre in Chile
Die achte Symphonie
Achterberg, Richard
78 Farberei-Geheimnisse   ɟachtundsiebzigɹ
Die 48er Demokratie und der Völkerbundgedanke   ɟachtundvierzigerɹ
1813; Blücher und Bonaparte   ɟachtzehnhundertdreizehnɹ
1806. Das preussische Offizierkorps   ɟachtzehnhundertsechsɹ
Der 18. Oktober; ein Schauspiel   ɟachtzehnteɹ

Hundert Frauen
Hundert Jahre grieschische Landwirtschaft
100 Jahre italienischer Geschichte   ɟhundertɹ
Hunderteinundsechzig merkwürdige Geschichten
Hundertfünzig Jahre deutscher Kunst
150 kleine Gärten   ɟhundertfünfzigɹ
Der hundertjährige Calender

C. Numerals following given names in titles. Arrange a numeral following a given name in a title as if spelled out in the language of the rest of the title, as spoken. In English and German the numeral is read as an ordinal preceded by the definite article; in French, the ordinal is used for the first only and cardinals for all others; in Spanish, ordinal numbers are used through ten and cardinal numbers for all others. An exception to this is a series of titles under the same author entry in which the numbers form a numerical sequence (e. g., the kings in Shakespeare titles); these are better arranged in numerical order (see footnote 43, p. 142). For numerals in given name headings see Rule 25.

Examples:	*File as:*
English	
Charles V	Charles the Fifth
Henry VIII	Henry the Eighth
Louis IX	Louis the Ninth
Louis XIV	Louis the Fourteenth
French	
Charles Ier	Charles Premier
Louis IX	Louis Neuf
Louis XIV	Louis Quatorze
German	
Louis XVI	Louis der Sechzehnte
Spanish	
Napoleón III	Napoleón Tercero
Alfonso XIII	Alfonso Trece

Examples of entries:

The Henry James reader
Henry V, King of England, 1387–1422   ˻Henry King of England, 5˼
Henry VIII, King of England, 1491–1547   ˻Henry King of England, 8˼
HENRY MOUNTAINS, UTAH

    Henry VIII   ˻Henry the Eighth˼
Shakespeare, William

    Henry VIII   ˻drama title˼
Vernulz, Nicolas de

    Henry VIII. and his court.   1867.   ˻Henry the Eighth˼
Mundt, Klara Müller

    Henry the Eighth and his court.   ˻c1898˼
Mundt, Klara Müller

Henry VIII and his wives
Henry VIII's fifth wife   ˻Henry the Eighth's˼

    Henry V   ˻Henry the Fifth˼
Shakespeare, William

Henry, the uncatchable mouse

Louis, Paul
The Louis Bromfield trilogy
Louis XVI und Empire; eine sammlung   ˻Louis der Sechzehnte˼
Louis XII, père du peuple   ˻Louis Douze˼
Louis IX, King of France, 1214–1270   ˻Louis King of France 9˼
Louis XIV, King of France, 1638–1715   ˻Louis King of France 14˼
Louis-Lucas, Pierre
Louis Napoléon and the genesis of the Second Empire

Louis IX en Égypt	⌈Louis Neuf⌉
Louis Norbert; a twofold romance	
Louis XIV et le Masque de fer	⌈Louis Quatorze⌉
Louis XV et sa cour	⌈Louis Quinze⌉
Louis XVI et la révolution	⌈Louis Seize⌉
Louis Sinclair; or, The silver prize medals	
Louis the Fifteenth and his times	
Louis XIV in court and camp	⌈Louis the Fourteenth⌉
Louis XVI furniture	⌈Louis the Sixteenth⌉
Louis the unfortunate	

D. Names of things that include a numeral. Arrange the names of classes of aircraft, boats, etc. in which a numeral is an integral part of the heading, e. g., P-40 (FIGHTER PLANES), S-51 (SUBMARINE), alphabetically as spoken, i. e., P-forty, S-fifty-one.

Example:

B., F. J.	
BF 109 (FIGHTER PLANES) *see* . . .	⌈one-oh-nine⌉
B. F. V.	
B-58 BOMBER	⌈fifty-eight⌉
B-58 HUSTLER (BOMBERS) *see* B-58 BOMBER	
B. G.	
B. S.	
B-17 BOMBER	⌈seventeen⌉
BTG	
B-24 BOMBER	⌈twenty-four⌉
B-29 BOMBER	⌈twenty-nine⌉
B. V.	
Baab, August	

Some things that are designated by numbers are better arranged in a numerical sequence (according to Rule 36). In the following example arrangement is first alphabetical by the words, then numerical.

Example:

IBM APERTURE CARD SYSTEMS, *see* . . .
IBM 650 (COMPUTER)
IBM 1401 (COMPUTER)
IBM 1401 (COMPUTER)—PROGRAMMING
IBM 1620 (COMPUTER)
IBM 7030 (COMPUTER)
IBM—FRANCE
IBM STRETCH COMPUTER, *see* . . .

For specific names of individual things with distinguishing numerals (e. g., EXPLORER II (BALLOON)), see Rule 36D.

VARIANT FORMS (RULES 10–12)

Introductory notes. Because language is not static and because there are variations even in the same language as used at different times and in different countries, there will be many cases of the same word being spelled differently or written in different forms. According to the rules for descriptive cataloging, titles and other information are given as presented by the work itself. Although it would be simpler to file every heading exactly as written, it seems likely that the user will be better served if the variants are brought together under one form, because the exact form of the particular item desired may not be known and similar entries would otherwise be separated. Therefore rules 10 and 11 recommend interfiling of the same words spelled differently and of the same compound words written differently, when more than one form appears in the catalog. For words spelled differently a choice must be made, according to the criteria given below; two-word (or hyphened) forms are always filed under the one-word form. Rule 12 recommends that dialect, colloquial, and humorous forms be arranged as written, but that in some cases additional entries be made under the full, standard form to aid in locating the items.

Great care must be taken when filing new cards in a catalog in which different spellings and forms are interfiled not to start a second alphabet. In order to forestall this, the form under which the heading is to be filed may be added in the upper right corner of the card or above the corresponding word or words. Filers must be constantly on the alert for possible variations in spelling and form and see that appropriate references are provided when needed. There will undoubtedly always be some such situations that are never discovered.

CRITERIA FOR CHOICE AMONG VARIANT SPELLINGS

When there is an established subject heading or subject cross reference under one of the spellings, choose that spelling (e. g., "Archaeology" rather than "Archeology," because "Archaeology" is the spelling of the subject heading; but "Encyclopedia" rather than "Encyclopaedia," because "Encyclopedia" is the spelling in the subject heading).

In other cases generally choose the most commonly accepted current usage. Consult the latest edition of standard general dictionaries. Also take into account the preponderant form in the entries.

When there is a choice between the American and English spellings, choose the American (e. g., "Color," rather than "Colour"). However, in countries in which the English rather than the American form of the language is dominant the English spelling will be preferred.

Choose the modern rather than the archaic spelling (e. g., "Complete" rather than "Compleat," "Mechanic" rather than "Mechanick").

DIFFERENT PARTS OF SPEECH

When there are several parts of speech based on the same word, the spelling or form chosen for the base word will apply to all (e. g., "Coloured," "Colouring," "Colours," will file as though spelled "Colored," "Coloring," "Colors"), even though some of the words may appear only in the unused form.

REFERENCES FROM VARIANT FORMS

Explanatory references should always be made from the form or forms not chosen, and an explanatory note made under the form chosen. Because of the fluidity of catalogs, these explanatory references may be made in place of specific subject references, even when there are no entries under the form referred from to be interfiled at the time they are made. Usually reference need be made only from the base word; references from other parts of speech based on that word are needed only when they would not file consecutively with the base word. The suggested wording in the explanatory references and notes in the examples in Rules 10–11 is as generalized as possible so that form cards can be prepared for most of the situations.

10. Words spelled in different ways

See also Rule 11, Words written in different ways; Rule 18, Proper names spelled differently.

A. When different entries, including corporate names, begin with or contain the same word spelled in different ways (e. g., Color and Colour; Merry, Merrie, and Mery), choose one spelling, according to the criteria given in the introduction to this section, p. 49, Criteria for choice among variant spellings, and file all entries under that spelling. File an explanatory reference under the other spelling or spellings, and an explanatory note preceding all entries under the spelling chosen, but following a surname entry. If there is only one of the possible spellings in the catalog, generally file it as spelled, without references, until such time as the other spelling appears.

Examples:
> Color
>> Here are filed all entries beginning with the words "Color" and "Colour."
>
> COLOR
> Color harmony and pigments
> Colour harmony in dress

Color harmony spectrum
Colorado
COLORED GLASS, *see* . . .
Coloured glasses
COLORED METHODISTS, *see* . . .
Colourfacts series
Colorful Colorado
COLORING MATTER
Colouring, tinting and toning photographs
Colours of good and evil
Colors: what they can do for you
The colossus again
Colour
> For entries beginning with the above word see the spelling "Color."
Colowick, Sidney P

In defence
> For entries beginning with the above words see the spelling "In defense."
In defense
> Here are filed all entries beginning with the words "In defense" and "In defence."
In defense of ignorance
In defence of letters
In defense of liberty

In old
> Here are filed all entries beginning with the words "In old" and "In olde."
In old Bellaire
In olde Connecticut
In old New York
In olde
> For entries beginning with the above words see the spelling "In old."

Example of corporate entry interfiled:
ALUMBRADOS
Aluminium
> For entries beginning with the above word see the spelling "Aluminum."
Aluminum
> Here are filed all entries beginning with the words "Aluminum" and "Aluminium."
ALUMINUM
Aluminium alloy castings, their founding and finishing

ALUMINUM ALLOYS
Aluminium and its alloys in electrical engineering
Aluminum Company of America
Aluminum construction manual
Aluminium Development Association
ALUMINUM FOUNDING
ALUMNI

B. When the spelling not chosen for interfiling is also a proper name, file the entries in which it is used as a proper name under the name as spelled. Make appropriate explanatory notes.

The following example also illustrates the situation in which there is a subject reference from one of the spellings to a different heading. A combined explanatory note and reference may be filed under both spellings, thus eliminating the separate subject reference (see 10D below).

Example:

Armor, Samuel
Armor

> Here are filed all entries beginning with the words "Armor" and "Armour," except that when "Armour" is a proper name it is filed as spelled.
>
> For subject material see the heading ARMS AND ARMOR.
>
> (*This form in place of* ARMOR, *see* ARMS AND ARMOR)

Armor and weapons in the middle English romances
Armour in England from the earliest times . . .
The armor within us
ARMORERS
The armourer's house
The Armorial who is who
Armour

> Entries beginning with "Armour" as a proper name are filed here as spelled.
>
> For entries beginning with the above word meaning armor, see the spelling "Armor."
>
> For subject material, however, see the heading ARMS AND ARMOR.

Armour, Tommy
Armour Research Foundation, Chicago
ARMOUR RESEARCH REACTOR
Armourers

> For entries beginning with the above word see the spelling "Armorers."

Armour's almanac
Arms, Dorothy Noyes

C. If the unused English spelling is also standard spelling in another language, the foreign words may be interfiled with the English if foreign languages are not emphasized.

Example:

Center, Stella Stewart
Center
      Here are filed all entries beginning with the words "Center" and
"Centre."
CENTER COUNTY, PA.
Centre crew
Le Centre européen de la Division . . .
Center-field jinx
Centre for Urban Studies, London
Center ice
Centre international de gestion et d'organisation, Brussels
The center of the world
Centre Street Congregational Church, Machias, Me.
Centerburg tales
Central
Centre
      For entries beginning with the above word see the spelling "Center."
Centrifugal

1. Alternative. If it is preferred to file the foreign words as spelled, then the corresponding English words should also be filed as spelled. In this case make reciprocal *see also* references.

Example:

Center, Stella Stewart
Center, *see also* the spelling "Centre"
CENTER COUNTY, PA.
Center-field jinx
Center ice
The center of the world
Centerburg tales
Central
Centre, *see also* the spelling "Center"
Centre crew
Le Centre européen de la Division . . .
Centre for Urban Studies, London
Centre international de gestion et d'organisation, Brussels
Centre Street Congregational Church, Machias, Me.
Centrifugal

2. Foreign words that vary slightly from the English spelling of the same word are always filed as spelled if there is no corresponding spelling in English.

Example:

Mariacher, Giovanni
Mariage américain
Un mariage dans le monde
Marian
Marret, Mario
MARRIAGE
Married
Marriott

D. When there is a subject reference from one spelling to another and there are titles, etc. to be interfiled, the subject reference may be replaced by an explanatory reference.

Example:

Arch of triumph
Archaeological
      Here are filed all entries beginning with the words "Archaeological" and "Archeological."
Archaeological discoveries in South America
Archeological exploration of Fishers Island
Archaeological Institute of America
Archaeologists
      Here are filed all entries beginning with the words "Archaeologists" and "Archeologists."
ARCHAEOLOGISTS
Archeologists and what they do
Archaeology
      Here are filed all entries beginning with the words "Archaeology" and "Archeology."
ARCHAEOLOGY
Archeology of eastern United States
The archaeology of New York State
The archaic gravestones of Attica
Archangel, Russia
Archäologische Gesellschaft zu Berlin[18]
Archard, Theresa
ARCHEGENESIS
Archeology
      For entries beginning with the above word see the spelling "Archaeology."

---

18. For arrangement of umlauts see Rule 2A.

(*This form in place of* ARCHEOLOGY, *see* ARCHAEOLOGY)
Archer, Charles

E. If the first letter is different the words should be filed as spelled, with reciprocal *see also* references.

Examples:

Enquiries [Enquiry, etc.]
　　see also the spelling "Inquiries," etc.
Enquiries into religion and culture
An enquiry into industrial art in England

Inquiries [Inquiry, etc.]
　　see also the spelling "Enquiries," etc.
Inquiries into human faculty and its development
The inquiring mind
Inquiry into inquiries

F. Misspelled words. Arrange misspelled words in titles, indicated by [sic] or [!], as if spelled correctly, disregarding [sic] and [!].

It is recommended that the correct spelling be used in typing title added entries.

If the misspelling of an author's name is not obvious, a reference from the misspelled form to the correct form may be useful.

11. Words written in different ways

Preliminary note. This rule covers compound words that are written in different ways—as two separate words (e. g., Hand book), as hyphemes (e. g., Hand-book), and as solidemes (e. g., Handbook).

For compound and hyphened proper names, see Rules 13–16. For hyphens between the separate letters or syllables of a single word (a typographical device), see Rule 8B3.

A. Basic rule—for compound words that appear in the catalog in only one form

1. Arrange hyphened words as separate words when the parts are complete words, i. e., when each part can stand alone as a word in the context of the combined word (e. g., Epoch-making, but not Co-operative or A-boating). The hyphen is treated as a space for filing purposes and arrangement is word by word.

Example:

An epoch in life insurance
Epoch-making papers in United States history
The epoch of reform

2. Arrange as two words compound words written as two separate words.

3. Arrange as one word compound words that are written as one.

B. Same word written differently

1. In the case of compound words that appear in the catalog written both as two separate words (or hyphened) and as a single word, interfile all entries, including corporate names, under the one-word form. This applies to subject headings and subject cross references also. File an explanatory reference under the two-word form, and an explanatory note preceding all entries under the one-word form. These special references and notes may take the place of specific subject *see* references either from one form to the other or from one or both forms to a different subject heading, and may even be used when there are no entries under the two-word form.

Examples:

Home carpentry
Home comers
　　　For entries beginning with the above words, written with or without a hyphen, see the one-word form "Homecomers."
Home coming
　　　For entries beginning with the above words, written with or without a hyphen, see the one-word form "Homecoming."
Home cookery
Homebrew and patches
Homecomers
　　　Here are filed all entries beginning with the words "Homecomers," "Home comers," and "Home-comers."
The home-comers
Homecoming
　　　Here are filed all entries beginning with the words "Homecoming," "Home coming," and "Home-coming."

　　　Homecoming
Bradbury, Ray

　　　The home-coming
Doyle, Sir Arthur Conan

　　　Homecoming
Seifert, Elizabeth

Homecomings
Homecrafts in Sweden

Corporate name interfiled:

Camp dramatics
Camp fire
　　　For entries beginning with the above words, written with or without a hyphen, see the one-word form "Campfire."

Camp grub
Campbell
The camper's bible
Campfire
      Here are filed all entries beginning with the words "Campfire,"
"Camp fire," and "Camp-fire."
Campfire adventure stories
Camp-fire and cotton-field
Campfire and trail
Camp Fire Girls
The Campfire girls flying around the globe
CAMPFIRE PROGRAMS
Camp-fire verse
Campfires and battlefields
The camp-fires of Napoleon
CAMPING

Subject heading—no subject reference to it from variant form:[19]

SEA POETRY
Sea power
      For entries beginning with the above words, written with or with-
out a hyphen, see the one-word form "Seapower."
A sea ringed with visions
Seaports and people of Europe
Seapower
      Here are filed all entries beginning with the words "Seapower,"
"Sea power," and "Sea-power."
SEA-POWER
Sea power in the machine age
Seapower in the nuclear age
Sea-power in the Pacific
Search

Subject heading—subject reference to it from variant form:

Thunder stone
Thunder storm
      For entries beginning with the above words, written with or with-
out a hyphen, see the one-word form "Thunderstorm."
         (*This form in place of* THUNDER-STORMS, *see*
         THUNDERSTORMS)
Thunder wings

---

19. In this and the following subject heading examples the subject reference situation
is as it exists in the Library of Congress *List of subject headings* as of 1967.

The thundering herd
Thunderstorm
> Here are filed all entries beginning with the words "Thunderstorm,"
"Thunder storm," and "Thunder-storm."

Thunderstorm   [fiction title]
Thunderstorm electricity
THUNDERSTORMS
Thurber, James

*Subject reference to a different subject heading from one of the forms but
not from the other:*

Teeling, William
Teen age
> For entries beginning with the above words, written with or with-
out a hyphen, see the one-word form "Teenage."
> For subject material, however, see the heading ADOLESCENCE.
> (*This form in place of* TEEN-AGE, *see* ADOLESCENCE)

Teen talk
Teenage
> Here are filed all entries beginning with the words "Teenage,"
"Teen age," and "Teen-age."
> For subject material, however, see the heading ADOLESCENCE.

Teen-age baseball stories
The teenage chess book
Teen-age clothes
TEEN-AGE DRIVERS
Teenage health
Teen age sketches
Teenagers ask more questions
The Teenie Weenies
Teens . . . how to meet your problems

Subject references to a different subject heading from both forms:

Live out your years
Live stock
> For entries beginning with the above words, written with or with-
out a hyphen, see the one-word form "Livestock."
> For subject material, however, see the headings DOMESTIC ANI-
MALS; STOCK AND STOCK-BREEDING.
> (*This form in place of* LIVE STOCK, *see* . . .)

Liverpool
Livestock
> Here are filed all entries beginning with the words "Livestock,"
"Live stock," and "Live-stock."

For subject material, however, see the headings DOMESTIC ANI-
MALS; STOCK AND STOCK-BREEDING.
　　(This form in place of LIVESTOCK, *see . . .)*
Live-stock and poultry diseases
LIVE STOCK ASSOCIATIONS
LIVESTOCK BREEDING RESEARCH
LIVE STOCK EXHIBITIONS
LIVESTOCK, FERAL, *see* FERAL LIVESTOCK
　　(Omit reference from LIVE STOCK, FERAL)
Livestock health encyclopedia
LIVE STOCK INSURANCE, *see* INSURANCE, AGRICULTURAL—
　　LIVE STOCK
Live stock journal annual
LIVESTOCK MARKETING, *see* MARKETING OF LIVESTOCK
Livingston

2. There are some cases in which the words written separately may have a
different meaning from the compound form. If the distinction can be made,
arrange them separately.

Example:
AIR MEETS
Air, men and wings
Air men o'war
The air menace and the answer
Airman's world
The airmen
Airmen speak
Airne, Clement Wallace

If such distinctions would be difficult to make, all entries may be filed under
one form.

Example:
Wild justice
Wild life
　　For entries beginning with the above words, written with or with-
　　out a hyphen, see the one-word form "Wildlife."
　　　　(Omit reference WILD LIFE CONSERVATION, *see* WILDLIFE
　　　　CONSERVATION)
Wild like the foxes
WILDINGS
Wildlife
　　Here are filed all entries beginning with the words "Wildlife,"
　　"Wild life," and "Wild-life."
Wild life　　　　　　　　　　　　　　　　　　　　　　　[fiction title]

Wild life at home	ɾanimals, etc.ɿ
Wildlife biology	ɾanimals, etc.ɿ
WILDLIFE CONSERVATION	
Wild life in Oregon	ɾnot animals, etc.ɿ
Wild life in South Africa	ɾanimals, etc.ɿ
Wild life in the Rocky Mountains	ɾnot animals, etc.ɿ
WILDLIFE MANAGEMENT	
Wildman, A B	

Since the combinations with the word "every" are so numerous, one explanatory note may serve for all.

Example:

Every, Edward Francis
Every
      All entries (except surname entries) beginning with the word "Every" are interfiled, whether it is written as a separate word, with a hyphen, or combined with the next word as a single word.
The Every body's album
Everybody's ancestry
Everychild; an American ideal
Every ᴄhild in school
Everychild's series
Every church its own evangelist
Every day
The everyday Bible
Every-day educator
An everyday girl
Every day heroes
Every living creature
Everyman, Mr., *see* Mr. Everyman
Everyman   ɾuniform title headingɿ
Everyman a capitalist
Every man's religion
Every woman's magazine
Eves, Charles Kenneth

C. Combining forms

1. Arrange as one word, words beginning with a prefix or combining form (i. e., words in which the first part cannot stand alone as a word with the meaning it has in the combined word), whether written with a hyphen, as two separate words, or as one word, except as specified in 11C5 below. Interfile all the variant forms of a word, including those in corporate names, in one alphabetical file. Make an explanatory note under the prefix and file it preceding all entries that begin with the prefix, including those in which it is a separate word with a different meaning, but following a surname entry.

2. *Caution:* Since some prefixes may also be words in themselves with different meanings, care must be taken to distinguish the usage in each particular instance. For example, "post" the separate Latin word and "post" meaning "mail" are filed as separate words before the longer words in which "post" is a prefix meaning "after."

3. List. Following is a list of the more commonly encountered prefixes and combining forms: A- (see Rule 12A), ante-, anti-, audio-, bi-, bio-, co-, demi-, dis-, electro-, ethno-, ex-, extra-, fore-, historico-, hydro-, infra-, inter-, magneto-, micro-, mid-, multi-, neo-, non-, pan-, pari-, photo-, post-, pre-, pro-, pseudo-, psycho-, re-, semi-, sesqui-, sub-, super-, tele-, trans-, tri-, ultra-, un-.

Example:

> Post, Wiley
> Post-
> > Words beginning with the above combining form are alphabetized as one word.
> Post-bag diversions
> Post biographies of famous journalists
> Post liminium
> POST-OFFICE, *see* POSTAL SERVICE
> The Post reader of Civil War stories
> POST-ROADS
> POSTAGE-STAMPS
> Post-Biblical history of the Jews
> Posted missing
> POST-IMPRESSIONISM (ART)
> POSTURE
> Post-war British cars
> Postwar British fiction
> The post-war condition of Britain
> Postwar youth employment
> Posy

Example of corporate entry interfiled:

> Pan-
> > Words beginning with the above combining form are alphabetized as one word.
> Pan   ⌐title⌐
> Pan in ambush
> Panama
> Panamerica comercial   ⌐title⌐
> Pan American Coffee Bureau, New York
> Pan-American Congress of Mining and Geology
> PAN AMERICAN DAY
> El Panamericanismo y las relaciones Dominico-Haitianas

Pangborn, Mark White
Pan-German League, 1890–1914
PANGERMANISM
Pan-Germanism versus Christendom
Pangonis, William J

4. When a prefix or combining form is the first of a sequence of such forms and is not followed immediately by the word it modifies, file it as a separate word.

Examples:

Fore-
> Words beginning with the above combining form are alphabetized as one word.

Fore-and-aft rig
Fore!   The call of the links
Fore-armed
Forecasting
FORE-EDGE PAINTING
Foreign
Fore-room rug
Forest

Hydro-
> Words beginning with the above combining form are alphabetized as one word.

Hydro- and aero-dynamics   [title]
HYDRO-AEROPLANES
HYDROCARBONS
Hydroelectric developments and engineering
HYDRO-ELECTRIC PLANTS
Hydro electric power from the Missouri River
HYDROFLUORIC ACID

Reichs-, Landes- und Provinzialordnungen
Reichs- und Freikonservative Partei
Reichsärztekammer

5. Combining forms made from the names of countries and peoples (e. g., Anglo-, Franco-, Greco-, Serbo-, etc.) are an exception to the rule for arrangement of combining forms, 11C1 above. File them as separate words before longer words beginning with the same letters. However, if such forms also appear in the catalog written in one-word form, interfile the two-word form with the one-word form in the position of the one-word form, according to 11B1 above.

Examples:

Franco, Victor
Franco-American Audio-Visual Distribution Center, New York
Franco Bahamonde, Francisco
FRANCO-CHINESE WAR, 1884–1885
Franco de Colonia
FRANCO-SPANISH WAR, 1635–1659
Francoeur, Robert Alfred

Serbo-Croatian
    For entries beginning with the above words, see the one-word form
  "Serbocroatian."
SERBO-TURKISH WAR, 1876
Serbocroatian
    Here are filed all entries beginning with the words "Serbocroatian"
  and "Serbo-Croatian."
SERBO-CROATIAN DRAMA
Serbocroatian heroic songs
SERBO-CROATIAN LANGUAGE
SERBS

D. Hyphen versus dash. It is not necessary to distinguish between the dash
separating a subject from a subdivision of that subject[20] and the hyphen separating two parts of a compound word, except when the hyphen appears in a
word which, according to the above rules, would be arranged as a single word.
In the first example below, filing is alphabetical by the word following
"Sound," whether that word is preceded by a dash for a subject subdivision
or a hyphen for a compound word. In the second example, it should be noted
that the marks are all hyphens following a combining form, therefore the
words are to be filed as one word.

Examples:

SOUND
SOUND—COLLECTED WORKS
Sound currency
Sound-film reproduction
SOUND—MEASUREMENT
Sound spending
SOUND-WAVES
Sound your horn!

MICROBIOLOGY
Micro-diffusion analysis and volumetric error

---

20. For the arrangement of subject headings see Rule 32.

MICRO-ORGANISMS
MICROPALEONTOLOGY

12. Dialect, colloquial, humorous forms

A. General rule. Arrange words in dialect, colloquial, and humorous forms and spellings as written. This includes the forms "de" and "ye" when used as articles for effect, even as initial articles. Elisions and contractions containing an apostrophe are filed according to the rule for Elisions, possessives, etc. (Rule 7).

The form compounded with "A-" or "A'" (colloquial or dialect, originally a preposition), as "A-boating," "A'piping," is filed as one word under "A," because here "A" is not an article but a prefix. For example of explanatory note regarding this see Rule 14A2.

"℞" is filed as the letter "R" with initials, but a reference from "℞" is filed as "Rx," and the term "Rx" is filed as written (see Rule 6F, Abbreviations). "'R'" meaning "are" is filed with the initials. In such cases the cataloger should provide additional entries to aid in locating the item, either partial titles or the full word for which the special form stands, as ⌈Prescription⌉ ... , ⌈Are⌉ ...

Examples:
>   Aboard the Flying Swan
>   A-boating we will go
>   The abode of love
>   ⌈Are⌉ you listenin'? by Tony Wons
>   "Are you listening?" by J. P. McEvoy
>   Betazzi, Enrico
>   Betcha can't do it
>   Betche, Ernest
>   De natura deorum
>   De night in de front
>   De nuestro Mexico
>   "De ole plantation"
>   De re metallica
>   Delzons, Louis
>   Dem good old times   ⌈Dem = Them⌉
>   Dem Pol entgegen
>   Demachy, Edouard
>   Ohya, A.
>   Oi, such a family!
>   Oigga, Vasile
>   ⌈Prescription⌉ for slimming
>   R. F. R.
>   ℞ for slimming

R. G.
R. Y. A.
'R' you listenin'? by Tony Wons
R. Z. T.
Ydewalle, Charles d'
Ye gods and little fishes
Ye olden time
Ye that thirst
Yea and nay
Yeager, George

B. Phonetic spellings. Arrange words spelled phonetically as they are written.

Example: *File as:*
    Iz the sol a substans?   Iz . . . (not Is)

NAMES—ALPHABETIZATION (RULES 13–18)

This section covers the alphabeting rules for special types of proper names, both personal and geographical (with a few cases of analagous corporate names, in Rules 14C and 15A5). Some of the examples are given only in full enough form to show the alphabetical position, with a comma at the end indicating a surname. For details of arrangement of entries under proper names, see Rules 20–25, Personal name entry arrangement.

13. Compound proper names

Preliminary note. A compound proper name is a name consisting of two or more separate words, with or without a hyphen. This includes names composed of more than one proper name (e. g., Martin-Leake), names with parts connected by a conjunction or preposition (e. g., Martín de Almagro), and names beginning with New, Old, East, North, Saint, San, Santa, etc.

The following types of names are not considered as compound names; treat them according to the rule referred to:
    1) Names beginning with a prefix (see Rule 14)
    2) Hyphenated American Indian names (see Rule 16)
    A. Arrange compound proper names as separate words. Alphabet with regard to all words in the name, including articles, conjunctions, and prepositions within the name, even treating as separate words prefixes within the name which would make the name one word when they occur at the beginning of the name (according to Rule 14). However, if an internal part of the name contains an elided prefix, that part is filed as one word.

65

Note. Note that Saint, San, Santa, etc. (all the forms of Saint in the various languages) are filed as separate words and not as prefixes, because they are adjectives, not particles. The abbreviations of Saint[21] are filed as if spelled out in the language of the name, according to the provisions for abbreviations in Rule 6. The elided form "Sant'" is arranged as a separate word when followed by a capital even when there is no space between the words.

B. When the same name is currently written both as one word and as two words, with or without a hyphen (e. g., San Román and Sanromán), arrange as written, with *see also* references from one form to the other. However, names combined with New that were written at some time as one word but are now established as two-word names should be interfiled under the two-word form, with an explanatory note preceding the entries, and an explanatory reference under the one-word form (cf. Rule 11B1), especially in the case of place names.

Examples for Rule 13:

Hall Co., Tex.
Hall-Edwards,
Hall of fame
Hall-Quest,
Hall Williams,
Hallam,

Martin-Dairvault,
Martín de Almagro,
Martín de la Escalera,
Martín de Yaniz,
Martin-Decaen,
Martín del Campe,
Martin des Pallières,
Martin Deslandes,
Martin du Gard,
Martin-Dubois,
Martin-Le Dieu,
Martin Le Roy,
Martin-Leake,
Martín Llorente,

New England
       Here are filed all entries beginning with the words "New England," "New-England," and "Newengland."
New Hampshire
New Jersey

---

21. For a list of some of the full forms for the abbreviations of Saint, see Rule 6A3.

A new way of life
New York
Newark
Newberry
Newengland
      For entries beginning with the above word see the two-word form
  "New England."
Newfoundland

North Africa
North to the Orient
North Yarmouth, Me.
Northampton

Saint, Lawrence Bradford
Saint among the Hurons
Saint-Gaudens,
St. Petersburg
Saint Vincent
Saintaux,
La sainte amante de Jésus
Sainte-Beuve,
Ste. Genevieve Co., Mo
Saintes,
San, Salih
San Antonio
San Cristóval,
San Francisco
San José scale
San Román, *see also* the one-word form "Sanromán"
San Román, Francisco J
San Salvador
Sanborn,
Sankin, S. L.
S. Albon und Amphabel   ɩSanktɩ
Sankt Florian, Austria
Sanromán, *see also* the two-word form "San Román"
Sanromán, Mario
Sant, Clarence Rowley van
Sant' Ambrogio (Church) Genoa
Sant'Ambrogio (Church) Milan
Sant'Anna,
Sant Feliu de Guíxols, Spain
Sant'Iago, *see also* the one-word form "Santiago"
Sant'Iago, João
Sant'Jorge,
Sant-Martí,

67

Sant'Tago, João, *see* Sant'Iago, João
Santa, Beauel M
Santa Anna,
Santa Rosa,
Santacana,
Santangelo,
Santiago, *see also* the two-word form "Sant'Iago"
Santiago
Sant'iago-Prezado,
São Paulo, Brazil
São Thomé (Island) West Africa
Saone River

Thomas à Becket
Thomas Aquinas
Thomas-Caraman,
Thomas Co., Ga.
Thomas de Saint Laurent,
Thomas Paine Historical Association
Thomas' register of American manufacturers
Thomas-San-Galli,
Thomas' wholesale grocery and kindred trades register

Visser,
Visser-Hooft,
Visser-Roosendaal,
Visser 't Hooft,[22]
Visser van Nieuwpoort,
Visserman,

(For additional examples see p. 103–5)

14. Proper names with a prefix

Preliminary note. A name with a prefix is one that begins with a separately written particle consisting of an article (e. g., La Crosse, L'Estrange), a preposition (e. g., De Morgan), a combination of a preposition and an article (e. g., Del Mar, Van der Veer), or a term which originally expressed relationship (e. g., Ap Richard, O'Brien), with or without a space, hyphen, or apostrophe between the prefix and the name.

A. Arrange proper names with a prefix as one word, whether the name is used as a heading or as a reference. Disregard a space or hyphen between parts of the name, and an apostrophe in an elided prefix.

This rule applies to place names of foreign origin whether the place is located in the country of its linguistic origin or in some other country.

---

22. Erroneously printed on some Library of Congress cards as Visser't Hooft. That form places the name, incorrectly, after Visserman.

Exceptions: The following categories are treated differently, as indicated briefly (more fully described in the rules referred to):

1) San, Saint, Old, New, East, North, etc.—consider as separate words (see Rule 13)
2) Prefix uncapitalized—disregard the prefix (in subject headings typed in all capitals these prefixes should be typed in lower case)
   a) the initial articles "al-" and "el-," etc. in Islamic names (see Rule 15A1)
   b) the initial articles "ha-" and "he-" in Hebrew names (see Rule 15A1)
   c) the Dutch "'s" at the beginning of a place name (see 14E below)
   d) the preposition "z" in a Czech or Slovak name (see 14C below)
   e) initial articles in Tibetan names (see Rule 15C5)
3) Expressions of relationship in Arabic and Hebrew names, e. g., Abd, Abu, Ben, etc.—regard the prefix, but file as separate words (see Rule 15A7)
4) Initial article in nicknames—disregard (but see Rule 17B)
5) The initial article "The" in place names in the English language (see 14D below)

Names in which such particles occur as separate words *within* the name are considered as compound names (see Rule 13A).

1. *Caution:* When such particles are used as prepositions, pronouns, etc., not part of a proper name, they are to be filed as separate words.

Initial articles in titles and other types of entries are disregarded (see Rule 4), but for a special exception for corporate names see 14G.

2. References. An explanatory note should be made under the prefix. If the prefix is also used as an initial article in other types of entries, in which it is disregarded, add a note explaining the filing rule for that situation. File the note card preceding all entries that begin with the prefix, including those in which it is a separate word with a different meaning, but following a single surname entry that is the same as the prefix alone. When the prefix on the explanatory note card consists of two words (e. g., De la) file the parts as separate words.

Examples:

Le
> Proper names beginning with the above prefix are alphabetized as one word.
> When the above word is used as an initial article in other types of entries, it is disregarded and the entry is filed under the word following it.

A
> When A is used an an initial article it is disregarded and the entry is filed under the word following it. *(continued on p. 70)*

Proper names beginning with the prefix A or A' (e. g., A'Becket), and colloquial or dialect words combined with A- or A' (e. g., A-boating, A'piping), are alphabetized as one word.

3. Comprehensive list of prefixes[23]

A, A'	Dell'	Los
Af	Della	M'
Am	Delle	Mac
Ap	Delli	Mc
At	Dello	Ne
Aus der	De Lo	Ní
Aus'm	De los	O', Ó
Av	Den	Op de
D'	Der[24]	Ten
Da	Des	Ter[24]
Dagli	Di	Ua
Dai	Du	Van
Dal	El	Van den
Dalla	Fitz	Van der
Dalle	Fon	Vander
De	Im	Van 't [or Van't]
Degl'	L'	Ver
Degli	La	Vom
Dei	Las	Von
Del	Le	Von der
De la	Les	Von und zu (file as separate words)
De las	Li	Zu
De li	Lo	Zum
		Zur

The following are examples of words having the appearance of prefixes but which actually are not prefixes:

Dos (Spanish)[25]
Pi (Spanish)
Ven (Dutch)[26]

---

23. Some may appear at the beginning of a name only in a reference from the prefix.
24. The *National Union Catalog* now files "Der" as a separate word when it is part of an apparently Armenian name, and "Ter" when it is part of a Russian compound name. Because of the difficulty of making such linguistic distinctions, for both the filer and the user, it is recommended that no exceptions be made.
25. "Dos" has generally been treated as a prefix. Since 1963 the policy of the *National Union Catalog* has been to treat it as a separate word and this seems better (see example, p. 71).
26. For example, in the name Ven-ten Bensel, Elise Francisca Wilhelmina Maria van der, "Ven-ten Bensel" is a compound surname consisting of the two names "Ven" and "ten Bensel." For filing of this name see Examples, p. 74.

Examples for 14A:

Abe Lincoln in Illinois
A'Becket, John J
À Beckett, Arthur William
Abeel,
A-boating we will go
Après la victoire
Appy,
Ap Rees,
Après moi
AtKisson,
Atlee, Philip
At Lee, Samuel Yorke
Atlee, William Yorke

De   [explanatory note]
De la   [explanatory note]
De laudibus Dei
De Scribe à Ibsen
De senectute
De Alberti, Amelia
Defoe,
Del siglo de oro
De la Ramée,
De la Roche,
Delaware
Delmar, Dora
Del Mar, Eugene
Delmas,
De Luxe Building Company
Democracy
De Morgan,
Demosthenes

Doody,
D'Ooge,
Dooley,

Dos, Antoine
Do's and don't's for hockey players
Dos brasas   [title]
Dos Passos, John
Los Dos primeros poetas coloniales cuatorianos   [title main entry]
DOS PUEBLOS RANCH
Dos Santos, Eduardo
Dosey, William H

El
>Proper names beginning with the above prefix are alphabetized as one word.
>
>When the above word is used as an initial article in other types of entries, it is disregarded and the entry is filed under the word following it.

el-
>For Arabic names beginning with the article "el-" (lower case e), see under the part of the name following the article, e. g.,
>
>el-Badry (filed as Badry)
>
>On the other hand, Arabic names beginning with "El" (capital E) are filed under El as a prefix, the whole name as one word, e. g.,
>
>El-Wakil (filed as Elwakil)

Elagin, Ivan

EL ALAMEIN, BATTLE OF, 1942 ⌐Arabic place name⌐[27]

Elam, Elizabeth

El Cajon, Calif. ⌐Spanish place name⌐

Eldon,

El Dorado, Ark. ⌐Spanish place name⌐

Eldorado, Neb.

El Hakim, pseud., *see* . . . ⌐Arabic personal name⌐

El Paso, Tex. ⌐Spanish place name⌐

Elrod,

Elwakil, Chams Eldine, *see* al-Wakīl, Shams al-Dīn

El-Wakil, Mohamed Mohamed ⌐Arabic personal name⌐

Elwell,

Labrador

La Crosse, Herman Thomas

Lacrosse, Jean Baptiste Raymond, Baron

LACROSSE

La Crosse, Wis.

Lacroze,

Le   (For position of explanatory note in relation to other entries, see example on p. 88)

Lester,

Les Tina,

L'Estrange, Alfred

Le Strange, Guy

L'Estrange, Roger

Leyland,

Los   ⌐explanatory note⌐

Los que viven por sus manos

---

27. For the Arabic names see Rule 15A2.

Losa, José Joaquín Cuerda
Los Alamos, N. M.
Los Angeles
Losano,

O pioneers
Obrie,
O'Brien,
Obrig,
Ó Cuilleanáin,
Ocular surgery
Ohnet,
Ó hÓgáin, Seán
Ohr,

Ter   [explanatory note]
Ter bescherming van de engelen
Tera, Harry
Ter-Akopov, G   D
Teramo, Gaspare
TER DOEST, BELGIUM (CISTERCIAN ABBEY)
Terence
Ter Goes, *see* Goes, Netherlands
Ter Haar, John Albert Anton
Terhune,
Ter-Oganezov, V   T
Terry,
TER SCHELLING (SHIP)
Tersman, Rune

Van, John Tee-, *see* Tee-Van, John
Van   [explanatory note]
Van Icarus tot Zeppelin
VANADIUM
Van Aken,
Vanamee,
Vandera, Alonso Carrió de la, *see* . . .
Van der Aa, Pieter, *see* . . .
Vanderbilt,
Van der Veer, Judy
Van Derveer, Lettie C.
Vandervelde,
Van der Veldt,
Van der Ven-ten Bensel, Elise Francisca Wilhelmina Maria, *see* Ven-ten
        Bensel, Elise Francisca Wilhelmina Maria van der
Vanderwalker,
Vanderwilt,

Vander Zanden,
Van der Ziel,
Van de Velde,
Vandiver,
Van Dyke,

Ven, Paul van der
Ven-ten Bensel, Elise Francisca Wilhelmina Maria van der
Venable, Charles L

B. M', Mc, Mac. Arrange names beginning with the prefixes M' and Mc as if written Mac. This is because they are so pronounced and the three prefixes are identical in meaning (M' and Mc are abbreviations of Mac) and are used interchangeably with the same surnames.

Examples:

Mach,
McHale,
Machen,
McHenry,
Machiavelli,
Machinery
MacHugh, Augustin
McHugh, James Gorman
Machuron,

MacLaren, Hale
Maclaren, Ian
MacLaren, J
M'Laren, J   Wilson
McLaren, Jack
MacLaren, James

1. *Caution:* Care must be taken with names that are pronounced the same but spelled differently after the M', Mc, or Mac, especially those with double "c's."

Example:

Macalister, Alexander
McAlister, Edward Dorris
MacAlister, James
McAll, Reginald Ley
McAllister, James Gray
Macaulay, James
McAuley, Mary Faith
McBurney, Ralph
McCalister, Wayde Hampton

McCall, Arthur Gillett
McCallister, James Maurice
McCall's magazine
MacCauley, Clay
Macdonald,

2. *Exception:* File the prefix M' in African names as part of the following word, e. g.,

M'bala *file as* Mbala

3. References. Explanatory references should be made from each of the abbreviated forms of Mac to the full form, as:

Mc
> Names beginning with Mc are filed as if spelled "Mac," e. g., McLaren is filed as Maclaren.

M'
> Celtic names beginning with M' are filed as if spelled "Mac," e. g., M'Laren is filed as Maclaren.
> African names beginning with M' are filed as one word as spelled, e. g., M'bala is filed as Mbala.

These abbreviated forms are filed strictly alphabetically by M and Mc respectively. For position of M', see example on p. 17.

C. Disregard the uncapitalized preposition "z" at the beginning of a Czech or Slovak name.

Example:
> Zeromski,
> z Žerotína,
> Zerr,

D. Disregard the initial article "The" in place names in the English language.

Example:
> Barber of Seville
> The Bend, Ohio
> Boy Scouts of America
> Butterworth,
> The Buttes, Mont.
> Buxton,

E. Disregard the Dutch "'s" at the beginning of a place name. For explanation of "'s," see Rule 4A2.

Examples:

Gravengaard,
's Gravenhaagse courant
's Gravenhage, *see* Hague
's Gravenhage voorheen en thans
Gravenhorst,

Hertog,
's Hertogenbosch, Netherlands (Diocese)
Hertogh de Bertout,

F. Disregard the inverted article in a place name reference.

Example:

Mans, Abraham des
Mans, Le, *see* Le Mans
Man's adaptation of nature

G. Corporate names. Occasionally a foreign language corporate name that begins with an article has been adopted in English usage as a unit, the article being considered an integral part of the name. In such a case arrange the name as one word under the article.

Example:

Lafond, Eddie
LA FONDA HOTEL, SANTA FE, N. M.
Lafont, Robert

15. Oriental names

Includes personal, corporate, and geographical names.
A. Islamic and Hebrew names
Includes Arabic, Aramaic, Hebrew, Persian, Syriac, and Turkish names.
1. Uncapitalized initial articles. Disregard the uncapitalized initial articles "al-" or "el-" (or the assimilated forms "ad-, an-, ar-, as-, az-," etc., if used) prefixed with a hyphen to Arabic, etc., names (e. g., al-Jundi, el-Amrousi) and the articles "ha-" or "he-" prefixed to Hebrew names (e. g., ha-Cohen).

> *Note.* This rule is based on the practice of Arabic and Hebrew bibliographies. Since a large percentage of Arabic names begin with an article, alphabeting by the part following the article eliminates congestion under the article in the catalog. Since 1965 Library of Congress cards have shown an uncapitalized initial article that is to be disregarded in filing in Roman type in contrast with the boldface of the following word.

When the prefix and name are written as one word, arrange as one word, alphabeted under the first letter (e. g., Hacohen). (Hebrew names are now commonly written as one word.)

Examples:
> Jund, Trinedad
> al-Jundī, Ad'ham
> June

> Amrouche, Marcel
> el-Amroùsi, Sayed
> Amṛta Rāya, *see* . . .

> Cohen, Marcel Samuel Raphaël
> ha-Cohen, Mordchai, *see* Hacohen, Mordchai
> Cohen, Morris

> Hackney, Thomas
> Hacohen, Mordchai
> Hacout, E

For articles that come between the parts of a name, see 15A6 below.

2. Capitalized "Al" and "El." "Āl" at the beginning of an Arabic name is to be regarded and filed as a separate word. "Al" and "El" (capitalized), with or without a hyphen, are to be regarded but treated as prefixes, the name being filed as one word (except those beginning "Al-i- . . ."). (Either the word is not a definite article, e. g., Āl signifies "family, dynasty," or the writer uses this form and wishes the word to be observed.) The same rule applies to place names beginning with "Al" or "El."

Examples:
> Al Sherman Enterprises, New York
> Āl Waṣfī, Waṣfī
> Alabama

> Alhambra
> Al Hamza, pseud., *see* el Hamza, pseud. (filed as Hamza)
> Alhazen, 965–1039

> Aljian, George W
> AL JIB, JORDAN
> Alken, Henry Thomas

3. References. An explanatory reference should be made under the article, as:

> el-
>> For Arabic names beginning with the article "el-" (lower case e), see under the part of the name following the article, e. g.,
>> el-Badry (filed as Badry)
>> On the other hand, Arabic names beginning with "El" (capital E) are filed under El as a prefix, the whole name as one word, e. g.,
>> El-Wakil (filed as Elwakil)

al-

> For Arabic names beginning with the article "al-" (lower case a), see under the part of the name following the article, e. g.,
> al-Jundī (filed as Jundi)
> On the other hand, Arabic names beginning with "Al" (capital A) are filed under Al as a prefix, the whole name as one word, e. g.,
> Al Nur (filed as Alnur)
> Arabic names beginning with "Āl" (capital Ā) are filed under Āl, as a separate word, e. g.,
> Āl Waṣfī (filed as two words under Al)

For the filing position of the note under "el-" in relation to the note under "El," see examples on p. 72.

4. Initial article in subject headings. If subject headings are typed in all capitals, it is recommended that the uncapitalized initial article be typed in lower case so that the distinction between lower case and capital in the first letter will be apparent for filing purposes, e. g.,

al-KHANDAQ, BATTLE OF, 627, *see . . .*   ₍to be filed under K₎
ĀL BŪ SAʿĪD DYNASTY   ₍to be filed under A₎

If this distinction is not made in typing, the filer must be alert to determine under which element the heading should be filed.

5. Article at beginning of subheading. In a corporate entry disregard the initial article when it occurs at the beginning of a subheading, preceded by a period.

Examples:

Egypt. Maktab al-ʿAmal
Egypt. al-Markaz al-Qawmī lil-Buḥūth
Egypt. Maṣlaḥat al-Āthār

Israel. Misrad mevaker ha-Medinah
Israel. ha-Moʿatsah ha-madaʿit
Israel. National Commission of UNESCO

6. Parts of a name. Within a heading, treat each part of a name, including articles, as a separate word, except an article at the beginning of a subheading (see 15A5 above).

Examples:

Abū ʿAbd Allāh Muḥammad
Abū ʿAbdallāh Ḥarīth ibn Asad
Abū ʿAbdallāh Muḥammad ibn ʿAbdūs
Abū al-ʿAlā
Abu al-Walīd Marwān ibn Janāḥ
Abū ʿAlī al-Ḥasan

Abū Bakr
Abū saʿīd
Abud, Salomón

Judah, Theodore Dehone
Judah Aryeh Loeb, of Gora, *see* . . .
Judah ben Isaac
Judah ben Solomon Charizi, *see* . . .
Judah, ha-Levi
Judah Ḥasid ben Samuel, *see* . . .
Judah ibn Verga, *see* . . .
Judah Sir Leon, *see* . . .

7. Prefix expressing relationship. When an Islamic or Hebrew name begins with a part expressing relationship (e. g., the Arabic "Abd, Abu, Ibn"; the Hebrew "Ben"; the Syriac "Bar"), alphabet under the prefix and file the parts as separate words.

Example:

Ben, Victor Ralph
Ben and me
Ben-Ardot, David
Ben Avigador, Aaron
Ben-Gurion, David
Ben-Hur
Ben no Naishi, 13th cent.
Ben-Oni, Asher
Ben Paris Pacific Northwest fishing guide and hunting guide
Ben rishonot la-ḥadashot   [Hebrew title]
Ben, Uncle, pseud.
Ben-Zion, S., pseud.
Ben Zion ben Israel, pseud.
Bena, Eduard

8. Arrangement of Islamic name headings

Introductory notes. The use of surnames in Islamic countries is of recent origin and still limited. The use of family names currently prevails in Iran, Lebanon, Syria, and Tunisia. In other countries in the Islamic area, usage varies.[28] When the name does not include a surname or a name used by the bearer as a surname, the elements of the name are arranged in a prescribed order. When the whole heading is in the prescribed order, the name is considered to be in direct order and no

---

28. U. S. Library of Congress. Processing Dept. *Cataloging Service*. Washington, D. C. Bulletin 67, Nov. 1964, p. 2.

punctuation is required; otherwise, a comma is inserted after the entry element.[29]

A name in which only one name precedes the first comma should be considered as a single surname, even though some of these single names may not actually be surnames. Names with more than one name before the first comma should all be considered as given names for filing purposes, since relatively few such names are actually compound surnames. These somewhat arbitrary decisions may be justified by the special character of Islamic names and the impossibility of making valid distinctions for filing on the basis of the heading alone.

Arrange Islamic name headings that begin with a single name followed by a comma as single surname headings, i. e., before longer entries beginning with the same name (according to Rule 20B). Arrange Islamic name headings consisting of more than one name before the first comma as given name headings, i. e., in the group following single surnames, alphabeting with regard to every word in the heading, disregarding punctuation (according to Rule 25B). An uncapitalized article, as "al-," within a personal name is regarded even when it is the first word in an element following a comma, and designations such as "Sultan of," "the prophet," and "called" or "calling himself" are interfiled with names. Interfile the Islamic names alphabetically with other entries beginning with the same word, regardless of kind of entry, form of heading, language, etc.

Examples:

Al, Bernardus Silvester Alfonsus	[Dutch]
Al', D., pseud., *see* Al'shits, D	
'Al admatam	[Hebrew title]
Āl al-Faqīh al-'Āmilī, Muḥammad Taqī	
Al amishmar	[Hebrew title]
Al-Anon Family Group Headquarters, inc.	
Āl Baḥr al-'Ulūm, Muḥammad Ṣādiq	
Al encuentro de Dios	[Spanish title]
Al-i-Ahmad Suroor	
Āl Jundī, Ad'ham, *see* al-Jundī, Ad'ham (filed as Jundī, Ad'ham)	
Al Kane Productions, inc., Philadelphia	
Āl Kāshif al-Ghiṭā', 'Alī ibn Muḥammad Riḍā	
'Al Profesor Rikhard Mikha'el Kevner	[Hebrew title]
Al Sherman Enterprises, New York	
Āl Waṣfī, Waṣfī	
al-'Alā', al-Ma'arrī Abū, *see* Abū al-'Alā', al-Ma'arrī	
Ala, Alireza Parviz	
Ala, Gordon	

---

29. *Anglo-American Cataloging Rules* 54.

al-'Alā, I   A   Abū, *see* Abū al-'Alā, I   A
'Alā' al-Dīb, *see* al-Dīb, 'Alā'
'Alā' al-Dīn 'Aṭa Malek, Joveynī, *see* Joveynī, 'Alā' al-Dīn 'Aṭā Malek
L'Ala d'Italia   [Italian title]
Ala-Könni, Erkki   [Finnish]
Alabama

Ali, A
Ali, Ahmad, Syed, *see* Ali, Syed Ahmad
'Alī, Ahmad Sa'd, *see* Ahmad Sa'd 'Alī
'Alī, al-Sayyid
'Alī, 'Alī Ahmad
Ali, Amir, syed
'Ali, pasha, of Janina
al-'Alī, Ṣāliḥ Ahmad
'Alī, Sayyid
Ali, Syed Husin, *see* Husin Ali, Syed
Ali, Syed Mujtaba
'Alī, Zakī
'Alī al-Dīn, Muftī
'Alī Āl Thānī, Sheikh of Qatar
'Alī 'Alā' al-Dīn ibn Muḥammed al-Kūṣçī, *see* Ali Kuşci
Ali Baba
'Alī ibn Ibrāhīm al-Ḥalabī, *see* Nūr al-Dīn al-Ḥalabī, 'Alī ibn Ibrāhīm
'Alī ibn Muḥammad, Abū Ḥaiyān, al-Tauḥīdī, *see* Abū Ḥayyān al-Tawḥīdī,
    'Alī ibn Muḥammad
'Alī ibn Muḥammad al-Āmidī, *see* al-Āmidī, 'Alī ibn Abī 'Alī
'Alī ibn Muḥammad, al-Khazrajī, *see* al-Khazrajī, Ḍiÿa' al-Dīn 'Alī ibn
    Muḥammad
'Alī ibn Muḥammad al-Lakhmī, *see* al-Lakhmī, Abū al-Ḥasan 'Alī ibn
    Muḥammad
'Alī ibn Muḥammad, al-Ushmūnī, *see* al-Ushmūnī, 'Alī ibn Muḥammad
'Alī ibn Muḥammad, called Ibn al-Athīr, *see* Ibn al-Athīr, 'Izz al-Dīn
'Alī ibn Muḥammad, called Saiyid Sharīf, al-Jurjānī, *see* al-Jurjānī, 'Alī ibn
    Muḥammad, al-Sayyid al-Sharīf
'Alī ibn Muḥammad ibn 'Arrāq, *see* Ibn 'Arrāq, 'Alī ibn Muḥammad
'Alī ibn Muḥammad Riḍā Āl Kāshif al-Ghiṭā', *see* Āl Kāshif al-Ghiṭā', 'Alī
    ibn Muḥammad Riḍā
Ali Khan, Anwar, *see* Khan, Anwar Ali
'Alī Khān ibn Aḥmad ibn Muḥammad Ma'ṣūm, *see* Ibn Ma'ṣūm, 'Alī ibn
    Aḥmad
Ali Khan, Jafar, *see* Jafar Ali Khan, Nawab of Bengal
'Alī Khān, Jā'far, Mirza, *see* Khān, Jā'far 'Alī, Mirza
Ali Khan, Liaquat, *see* Khan, Liaquat Ali
Ali Khan, Prince, *see* Khan, Ali Solomon
Ali nuove   [Italian title]

Ali-Özkardeş, M, *see* Özkardeş, M   Ali-
Ali-Rājpur, India (State), *see* Alirājpur, India (State)
'Alī shīr, Mīr, called al-Nawā'ī
Ali the Lion, *see* 'Ali, pasha, of Janina
'Ali-ud-din, Mofti, *see* 'Alī al-Dīn, Muftī
Ali-Zade, Z   I   , *see* Alizade, Z   I
Alia, Ferdinando Stassi d', *see* Stassi d'Alia, Ferdinando

9. **Hebrew initialisms.** Some Hebrew writers are known by initialisms, i. e., a combination of the initials of their personal names and appellatives, written in capitals with the auxiliary letters in lower case. Treat these as a word.

Example:

Rashevsky, Nicholas
Rashi, P   M
RaSHI, *see* Solomon ben Isaac, called RaSHI
Rashi and the Christian scholars
Rashi Fein, *see* Fein, Rashi
Rashid,

B. Chinese and Japanese names
Examples follow 15B6 below.
1. Arrange Chinese and Japanese names by the first part (i. e., the family name) whether it is separated from the rest of the name by a comma or not (e. g., in the author entries "Li Chang" and "Li, Chi," both authors belong to the Li family, Chang and Chi being forenames).
>   *Note.* Entries without the comma are relatively rare now, as the comma has been inserted in the proper place in Library of Congress headings for Chinese and Japanese names at least since 1941. Since the name preceding the second capitalized name is not always a surname, the mental insertion of the comma should be confined to headings found on pre-1941 cards and then only if there are no cards of later date with the same heading minus the comma.
2. Names of members of a Chinese family having occidental personal names are interfiled with the strictly Chinese names, but if a Chinese family name, combined with occidental personal names, has the appearance of being a compound surname, it is filed as such (e. g., Chen Tsen I, Pierre Claver).
3. An old Chinese name that consists of only two hyphened syllables (e. g., Lao-tzŭ, meaning the Old one) is arranged as a two-word phrase. If it is also written as one word, make a reference from the one-word to the two-word spelling.
4. Arrange alphabetically by individual words. Assume that a hyphen

always separates two distinct words, even though this rule is not strictly accurate for certain names.

5. Interfile Chinese names spelled with the same letters, ignoring the aspirate and all modifications of letters. When names are identical except for an aspirate or modified letter, arrangement is by date or designation (see Rule 2A3).

6. Arrange entries according to the regular rules for surname entries (Rules 20 and 21) and given name entries (Rule 25).

Examples for 15B1–6:

Chinese:

Chen', Chan-khao, *see* Ch'ên, Ch'ang-hao
Ch'ên, Ch'ang-hao
Chen, Chen Chong
Chen Chi
Ch'ên, Chi, writer on botany
Ch'ên, Ch'i, fl. 1773
Ch'ên, Ch'i, 1872 or 3-1932
Ch'ên, Chi-t'ung
Ch'ên, Ch'i-yüan
Ch'ên, Chia-kan
Ch'ên, Chih-liang
Ch'ên, Ching
Ch'ên, Ching, novelist
Ch'ên, Ch'ing, writer on games
Ch'ên, Ch'un, 1153–1217
Ch'ên, Chun, 1902–
Chên, Chün, 1919–
Ch'en, Eugene
Chên, Graham Mien
Ch'ên, Hsi-ên
Chen Huan-Chang
Ch'ên, I-fêng
Chen, Jack
Chen, Wei
Chen Wei Lu, pseud., *see* Trace, Granville
Chen, Z. L., *see* Ch'ên, Shan-lin
CHEN CAERULESCENS (LINNAEUS), *see* BLUE GOOSE
Chên-chu
Chên-chung, pseud.
Ch'ên hsing chi
Chen-ki-souen, *see* Chenke-Seuen
Chên li ti ta pien
Chen Tsen I, Pierre Claver

CHEN WU KUAN PAGODA
Chen Zen, Sophia H., *see* . . .
Chenault, John Cabell

Chu, Chêng
    Lu Hsün chuan lüeh.
Ch'u, Ch'êng
    P'o miao li ti pi mi.
Chü, Chêng, 1876–1951

Lao-tzŭ
Laos
Laotzŭ, *see* Lao-tzŭ

Sun, Ching-chih
Sun, Ch'ing-ling Sung
Sun Ching-shi, *see* Sun, Ching-chih
Sun Hsi-chen
Sun, I
Sun, I-hsien
Sun, I-tu Jên
Sun', ĨAt-Sen, *see* Sun, Yat-sen
Sun, In'-Chzhu, *see* Sun, Yin-chu
Sun, Jan
Sun, John T
Sun, Wên
Sun, Yat-sen
SUN
The sun also rises
SUN LORE
Sun, sea and sky
Sun-Soong, Ching-ling, *see* Sun, Ch'ing-ling Sung
SUN-SPOTS
Sun-tzŭ
SUN WORSHIP
Sun Yat-sen versus communism   [title]
Sunaga, Katsumi

Japanese:
Saitō, Hidesaburō
Saitō, Hirosi
Saitō, K., pseud.
Saitō, Masakane
Saitō Musashi-bō Benkei, *see* Benkei, d. 1189
Saitō, R.
Saitō, Takeshi
Saitō, Zenemon

Saitō Gratitude Foundation
Saitō hō-on Kai

7. Exception to the general rules. The Chinese surname "I" presents a special problem. It would be practically impossible to apply simultaneously the two pertinent rules—(1) the rule for initials, to arrange initials before longer words, in one straight alphabetical file disregarding punctuation (Rule 5A and B), and (2) the rule for surnames, that a surname entry precedes all other entries beginning with the same word (Rule 20B). Because of this, and the difficulty of identifying the different types of entries involved because the headings are so similar, it is recommended that all entries beginning with "I" be interfiled word by word in one straight alphabetical file, disregarding punctuation, kind of entry, language, etc. An explanatory note should be filed at the beginning of the letter.

The same policy is recommended for the letter "U," which appears both as a Chinese surname and as a Burmese name and title of address.

Examples:

I

> All entries beginning with the letter "I," including the name "I," are interfiled in one alphabet, disregarding punctuation and kind of entry.

I., A.⎫
I. A. ⎬ interfile according to Rule 5F.

IAA

I, a stranger   ⌈title⌉
IAWA
I accuse!   ⌈title⌉
I AM MOVEMENT
I, An   ⌈name⌉
I, Anastasia   ⌈title⌉
I and Claudie   ⌈title⌉
I believe   ⌈title⌉
I. C.
I can wait   ⌈title⌉
I, Chia-yüeh
I, Chih
I, Chin
I-ching, 635–713   ⌈name⌉
I ching   ⌈uniform title⌉
I, Claudius   ⌈title⌉
I-chou, pseud.
IDF
I ditt ansikt sved
I Ging, *see* I ching

I give you my word   [title]
I., J.
I, Judy   [title]
I, Juan de Pareja   [title]
I., K. B.
I. K. U.
I, Keturah   [title]
I kid you not   [title]
I, Kiyon
I, Kʻo
I name thee Mara
I, Nan   [name]
I, Varina   [title]
Iams, Jack

U   [explanatory note]
U
U., A
U. A. R.
U, Ai, *see* Ai, Wu
The U and I cultivator
UBEA
U., B. W.
U Ba Tin, *see* . . .
U Ba U, *see* Ba U, U
U. C. C.
U, Chuan′-t̄sz͡ûn′, *see* Wu, Chʻuan-chün
U, Chzhao-ti, *see* . . .
U, Ha-yŏng
U., I.
U Khin, *see* Khin, U
U, Ki-do
U, Kyin, *see* Kyin U, U
U Le Lah
U., M., *see* Urban, Matej
UN
U, Nak-ki
"U No" letters
U Nu, *see* Nu, U
U. P. G.
U. S.
U. S. S. R.
U Shan Maung, Maung
U, Sŭng-gyu
U. T. C. D.
U temrîavi

U Thant, *see* Thant, U
U Thein, Wah
U, Tŏng-nin
U-TSzy, *see* Wu, Ch'i
U Tun Nyoe, *see* Tun Nyoe, U
U, U Ba, *see* Ba U, U
U, Zhuĭ
Uarov, M. I.

C. Other Oriental names

Includes Burmese, Indic, Indonesian, Thai, Tibetan, Vietnamese, etc.

Introductory note. Many names, especially the older ones, in the Southeast Asia countries do not contain a surname. Many consist of just one word, or a group of words in direct form, sometimes with hyphens, sometimes with parts not capitalized. Titles, terms of address and honorific words are frequently added to names. Sometimes these same words are used as names.

1. General rule. Arrange Oriental names according to the regular rules for order of entries, i. e., single surname entries first, followed by all other entries. Consider as a surname entry any heading that has the appearance of a surname entry according to the definition in Rule 20, *Preliminary note.*

2. When a name has a title of address in place of forenames, subarrange it alphabetically by the title of address.

3. Arrange compound and phrase names alphabetically by individual words. Disregard hyphens and treat each word as a separate word, whether capitalized or not. Compound surname entries precede longer entries beginning with the same combination of words.

4. *Caution:* When the same word, e. g., Le, appears both as a separate word in Oriental names and as a prefix in occidental names, care must be taken to distinguish between them.

Examples for 15C1–4:

Arya, Arnand Swarup
Arya, pseud.
Arya, V   P
Arya Bhata, *see* Āryabhaṭa
Āryabhadracarīmahāpraṇidhānarāja, *see* . . .
Āryabhaṭa

Ba, Amadou Hampaté
Ba., Ro
Ba, TSzin', pseud., *see* . . .
Ba Hkin, Maung, *see* . . .
Ba Swe, U
Ba U, Agga Maha Thiri Thudhamma, *see* Ba U, U
Ba U, U
Baa, Enid M

Das,
Das, Aubrey C
Das, Mati Lal
Das, Tara P
Das, Y   C
Das Basu, Durga, *see* Bose, Durgadas
Das Granthī, *see* Daswe<u>n</u> Pādshāh kā Granth
Das Gupta, Ajit
Das Gupta, Prodosh
Das-Gupta, Rabindra Kumar
Das ist unsere Erde
Das Konar, Narayan, *see* Konar, Narayan Das
Das Neves, Olavo, *see* Neves, Olavo Das
Dāsa, Ananta Kiśora
Dāsa-Gupta, Surendranātha, *see* Dasgupta, Surendra Nath
Daschner, Hubert
Dasgupta, Ajay
Dasgupta, Surendra Nath
Dash, Arthur Jules

Le, Ivan, pseud.
Le, She-chin
Lê, Thành-khôi, *see* Le-thành-Khôi
Lê, Van Hô
Le   ⌈explanatory note, see Rule 14A2⌉
Le-'Agnon shai   ⌈Hebrew title⌉
Lê-bâ-Khanh
Lê-bá-Kông
Le Thanh, Truong
Le-thành-Khôi
Lê-thanh-Tuong
Le-Van
Le-van-Chat
Le-Van-Hap
Le-zekher Devorah Radler-Feldman   ⌈Hebrew title⌉
Lea, Albert Miller
Le B
        Le voyageur curieux qui fait le tour du monde.
Leb, Hans
Lebanon
Le Bar, Lois Emogene
Lebaut, René
Letham, Daryl Lee
Lethành-Khôi, *see* Le-thành-Khôi
Lethbridge, Henry J
Levallois, Pierre

Le Van, Donald C
Levand, Leon P

Mi, Wên k'ai
Mi amigo
Mi-kee, pseud.
Mi Khaing, Daw Mi, *see* Mi Mi Khaing, Daw
Die Mi-Kultur der Hagenberg-Stämme
Mi-la-ras-pa, 1038–1122
Mi labor en servicio de México
Mi Mi Khaing, Daw
Mi primer diccionario
Mi-tz'ŭ-k'ai-wei-chih, *see* Mickiewicz, Adam
Mi yiten boker   ɪHebrew titleɪ
Mia, Abdul Jabhar
Mila 18   ɪMila eighteen—titleɪ
Mila-rä-pa, *see* Mi-la-ras-pa
Milan
Milaraspa, *see* Mi-la-ras-pa
Milarepa, *see* Mi-la-ras-pa
Milas, Nikodim

5. In Tibetan names disregard uncapitalized initial articles.

Examples:

San Sebastián
gSañ-ston, *see* Orgyan-pa
San-Tsang, *see* Hsüan-tsang
Sanabria

K'an Jen, pseud.
mK'an-po, *see* Orgyan-pa
Kan-su shêng, China
Kana, Geōrgiou A

6. Exception to the general rules. It is recommended that all Burmese name entries beginning with "U," either as a name or as a title of address, be inter-filed with entries beginning with the initial "U," according to Rule 15B7 above.

16. American Indian names

Arrange hyphenated American Indian names as one word.

Examples:

Absalom's conspiracy
Ab-sa-ra-ka, home of the Crows
Ab-sa-ra-ka, land of massacre
Absaroka Mountains, Ky.

Maung, Dwe
Maun-gwu-daus, Seneca chief
Maunier, René

17. Nicknames and sobriquets

A. Treat nicknames and sobriquets as words, not as personal names. Disregard an initial article and file by the word following it.

Example:

Duce, James Terry
"Il Duce," the life and work of Benito Mussolini
Ducèdre,

Note. In the future, some nicknames will be used as entry (e. g., El Greco), since the *Anglo-American Cataloging Rules* (40) provide that a person who is commonly identified by a nickname be entered under his nickname.

Example:

Gréciano,
El Greco, d. 1614
Grecu,

B. References. Since the filing position of nicknames beginning with articles is puzzling to users and filers alike, the catalog should provide an approach through both the key word and the article. Therefore, references from a nickname to a name heading should generally be made in duplicate, one to be filed under the key word and the other under the article. In the latter, consider the article a prefix and file as one word under the article. If entry is under the nickname, a reference in the same form should be made and filed under the article.

Examples:

Campert,
El Campesino, *see* González, Valentín R   ₍file under Campesino₎
Campfield,

Elbwart,
El Campesino, *see* González, Valentín R   ₍file as Elcampesino₎
Elcano,

Elgozy,
El Greco, *see* El Greco, d. 1614 (filed under Greco)
Elgström,

Theotocopuli, Dominico, *see* El Greco, d. 1614 (filed under Greco)

Note. A heading with an initial article that is to be disregarded in filing is printed on a Library of Congress card with the article in Roman type in contrast with the boldface of the following word. This was started in 1965.

18. Proper names spelled differently

A. General rule. Arrange separately proper names that differ in spelling, however slightly. References between the different spellings are desirable, filed before the first entry under each variant spelling.

Exceptions:

1) Names beginning with M', Mac, Mc (see Rule 14B)
2) Names with the same prefix written differently (see Rule 14A)
3) Names in which the only difference is the modification of a letter or use of an aspirate (see Rules 2A3 and 15B5)

For compound proper names that are written differently, i. e., both as one word and as two words, see Rule 13B.

Examples:

Andersen, *see also* the spellings Anderson, Anderssen, Andersson
Andersen, Anders
Andersen, Hans Christian
Anderson, *see also* the spellings Andersen, Anderssen, Andersson
Anderson, Arthur
Anderson, James
Anderssen, *see also* the spellings Andersen, Anderson, Andersson
Anderssen, Adolf
Anderssen, Walter
Andersson, *see also* the spellings Andersen, Anderson, Anderssen
Andersson, Axel

Clark, *see also* the spelling Clarke
Clark, Allen Culling
Clark, Howard Walton
Clark University
Clarke, *see also* the spelling Clark
Clarke, Adam

Caterina da Siena, Saint
Catharina, Saint, of Alexandria
Catharine, *see also* the spellings Catherine, Katharine, Katherine, etc.
Catharine II, Empress of Russia
Cather, Willa Sibert
Catherine, *see also* the spellings Catharine, Katharine, Katherine, etc.
Catherine de Médici, consort of Henry II, King of France
Katharina von Bora
Katharine, *see also* the spellings Katherine, Catharine, Catherine, etc.

Katharine, pseud.
Katherine, *see also* the spellings Katharine, Catharine, Catherine, etc.
Katherine of Aragon

Allegany, *see also* the spellings Alleghany, Allegheny
Allegany Co., Md.
Alleghany, *see also* the spellings Allegany, Allegheny
Alleghany Mountains
Allegheny, *see also* the spellings Allegany, Alleghany
Allegheny Co., Pa.

The variations should also be carefully observed when they occur in fore-names following a surname.

Example:

Weber, Herman Carl
Weber, Hermann
Weber, Herrmann

B. Exception for certain place names. In the case of variant spellings for the same place name the entries may be interfiled under one spelling, with appropriate explanatory notes and references, according to the rules for words spelled in different ways (Rule 10).

Example:

Bagdad
> Here are filed all entries beginning with the words "Bagdad" and "Baghdad."

BAGDAD
Baghdad-by-the-Bay
BAGDAD RAILROAD
Baghdad sketches
Bagdikian, Ben H
Baghdad
> For entries beginning with the above word see the spelling "Bagdad."

PART II

Order of entries
(Rules 19-37)

This part covers the rules for the order of different kinds of entries beginning with the same word.

---

19. Order of entries under same word—General rules

Introductory note. In a dictionary catalog all types of entries (author, subject, title) are interfiled to form a single alphabet. There should be as few deviations from the straight alphabetical order as possible, even when there are many entries beginning with the same word, and these should be made only when the resulting order is deemed more practical from the point of view of use.

A. General rule. When the same word, or combination of words, is used as the heading of different kinds of entry, arrange the entries in two main groups as follows:

   1) Single surname entries, arranged alphabetically by forenames

   2) All other entries, arranged alphabetically word by word, disregarding kind of entry, form of heading, and punctuation

   Note. Grouping all of the single surname entries at the beginning of the file will facilitate searching, especially when complete names are not known. A small number of surname entries would be rather lost scattered through long files of subject, place name, and/or other entries beginning with the same word.

B. Summary of specific rules for different kinds of entries under the same heading. In each of the two main groups (see 19A above) there are a few subgroupings and specific rules that apply to different kinds of entries under the same heading. These are summarized here. For details and fuller examples, see the rules for the specific topics that follow in this part.

93

1. Single surname entries. Arrange different kinds of entries under the same single surname heading in groups in the following order:
1) Author (main and/or added entry)
2) Subject, without subdivision
3) Subject, with subdivision

2. All other entries

a. Personal name entries (compound names, given names). Arrange different kinds of entries under the same compound or given name heading in three groups the same as under single surname headings (19B1 above).

b. Corporate entries (corporate names, place names, uniform titles). Arrange different kinds of entries under the same corporate name in groups in the following order:
1) Author (main and/or added entry) without subheading
2) Subject without subdivision, and identical title added entries, interfiled and subarranged alphabetically by their main entries
3) Name with corporate and/or subject subdivisions, the subdivisions interfiled alphabetically with each other and with titles, etc., disregarding punctuation; each corporate author heading followed by its own subject entries.

c. Title and subject entries identical. Interfile title added entries and subject entries that are identical and subarrange alphabetically by their main entries. Title main entries precede identical entries with an author.

Examples for Rule 19:
Love, John L.
LOVE, JOHN L.
Love, William

    Love   [title]
Bowen, Elizabeth

    LOVE
Magoun, F. Alexander

    Love   [title]
Mamis, Justin

    LOVE
Martinez de Toledo, Alfonso

Love and beauty
Love is a many-splendored thing
LOVE, MATERNAL
LOVE POETRY
LOVE—QUOTATIONS, MAXIMS, ETC.
Love songs, old and new
LOVE (THEOLOGY)
Love your neighbor

London, Jack, 1876–1916
LONDON, JACK, 1876–1916
LONDON, JACK, 1876–1916—BIBLIOGRAPHY
London   ɩplace as authorɩ
    The case of the city of London . . .
London; a guide to the public buildings . . .   ɩtitle main entryɩ

    LONDON
Harrison, Frederic

    London   ɩtitle of a poemɩ
Johnson, Samuel

    LONDON
Loftie, William John

LONDON—ANTIQUITIES
London as it is today
LONDON BRIDGE
London.   Central Criminal Court   ɩauthorɩ
LONDON.   CENTRAL CRIMINAL COURT
LONDON—DESCRIPTION
London (Diocese)
LONDON IN LITERATURE

PERSONAL NAME ENTRY ARRANGEMENT
(RULES 20–25)

This section covers the rules for the filing position of personal name entries in relation to other entries in the catalog and to each other.

20. Surname entries—General rules

The following rules apply to all kinds of surnames, i. e., single surnames, compound surnames, surnames with prefixes, etc.

Preliminary note. A surname in a personal name entry is the part that precedes the first comma in the entry, when the comma is followed by:

1) A forename or forenames
2) A forename initial or initials
3) A title of polite address, honor or distinction, such as "Mr.," "Mrs.," "Mother," "Captain," "Professor," or designation such as "pseud." But see exception for names with the appearance of a given name in the following paragraph, no. 1.
4) A blank space or a long dash (in rare instances the comma may be omitted before the long dash, e. g., ɩSmithɩ———)

It is not always possible to determine whether a single name, especially one that has the appearance of a given name, is a given name or a surname.

When the distinction is not clear, treat the name as a given name, even though it may actually be a surname in some cases. The following categories are to be treated as given names and filed accordingly (see Rule 25):

1) A single name that has the appearance of a given name (e. g., Charles, Henry, John, Thomas), when followed by a designation of a religious character or family relationship such as "Brother," "Father," "Mother," "père," "mère," etc., also the designation "pseud."

2) A single name without any designation, that has the appearance of a given name, whether used as a heading or a *see* reference

3) Single names of the classical type, e. g., Homer, Horace

The comma has sometimes been omitted after the surname in certain Oriental names but the names are to be filed as if the comma were present, i. e., as surnames (see Rule 15B1).

The comma is omitted after the surname in certain corporate names when the forenames or initials are enclosed in parentheses, but the names are to be filed as surnames (see Rule 23A).

A. General rules relating to form of headings (**applicable to all surname entries**)

1. Disregard square brackets around a name.

2. Disregard parentheses around a woman's maiden name. These will not be used in entries established according to the *Anglo-American Cataloging Rules*. Entries for the same name in both the old and new forms may be interfiled.

3. Disregard designations which show the relationship of a person to one particular work (see Rule 26B3).

4. The designation "pseud." will not be used in headings established according to the *Anglo-American Cataloging Rules*. However, since there will still be entries with "pseud." in catalogs, examples are included here. Its filing position requires no special rule—when there are no dates in the heading, "pseud." simply interfiles alphabetically with other designations in the group of names without dates. Thus, those pseudonymous names without dates which are not designated as such will probably precede other entries for the same name, while those that are designated will be interfiled with other designations. (If there is any confusion in a particular situation, or new entries for a name that previously had "pseud." omit it, it is recommended that "pseud." be removed from the old entries.)

5. Disregard titles of office (e. g., Pres. U. S.) following a name. Such designations will not be used according to the new cataloging rules. Entries for the same name in both the old and new forms may be interfiled.

B. Filing position. A surname entry precedes all other entries beginning with the same word or combination of words. A single surname is always the first entry under that word. (For the filing position of compound surnames, see Rule 21.) In relation to other entries in the catalog consider only the surname, not the forenames or designations.

C. Order of entries under the same surname—General rule. Arrange headings of the same surname in groups in the following order:

1) Surname alone with nothing following it
2) Surname alone followed only by dates
3) Surname followed by designation, forenames, or initials

D. Order of entries under the same surname followed by designations, forenames, or initials

1. Arrange entries under the same surname followed by designations, forenames, or initials alphabetically by the designation, forename, or initial that follows the surname, all in one group. Disregard any designations, such as titles of nobility, honor, or address, or distinguishing phrases, that may precede or follow forenames unless it is necessary to distinguish between names that would otherwise be identical (for these, see 20D3, E2 and 5).

Example for 20C–D1:

Jones,
Jones,   fl. 1641
Jones, A
Jones, Captain
Jones, Chester Lloyd
Jones, Mr.   [Mr. = Mister]
Jones, Morris
Jones, Mother
Jones, Mrs.   [Mrs. = Mrs.]
Jones, Paul
Jones, pseud.
Jones, William

2. An initial precedes a fully written forename beginning with the same initial letter. Treat initials the same whether followed by open space (for later completion of name) or a period.

Example:

Adams, J
Adams, J   C
Adams, J   Duncan
Adams, J   F
Adams, J   Stacy
Adams, James
Adams, James C
Adams, James Clyde
Adams, James Donald
Adams, James E

3. Every word between the first comma and the next punctuation mark is to be regarded except a title of nobility, honor, or address preceding a forename. In inverted corporate names parentheses take the place of commas (see Rule 23A).

Examples:

> Warren, Henry Clarke, 1854–1899
> Warren, Henry de, comte
> Warren, Henry Pitt, 1846–1919

> Gordon, Charles
> Gordon, Lord George
> Gordon, John

Regard punctuation following forenames; disregard any titles or phrases following that punctuation except when needed to differentiate entries with the same forename.

Examples:

> Smith, John, dealer in pictures, London
> Smith, John A

> Brown (John) and Company, of Sheffield, Eng.
> Brown, John A

When the surname is followed only by a second forename (after a space for the insertion of a first forename), arrange as though the second forename were the first forename.

Example:

> Pimental, Alfredo Mesquita
> Pimental, Luis
> Pimental,⠀⠀⠀⠀⠀Mattos

4. Arrange hyphened forenames as two words.

Example:	*File as:*
Menotti, Gian-Carlo	Menotti, Gian Carlo
Li, Fei-kan	Li, Fei kan

E. Order of entries when surname and forenames are the same

1. Arrange headings of the same surname and forenames in groups in the following order:

1) Names with neither dates nor designations
2) Names with designations (whether at end or within the entry) but no dates
3) Names with dates, or designations and dates

Examples:

Pearson, John
Pearson, John, of Ewell, Surrey, Eng.
Pearson, John, 1758–1826

Campbell, Mrs. John Charles
Campbell, John Charles, 1867–

2. Arrange the same names without dates but with designations, such as titles of nobility, honor, or address, or distinguishing phrases, alphabetically by the designations preceding or following the forenames.

Example:

Smith, John
Smith, John, dealer in pictures, London
Smith, John, LL.D.
Smith, Mrs. John
Smith, John, of Malton, Eng.
Smith, John, pseud.
Smith, Sir John

3. Arrange the same names with dates chronologically by the first date given, whether it is a birth date, approximate date, or death date. When some entries with the same name and birth date include a death date and some do not, interfile them. (This situation occurs because it is now common practice not to add death dates to name headings established before the person died.)

Example:

Smith, John, 1563–1616
Smith, John, b. 1573, pseud.
Smith, John, 1580–1631
Smith, John, d. 1612
Smith, John, 1618–1652
Smith, John, 1722–1771
Smith, John, fl. 1747
Smith, John, 1747–1807
Smith, John, 1797?–1837
Smith, John, 1798–1888
Smith, John, b. 1823
Smith, John, d. 1827
Smith, John, ca. 1837–1896
Smith, John, 1837–1922
Smith, John, d. 1861

4. When an exact date of birth or death, to the month and day, is given, to differentiate persons with the same name and year, arrange chronologically by the exact date.

Example:
> Smith, John, 1900 (Jan. 19)–
> Smith, John, 1900 (Mar. 2)–

5. When a name has both dates and some kind of designation disregard the designation unless needed to distinguish between entries otherwise identical. The arrangement is chronological by date then alphabetical by designation.

Examples:
> Pearson, John, of Ewell, Surrey, Eng.
> Pearson, John, Bp. of Chester, 1613?–1686
> Pearson, John, 1923–

> Smith, John, fl. 1673–1680, clockmaker
> Smith, John, fl. 1675–1711, rector of St. Mary's, Colchester
> Smith, John, fl. 1677, dramatist

> Smith, Sydney
> Smith, Sydney, 1771–1845
> Smith, Sydney, 1869–
> Smith, Mrs. Sydney, 1873–
> Smith, Sydney, 1880–

> Stevenson, James Henry, 1860–   assyriologist
> Stevenson, James Henry, 1860–   engineer

> Brown, John, 1847–
> Brown, Mrs. John, 1847–1935
> Brown, John, fl. 1854

6. Disregard the number in a title of nobility unless it is necessary to distinguish between names otherwise identical. When there are no dates, arrange numerically. When there are also dates, arrange chronologically by the dates (the result will probably be the same).

Examples:
> Campbell, John, 5th Duke of Argyll
> Campbell, John, 1708–1775

> Cavendish, William, 1st Duke of Devonshire, *see* . . .
> Cavendish, William, 2d Duke of Devonshire, *see* . . .
> Cavendish, William, 7th Duke of Devonshire, *see* . . .
> Cavendish, William, Duke of Newcastle
> Cavendish, Sir William, ca. 1505–1557
> Cavendish, William George Spencer, 6th Duke of Devonshire

> Stanhope, Philip Henry Stanhope, 4th Earl, 1781–1855
> Stanhope, Philip Henry Stanhope, 5th Earl, 1805–1875

Comprehensive example for Rule 20:[30]

Smith,
Smith,   fl. 1641
Smith, Adam
Smith, Captain
Smith, Chester Lloyd
Smith, Lord George
Smith, Henry Clarke, 1854–1889
Smith, Henry de, comte
Smith, Henry Pitt, 1846–1919
Smith, J
Smith, J   A   X
Smith, J   Alden
Smith, J   B
Smith, Jack Hayden
Smith, John
Smith, John, LL. D.
Smith, Mrs. John
Smith, John, of Malton, Eng.
Smith, John, pseud.
Smith, Sir John
Smith, John, surgeon and trading captain
Smith, Sir John, 1534?–1607
Smith, John, 1563–1616
Smith, John, b. 1573, pseud.
Smith, John, d. 1612
Smith, John, Bp. of Chester, 1613?–1686
Smith, John, 1618–1652
Smith, John, fl. 1675–1711, rector of St. Mary's, Colchester
Smith, John, fl. 1677, dramatist
Smith, John, 1722–1771
Smith, John, fl. 1747
Smith, John, 1747–1807
Smith, John, 1797?–1837
Smith, John, 1798–1888
Smith, John, b. 1823
Smith, John, d. 1827
Smith, John, ca. 1837–1896
Smith, John, 1837–1922
Smith, Mrs. John, 1847–1935
Smith, John, d. 1861

---

30. Illustrations of most of the preceding specific rules are included here so that the complete arrangement may be seen at a glance. Because no one surname would present actual examples of every situation, some forenames, titles, designations, and dates have arbitrarily been added to the surname "Smith."

Smith, John, 1900 (Jan. 19)–
Smith, John, 1900 (Mar. 2)–
Smith (John) and Son, ltd.
Smith, John A
Smith, Johnston
Smith, Mishael
Smith, Mr.   ₁Mr. = Mister₁
Smith, Mitchell
Smith, Mother
Smith, Mrs.   ₁Mrs. = Mrs.₁
Smith, Munroe
Smith, pseud.
Smith, William, 1st Duke of Devonshire, *see* . . .
Smith, William, 7th Duke of Devonshire, *see* . . .
Smith, Sir William, ca. 1505–1557
Smith   ₁fiction title₁
Smith and Jones   ₁fiction title₁
Smith College

SPECIAL TYPES OF SURNAME ENTRIES
(RULES 21–24)

21. Compound surname entries

Preliminary note. Compound surname entries are entries in which the surname consists of two or more separate words, with or without hyphen, which are to be filed as separate words according to Rule 13. Compound Oriental name entries are covered in Rule 15.

For definition of surname in a personal name entry, see Rule 20, *Preliminary note.*

A. Interfile compound surname entries alphabetically with the group of titles, etc. following entries for the first part of the name alone as a single surname. Alphabet with regard to all words in the surname part of the entry.

B. Compound surname entries precede other entries beginning with the same combination of words.

For examples for Rule 21 see Comprehensive examples for Rules 21 and 22, p. 103–5.

22. Names of clan, family, house, dynasty, etc.

A. General rule. Interfile a surname followed by "clan," "family," "House of," "Counts of," etc., alphabetically with the group of titles, etc. following all entries under the same name as a single surname. Alphabet with regard to all words in the heading, disregarding the comma in an inverted heading. Such an entry for a compound surname follows all surname entries for the same compound name. For use of a family name as an author entry see also Rule 37C, Manuscripts, no. 2.

B. Name of progenitor, etc. in heading. Interfile headings for family histories that include the name of a progenitor or other designation in parentheses with subdivisions of the family name, titles, etc., alphabeting by the forename of the progenitor or by the designation.

Examples:

   LEE FAMILY
   LEE FAMILY (BENJAMIN LEE, 1765–1828)
   LEE FAMILY (JOHN LEE, 1620–1690)

   STRAUSS FAMILY
   STRAUSS FAMILY (MUSICIANS)

   ADAMS FAMILY
   Adams family.   Archives
   ADAMS FAMILY (GEORGE MEREDITH ADAMS, 1829–1886)
   ADAMS FAMILY—JUVENILE LITERATURE

Comprehensive examples for Rules 21 and 22:

   Williams, Zedekiah Fletcher
   Williams and Orton Manufacturing Company
   Williams College
   Williams-Ellis, Amabel
   Williams-Ellis, Clough
   WILLIAMS FAMILY
   WILLIAMS FAMILY (ROGER WILLIAMS, 1604?–1683)
   Williams Library, London
   Williams-Wynn, Charles Watkin
   Williams-Wynn, Frances
   Williams-Wynn, Sir Watkin, bart.
   WILLIAMS-WYNN FAMILY
   Williamson

   Lloyd, William
   Lloyd Brothers, Cincinnati
   LLOYD FAMILY
   Lloyd George, David
   Lloyd George Adams Library
   LLOYD GEORGE FAMILY
   Lloyd guide to Australia
   Lloyd library
   Lloyd-Williams, Richard
   Lloyd's of London

Saint, Lawrence Bradford
St. Albans, Me.
The saint and the sword
Saint-Ange, Louis de
St. Clair, Arthur
A saint in the making
Saint-Martin, Louis Pierre
Saint-Pierre, Bernardin de
Saint-Pierre, Jacques
Saint-Pierre, Michel
Saint Pierre (Benedictine Abbey)
Saint Pierre (Island)
Saint Pierre, Martinique
SAINTS

Buckingham, Walter S
Buckingham and Chandos, Richard Grenville, 1st Duke of
Buckingham and Chandos, Richard Grenville, 2d Duke of
Buckingham and Chandos, Richard Grenville, 3d Duke of
BUCKINGHAM FAMILY
BUCKINGHAM PALACE
Buckingham, Pa.

Strauss, William Louis
Strauss and Company, Liverpool
Strauss Commission on Incentive-Hazardous Duty and Special Pays
STRAUSS FAMILY
STRAUSS FAMILY (MUSICIANS)
Strauss souvenir album
Strauss und Torney, Lothar von
Strauss und Torney, Lulu von
Strauss und Torney, Viktor von
Strauss, Vetter und Co., Deutsche Verlagswerke, Berlin
Strauss von Moltke, Johannes von

Gil, Peter Paul
Gil-Albert, Juan
Gil Blas   [title]
Gil de Rubio, Victor M
Gil Munilla, Ladislav
Gil-Robles, Enrique
Gil-Robles y Quiñones, José María
Gil Vicente   [title]
Gil y Pablos, Francisco
Gil y Robles, Enrique

Gil y Zárate, Antonio
Gil Yépez, Carlos
GILA RIVER

Medici, Lorenzo de', il Magnifico
The Medici art series
MEDICI, HOUSE OF
Medici-Tornaquinci, Alfonso Cosimo de'

(For additional examples, see p. 66–68)

23. Corporate name entries beginning with a surname

Preliminary note. This rule covers firm names and names of institutions, organizations, etc., in which the heading consists of:

1) a surname followed by a forename or one or more initials or abbreviations of forenames and further parts of the corporate name or a designation, e. g., Wilson (H. W.) Company; Witte (Friedrich) (Firm)
2) a surname without forenames or initials, followed only by a designation, e. g., Fraser (Firm)
3) a compound or phrase name beginning with a surname, e. g., Fraser, Smith, and Company

Note. According to the *Anglo-American Cataloging Rules* there will be no corporate entries in the form of surnames with forenames inverted (the only inverted entries will be for surnames with initials or abbreviations of forenames). However, since there may still be entries with full forenames in catalogs, and the form may still occur in cross references, examples are included here. Another change will be the omission of the type of business in the designation, unless it is an integral part of the name or is needed to distinguish between identical names.

A. Surname followed by forenames, etc.

1. Arrange a corporate name consisting of a surname followed by a forename or one or more initials or abbreviations of forenames in its alphabetical place among the personal names in the surname group. Arrange abbreviated forenames as written. Disregard the further part of the corporate name or the designation unless needed to distinguish between otherwise identical entries.

Disregard parentheses around the forename or initials; construe them as commas. (Older entries may not have parentheses as they have not always been used.)

Caution: Be alert to sequences of names in which the name following the first comma is not a forename, even though it may have the appearance of one, e. g., Strong, Carlisle and Hammond Company (for arrangement of this type of name see 23B below).

105

Examples:
 Witte, Eva Knox
 Witte (Friedrich) (Firm)
 Witte, Gaston François de

 Huebner, Robert J
 Huebner (S. S.) Foundation for Insurance Education
 Huebner, Solomon Stephen
 Huebner, Walther
 Huebner Foundation for Insurance Education, *see* . . .

 Burrow, Clayton
 Burrow (Ed. J.) & Co., ltd.
 Burrow, Edward John
 Burrow, F   R

2. If the corporate entry consists of a personal name followed by further parts of the corporate name and the name is the same as a personal name entry, arrange it after the same name with dates.

Example:
 Smith, John
 Smith, John, dealer in pictures, London
 Smith, John, 1798–1888
 Smith (John) and Son, ltd.
 Smith, John A

3. Arrange different corporate names that begin with the same personal name alphabetically by the terms following the personal name.

Example:
 Brown, John, 1907–
 Brown (John) and Company, ltd., Sheffield and Clydebank
 Brown (John) and Company, of Sheffield, Eng.
 Brown, John A

4. If the corporate heading contains two forenames connected by "and," alphabet with regard to all words in the name.

Example:
 Black, Adam, 1784–1874
 Black (Adam and Charles) (Firm)
 Black, Adam Elliott

B. Surname without forenames or initials
1. Arrange a corporate name consisting of a surname only, followed by a

designation, and compound and phrase names in their alphabetical place in the group of titles, etc. following the same name as a single surname. Alphabet with regard to all words in the heading, including "inc.," "ltd.," etc., and such phrases as "and Company," "(Firm)," etc.

Examples:

Fraser, Alice
Fraser, Arthur, 1893–
Fraser (Arthur) and Company
Fraser, Charles
Fraser, William
Fraser & Charles
FRASER FAMILY
Fraser (Firm)
Fraser-Knight, James
The Fraser murder case
Fraser, Smith, and Company

Prentice, William Reed
The prentice
Prentice-Hall book about inventions
Prentice-Hall, inc.
Prentice-Hall inheritance service
Prentice-Hall world atlas

Rolls, W.
ROLLS (IRON MILLS)
ROLLS-ROYCE AUTOMOBILE
Rolls-Royce, ltd.
Rolls series

Likewise, a corporate name beginning with a compound personal name is arranged after the surname entries for the same compound name.

Example:

Wenner-Gren, Marguerite Gauntier
Wenner-Gren Foundation for Anthropological Research, New York

2. When a firm name without a forename or initials following the surname has on the second line of the entry the date of the book cataloged and the exact corporate name of the firm on that date, subarrange entries chronologically by date then alphabetically by title when date and firm name are the same. This form usually indicates that the firm was known under different names at different periods of its existence. However, the Library of Congress discontinued this method of subdivision on December 9, 1949.

Example:
> Scribner (Firm, publishers) New York
>   (18– Scribner, Armstrong & Co.)
> Scribner (Firm, publishers) New York
>   (1898. Charles Scribner's Sons)
> Scribner (Firm, publishers) New York
>   (1920. Charles Scribner's Sons)

24. Place name followed by a personal name or personal title

A. Arrange entries for noblemen and prelates which consist of a place name combined with personal names among the personal surnames, not with places. Subarrange alphabetically by the personal names in the entry.

B. Arrange references from the name of a bishop's or archbishop's see, which omit the bishop's or archbishop's name but give the dates of his administration, among the personal surnames, not with places. Subarrange chronologically by date of administration.

Examples for Rule 24:
> Essex, Arthur
> Essex, Arthur Capel, 1st Earl of
> Essex, Richard Hamilton
> Essex, Robert Devereux, Earl of
> Essex [place, titles, etc.]

> Ely, Alfred
> Ely, Bishop of, 1506–1515, *see* Stanley, James, Bp. of Ely, 1465?–1515
> Ely, Bishop of, 1808–1812, *see* Dampier, Thomas, Bp. of Ely, 1748–1812
> Ely, Ezra Stiles
> Ely, Francis Turner, Bp. of, *see* Turner, Francis, Bp. of Ely
> Ely, Frank David
> Ely, John Kirby, Bp. of, *see* Kirkby, John, Bp. of Ely
> Ely, Joseph Allen
> Ely [place, titles, etc.]

25. Given name entries

Preliminary note. Personal name entries are treated as given name entries providing the name is *not* followed by:
>   1) A comma and a forename or forenames
>   2) A comma and a forename initial or initials
>   3) A comma and a title of polite address, honor, or distinction, such as "Mr.," "Mrs.," "Mother," "Captain," "Professor," or designation such as "pseud." But see exception for names with the appearance of a given name in the following paragraph, no. 1.

108

4) A comma and a blank space or a long dash (in rare instances the comma may be omitted before the long dash, e. g., ₎Smith₎————)

It is not always possible to determine whether a single name, especially one that has the appearance of a given name, is a given name or a surname. When the distinction is not clear, treat the name as a given name, even though it may actually be a surname in some cases. The following categories are to be treated as given names and filed accordingly:

1) A single name that has the appearance of a given name (e. g., Charles, Henry, John, Thomas), when followed by a designation of a religious character or family relationship such as "Brother," "Father," "Mother," "père," "mère," etc., also the designation "pseud."

2) A single name without any designation, that has the appearance of a given name, whether used as a heading or a *see* reference

3) Single names of the classical type, e. g., Homer, Horace

The comma has sometimes been omitted after the surname in certain Oriental names but the names are to be filed as if the comma were present, i. e., as surnames (see Rule 15B1).

The comma is omitted after the surname in certain corporate names when the forenames or initials are enclosed in parentheses, but the names are to be filed as surnames (see Rule 23A).

A. General rules relating to form of headings (applicable to all given name entries)

1. The rules for the following situations are the same as for the corresponding situations with surnames: (1) square brackets (Rule 20A1), (2) designations which show the relationship of a person to one particular work (Rule 20A3), and (3) "pseud." (Rule 20A4). It is especially recommended that "pseud." be removed from old given name entries because it is an artificial designation that would not be known to users of the catalog and entries arranged by it would not be readily found.

2. Disregard a numeral following a given name except when necessary to distinguish between given names with the same designation. Arrange first alphabetically by the designation, then when there is more than one numeral, numerically by the numerals.

Example:

Charles V, Emperor of Germany
Charles II, King of France
Charles I, King of Great Britain
Charles II, King of Great Britain

3. In headings for sovereigns, noblemen, and popes, disregard epithets such as "the Conqueror," "the Great," etc. and the title "Saint" when they come *between* the given name and the designation. A reference should be made from the name followed by the epithet, etc., especially in the English form, to be alphabeted by the epithet, etc.

> *Note.* According to the *Anglo-American Cataloging Rules* epithets are not to be used in given name headings for sovereigns, noblemen, and popes, nor "Saint" in headings for sovereigns and popes. The above rule and examples of the old-form headings are included because there will still be many such forms in catalogs. The same names are shown in the second example in their new forms, much simpler both to file and to use. The order of entries is the same regardless of form, therefore it would be possible to interfile the old- and new-form headings without changing the old if so desired.

Examples:

Headings in old form:

Charles, Count of Valois
Charles, le Téméraire, Duke of Burgundy
Charles, Duke of Orléans, Count of Angoulême
Charles the Bold, *see* Charles, le Téméraire, Duke of Burgundy (filed as Charles, Duke of Burgundy)

William, Father, pseud.
William I, the Conqueror, King of England, 1027?–1087
William, of Newburgh
William the Conqueror, *see* William I, the Conqueror, King of England, 1027?–1087 (filed as William I, King of England, 1027?–1087)

Leo of Rozmital
Leo I, the Great, Saint, Pope
Leo X, Pope
Leo S. Rowe Pan American Fund
Leo, Saint, Pope Leo I, *see* Leo I, the Great, Saint, Pope (filed as Leo I, Pope)
Leo Sibrandus
Leo the Great, Pope, *see* Leo I, the Great, Saint, Pope (filed as Leo I, Pope)

Same headings in new form (filing order same):

Charles, Count of Valois
Charles, Duke of Burgundy
Charles, Duke of Orléans, Count of Angoulême
Charles the Bold, *see* Charles, Duke of Burgundy

William, Father
William I, King of England, 1027?–1087
William, of Newburgh
William the Conqueror, *see* William I, King of England, 1027?–1087

Leo of Rozmital
Leo I, Pope
Leo X, Pope
Leo S. Rowe Pan American Fund
Leo, Saint, Pope Leo I, *see* Leo I, Pope
Leo Sibrandus
Leo the Great, Pope, *see* Leo I, Pope

4. Disregard a second given name or family name that comes *between* a numeral and a designation and alphabet by the designation; but if the second name *precedes* the numeral, consider as a compound given name and alphabet by the second name. In the case of a second name between a numeral and a designation, references should be provided as needed from the form without the numeral between the two names.

Examples:

Gustaf Adolf, crown prince of Sweden
Gustaf Adolf, King of Sweden
    Kings of Sweden with this name are entered in a single numerical
sequence together with all kings of Sweden with the first name Gustaf,
e. g.,
    Gustaf I Vasa, King of Sweden, 1496–1560
    Gustaf II Adolf, King of Sweden, 1594–1632
    Gustaf III, King of Sweden, 1746–1792
Gustaf-Janson, Gösta
Gustaf I Vasa, King of Sweden
Gustaf II Adolf, King of Sweden
Gustaf III, King of Sweden
Gustaf, Prince of Sweden and Norway
Gustaf Vasa, King of Sweden
    ⌊Same reference as under Gustaf Adolf above⌋

Victor Chemical Works
Victor Emmanuel II, King of Italy
Victor Emmanuel III, King of Italy
Victor Gaunt, master spy

B. Filing position of given name entries and order of entries under the same given name

1. Arrange all given name entries, both single and compound, after the single surname entries of the same name, interfiling alphabetically in the group of titles, etc. beginning with the same word. Alphabet with regard to all designations and words, articles and prepositions included (following the General rules in 25A above for choice of key word in certain instances), and disregard punctuation. If a given name heading and a different type of entry are identical (except that the name heading may include dates), the name heading precedes the other entry (cf. "I-ching" example, p. 85, and old-form Charlemagne example, p. 163).

2. When an ordinal numeral follows a given name in a title entry, arrange it as spoken (according to Rule 9C). This separates a title from the formal headings for the name, but places it with titles in which the number is spelled out.

Comprehensive examples for Rule 25:

Charles, David
Charles, Prof.
Charles, William
Charles, *see* Livry, Charles, marquis de
Charles   [title]
Charles A. Bennett Company, inc., Peoria, Ill.
Charles, abbé
Charles Ann, Sister
Charles Auchester   [title]
Charles, Brother
Charles City, Iowa
Charles, Count of Valois
Charles de Blois
Charles, Duke of Burgundy
Charles II, Duke of Lorraine
Charles IV, Duke of Lorraine
Charles, Duke of Orléans, Count of Angoulême
Charles II, Duke of Parma
Charles Edward, the Young Pretender
Charles V, Emperor of Germany
CHARLES FAMILY
Charles III, King of France
Charles I, King of Great Britain
Charles II, King of Great Britain
Charles X Gustavus, King of Sweden
Charles XII, King of Sweden
Charles XIV John, King of Sweden and Norway
The Charles men
CHARLES (NAME)
Charles of Sezze, Saint
Charles Ier empereur d'Autriche   [title] [Ier = premier]
Charles, pseud., *see* Rondeau, Charles
Charles-Roux, François
Charles Stewart Mott Foundation, Flint, Mich.
Charles the Bold, *see* Charles, Duke of Burgundy
Charles the Second   [title]
Charles II and his court   [Charles the second]

Charles II and Madame Carwell
Charles the Twelfth   [title]
CHARLES W. MORGAN (SHIP)

Homer, Winslow
Homer
Homer and history

AUTHOR ENTRY ARRANGEMENT
(RULES 26–27)

Introductory notes

DIFFERENT METHODS OF ARRANGEMENT

There are two different basic arrangements for titles under an author: (1) alphabetical by title page titles, or (2) organized, in which the collected works and selections are grouped and all editions and translations of a particular work are brought together. A library may apply either order consistently in all cases, or it may adopt a selective combination of the two. Arrangement of all works by title page title is suitable only for a small collection with relatively few titles under an author. An organized arrangement should be introduced in situations where the alphabetic order becomes difficult to consult because of the number and character of the titles, editions, translations, etc., as under classic and voluminous authors, and where the collection is used for research purposes.

Rule 26 covers the basic alphabetic arrangement under an author entry, including general rules that are applicable in Rule 27 also.

Rule 27 covers all situations where a uniform title is applied in order to secure a special organized arrangement of the titles, editions and translations.

EDITIONS

Libraries have varied widely in methods of arranging editions of the same title. Some of the systems in use are as follows:

1) Scientific, technical, and other factual material—by date, often in reverse order with latest edition first
2) Belles-lettres—alphabetical by name of publisher, editor, translator, illustrator, series, etc., either consistently by one of them or by whichever is most appropriate in a particular case
3) All types of material by date of publication, either with earliest date first or with latest date first

113

The following rules recommend the chronological order for all types of material, for the following reasons: (1) a uniform treatment of editions throughout the catalog is desirable, (2) arrangement by date is more precise (the other methods involve individual judgment decisions), (3) the pattern of arrangement will be more readily discernible to the user, and (4) it is the easiest and least complicated for the filer. The straight rather than the reverse order of dates is recommended because (1) it is the more normal sequence, (2) it is the order found in the Library of Congress printed catalogs, and (3) in this order, when analytics are interfiled with editions of the work they will normally not precede entries for the original edition of the work as a separate publication, as they would tend to do with dates in reverse order. This system will be more effective, especially in public libraries where many copies are added, if reprint dates are disregarded in cataloging, unless for bibliographical reasons the library actually wants each reprint filed separately.

26. General arrangement under author

Preliminary note. This rule applies to all types of author entries—personal names, corporate names, place names, uniform titles and periodical titles used as headings, etc.

A. Basic rule. Under an author heading arrange different kinds of entries in groups in the following order:

    1) Works *by* the author, subarranged alphabetically by their titles

    2) Works *about* the author, without subdivision, subarranged alphabetically by their main entries; except subject entries for individual works, which are arranged in group 1 immediately after the author entries for the same work (see 26B12 below)

    3) Works *about* the author, with subdivision, subarranged alphabetically by the subdivisions

B. Works *by* the author

1. Titles. Alphabet the titles according to the basic rules for alphabetical arrangement as they may apply. File titles for complete and selected works in their alphabetical places with other titles, by their title page titles.

Example:

    Hawthorne, Nathaniel
        The American notebooks.
        Complete short stories.
        Complete writings.
        Fanshawe.
        Hawthorne; edited by Bliss Perry.
        The scarlet letter.
        Selected tales and sketches.

Twice-told tales.
Works.

For special arrangements under classic and voluminous authors, see Rule 27; for music uniform titles, see Rule 37B.

2. Main and added entries. Interfile all main and added entries under the same author heading in one file. Subarrange alphabetically by the titles of the books. On added entries, disregard an author main entry, but alphabet by a title main entry; also, disregard a uniform title when there is one and alphabet by the title page title. Examples follow 26B3 below.

3. Designations following heading. In both main and added entry headings <u>disregard</u> designations that show the relationship of the heading to one particular work, as "comp.," "ed.," "illus.," "tr.," "joint author ɾeditor," etc.ɿ, "appellant," "defendant," "plaintiff," "praeses," "supposed author," "Spurious and doubtful works," etc. "Joint author ɾeditor," etc.ɿ and the last two will no longer be used according to the *Anglo-American Cataloging Rules*, but "supposed artist ɾlithographer," etc.ɿ will be used.

Examples for 26B2–3:

Pennell, Joseph, 1857–1926
    The adventures of an illustrator.

    Pennell, Joseph, 1857–1926, illus
Van Rennselaer, Mariana Griswold
    English cathedrals . . .

Pennell, Joseph, 1857–1926
    Etchers and etching . . .

    Pennell, Joseph, 1857–1926, joint author
Pennell, Elizabeth Robins
    The life of James McNeill Whistler.

    Pennell, Joseph, 1857–1926, illus.
Dark, Sidney
    London.

Pennell, Joseph, 1857–1926
    Our journey to the Hebrides.

American Society for Metals
    Age hardening of metals.

    American Society for Metals
French, Herbert James
    Alloy construction steels.

American Society for Metals
    Atom movements.

Beecher, Henry Ward, 1813–1887
  Norwood; or, Village life in New England.
Beecher, Henry Ward, 1813–1887, defendant
  Official report of the trial of Henry Ward Beecher.
Beecher, Henry Ward, 1813–1887
  Oration at the raising of "The old flag" at Sumter.

  Beecher, Henry Ward, 1813–1887
Our martyr President, Abraham Lincoln.   Voices from the pulpit of New
  York and Brooklyn.

Beecher, Henry Ward, 1813–1887
  Past perils and the perils of today.

  Landsberg, Helmut, 1906–   ed.
Advances in geophysics.

Landsberg, Helmut, 1906–
  Physical climatology.

  Hanson, Howard
American music for string orchestra.

Hanson, Howard
  ⌈Concerto, piano, op. 36, G major⌉
  Hanson, Howard
Gershwin, George
  ⌈Works, instrumental. Selections⌉ Phonodisc.
  Curtain up!   George Gershwin favorites.
    Howard Hanson, conductor of some of the works.

Hanson, Howard
  ⌈Symphony, no. 5, op. 43⌉

  Hanson, Howard
Kennan, Kent Wheeler
  ⌈Works, instrumental. Selections⌉ Phonodisc.
  Three pieces for orchestra.
    Howard Hanson, conductor.

  Hanson, Howard
    Works, instrumental. Selections. Phonodisc.
Americana for solo winds and string orchestra.

4. Same title in a main and added entry. If under an author heading the
title is the same in a main entry for a work by that author and in an added
entry under that author's name for a work by another author, or there is more
than one added entry with the same title by different authors, arrange the
entries for that title under the name as main entry first, followed by the added
entries arranged first by the title, then alphabetically by their main entries,
then, under the same main entry, chronologically by date.

Examples:

Browning, Robert, 1812–1889
    Pippa passes.
    Poems. ₍all editions₎

Browning, Robert, 1812–1889, comp.
Browning, Elizabeth Barrett
    Poems, selected and arranged by Robert Browning. 1892.

Browning, Robert, 1812–1889, comp.
Browning, Elizabeth Barrett
    Poems; selected and arranged by Robert Browning. ₍c1893₎

Browning, Robert, 1812–1889
    Pompilia.

U. S. National Science Foundation
    Organization of the Federal Government for scientific activities.

U. S. National Science Foundation
Conference on Training Science Information Specialists, Georgia Institute
   of Technology, 1961–1962
    Proceedings.

U. S. National Science Foundation
National Coastal and Shallow Water Research Conference
    Proceedings.

U. S. National Science Foundation
Symposium on Engineering Applications of Random Function Theory and
   Probability
    Proceedings.

U. S. National Science Foundation
    Programs for education in the sciences.

5. Shorter title before longer. Arrange different titles that begin with the same words by the title proper, the shorter title before the longer, disregarding any subtitle, alternative title, etc. that may follow the shorter title. Also disregard an author phrase ("by" or "of" followed by the author's name) when it appears after the title of the book in the body of the entry, even when it includes more than one name or is different in different editions of the work.

Examples:

Auslander, Joseph
    The winged horse; the story of the poets and their poetry.
    The winged horse anthology.

Kyne, Peter Bernard
    Cappy Ricks; or, The subjugation of Matt Peasley.
    Cappy Ricks comes back.

Nelson, Oscar Severine
    Accounting systems, by Oscar S. Nelson and Arthur D. Maxwell.
    Accounting systems and data processing ₍by₎ Oscar S. Nelson ₍and₎
Richard S. Woods.

Lamb, Charles
    The works of Charles Lamb.   ⎫
    The works of Charles and Mary Lamb. ⎬ File both as simply Works
                                        ⎭

Sherwood, John F.
    College accounting, by J. F. Sherwood, A. B. Carson ₍and₎ Clem Bol-
ing. 6th ed. ₍c1957₎
    College accounting, by A. B. Carson, J. F. Sherwood ₍and₎ Clem Bol-
ing. 7th ed. ₍1962₎

6. Author's name at beginning of title. At the beginning of a title the author's name, even in the possessive case, should be disregarded if it is simply
an author statement transcribed from the work. A joint author statement in
the possessive should also be disregarded (e. g., Mary and Russel Wright's
Guide to easier living). However, if the name in the possessive case is the
author's pseudonym, or if an author's name is an integral part of the title, do
not disregard it in filing. Do not disregard a name other than the author's. In
cases where the name is to be disregarded in filing it is suggested that some
local device, such as pencilled angle brackets ($<$ $>$), be employed to indicate this to the filers.

Examples:

Barlow, Peter
    An essay on magnetic attraction.
    $<$Barlow's$>$ tables of squares, cubes, square roots . . .
    A treatise on the strength of timber . . .

Shakespeare, William
    Selections from Shakespeare.
    The Shakespeare apocrypha.
    Shakespeare's wit and humor.
    Three tragedies.

Cicero, Marcus Tullius
    Cicero on oratory and orators.
    De re publica.
    $<$Cicero$>$ De senectute.
    $<$Cicero's$>$ epistles to Atticus.
    $<$M. Tulli Ciceronis$>$ Orationes.
    Orations of Cicero.
    $<$Cicero:$>$ select letters.
    $<$Cicéron:$>$ Traité du destin.

Croly, Jane Cunningham
    The history of the woman's club movement in America.
    Jennie Juneiana: talks on women's topics.
    Jennie June's American cookery book.   [pseudonym]
    Knitting and crochet.

    Beck, Frederick K   , joint author
Beck, Neill
    The Farmers Market cookbook.

Beck, Frederick K
    The Fred Beck wine book.
Beck, Frederick K
    73 years in a sand trap.   [seventy-three]

Lindsay, Howard
    Clarence Day's Life with father.
    The Great Sebastians.

Lawrence, Robert
    Carmen.
    Gilbert and Sullivan's H. M. S. Pinafore.
    Gilbert and Sullivan's The Gondoliers.
    Gilbert and Sullivan's The Mikado
    Haensel and Gretel.

There are times when a name other than the author's in the possessive case at the beginning of a particular title must be regarded on all entries, main and secondary, for that title except an added entry, i. e., when the added entry heading begins with the same name as the name in the possessive case in the title. In this situation, the angle brackets are added only on the added entry card.

Example:

Jordan, Emil Leopold
    Family circle's pictorial guide to national parks.
    Hammond's Guide to nature hobbies.
    Hammond's Nature atlas of America.
    Hammond's pictorial travel atlas of scenic America.
    Panorama do Brazil.

Hammond (C. S.) and Company
    Great cities of the world.

    Hammond (C. S.) and Company
Jordan, Emil Leopold
    <Hammond's> Guide to nature hobbies.

119

> Hammond (C. S.) and Company
Shepherd, William Robert
> Historical atlas.

> Hammond (C. S.) and Company
Jordan, Emil Leopold
> <Hammond's> Nature atlas of America.

> Hammond (C. S.) and Company
> <Hammond's> pictorial atlas of the world.

> Hammond (C. S.) and Company
Jordan, Emil Leopold
> <Hammond's> pictorial travel atlas of scenic America.

> Hammond (C. S.) and Company
> Reference atlas of the world.

7. Translations. Arrange each translation alphabetically by its own title.

Example:

> Mann, Thomas
> Joseph in Egypt.
> The magic mountain (Der Zauberberg)
> A man and his dog.
> La montagne magique (Der Zauberberg)
> Young Joseph.
> Der Zauberberg.

For the method of arranging translations immediately after the original title by language (by means of uniform titles), see Rule 27D.

8. Editions published under different titles. Arrange each edition or issue of a work that is published under a different title alphabetically by its own title.

Examples:

> Maugham, W. Somerset
> The circle.

> Fools and their folly.
> Originally published under title: Then and now.

> The moon and sixpence.

> Then and now.
> Later published under title: Fools and their folly.

> The trembling of a leaf.

> Cooke, Nelson Magor
> Basic mathematics for electronics. 2d ed. 1960.
> First ed. published in 1942 under title: Mathematics for electricians and radiomen.

Electronics dictionary.

Mathematics for electricians and radiomen. 1st ed. 1942.
    Second ed. published in 1960 under title: Basic mathematics for electronics.

For the method of arranging editions published under different titles under one uniform title, see Rule 27B.

9. Editions with the same title

cf. *Introductory notes* to this section, p. 113, Editions.

a. Basic rule. Arrange editions of all types of material, both factual and belles-lettres, that have the same title, in straight chronological order by dates of publication, with earliest date first, disregarding any subtitles or edition numbers.

Example:

Briscoe, Herman Thompson
    General chemistry for colleges. ɾc1935ɿ
    General chemistry for colleges. ɾc1938ɿ
    General chemistry for colleges. 3d ed. ɾ1943ɿ
    General chemistry for colleges. 4th ed. ɾ1949ɿ

For the arrangement of editions of the work as a separate in relation to other kinds of entries for the same work, see 26B13 below and Comprehensive examples for 26B9–13, p. 129–31.

(1) When there are two or more entries with the same date, subarrange first alphabetically by place of publication, then by publisher, then by number of volumes, special edition, etc.

(2) An edition without date (i. e., "n. d.") precedes the editions with dates. Arrange incomplete dates before complete dates in their relative place in the sequence. Regard only the first date in an imprint with inclusive dates for volumes. If the imprint has both a publication and a copyright date, use the publication date (e. g., for 1946 ɾc1945ɿ, use 1946). Disregard question marks and "c" for copyright. Example:

n. d.		1929	
1882	⎫ Disregard –88	193–?	
1882–88	⎭ and interfile	1930	
1899		1935	
19—?		1941	⎫ Interfile
1900		1941?	⎭

(3) **Facsimile reproductions.** Arrange entries for facsimile reproductions under the original date of publication, not under the date of reproduction. These entries follow the entry for the original work if there is one, but precede other editions of the work. If there are two or more entries for reproductions, subarrange them chronologically by their own dates of publication.

Example:

Sturt, Charles

> Two expeditions into the interior of southern Australia, during the years 1828, 1829, 1830, and 1831; with observations on the soil, climate, and general resources of the colony of New South Wales. London, Smith, Elder, 1833. ₍Adelaide, Public Library of South Australia, 1963₎ (Australiana facsimile editions, no. 4)

> Two expeditions into the interior of southern Australia, during the years 1828, 1829, 1830, and 1831; with observations on the soil, climate, and general resources of the colony of New South Wales. 2d ed. London, Smith, Elder, 1834.

b. Variations in wording. Slight variations in the wording of the title proper must be regarded. The presence of a subtitle, and variations in wording of subtitles, are disregarded, except when the subtitles show that the works are entirely different.

Examples:

Different main title:

Schultz, William John

> American public finance. 2d rev. ed. 1938.
>> Previous editions have title: American public finance and taxation.

> American public finance. 3d ed. 1942.
> American public finance and taxation. 1931.
> American public finance and taxation. Rev. ed. 1934.
>> Later edition has title: American public finance.

Subtitle disregarded:

Essipoff, Marie Armstrong

> Making the most of your food freezer; new ideas, new techniques, new recipes. ₍1951₎
> Making the most of your food freezer. ₍1954₎
> Making the most of your food freezer. Rev. and enl. by Edwina Jackson. ₍1961₎

Subtitle regarded:

Finney, Harry Anson

> Principles of accounting. 3d ed. 1946.
>> Contents: ₍1₎ Intermediate. ₍2₎ Advanced.

> Principles of accounting. 4th ed. 1951–52.
> Principles of accounting. 5th ed. ₍1958₎–60.
> Principles of accounting, introductory. 3d ed. 1948.
> Principles of accounting, introductory. 4th ed. 1953.
> Principles of accounting, introductory. 5th ed. 1957.

c. More than one work in book. If the book contains more than one work the entry is considered an edition of the first work named, e. g.,

>O'Neill, Eugene Gladstone
>>The Emperor Jones, Diff'rent, The straw.　ɾc1921ı

is filed as a 1921 edition of "The Emperor Jones."

>Stevenson, Robert Louis
>>Treasure Island and Kidnapped.　ɾn. d.ı

is filed as a "no date" edition of "Treasure Island."

>Browning, Robert
>>The pied piper of Hamelin, and other poems.　ɾc1897ı

is filed as an 1897 edition of "The pied piper of Hamelin."

d. Special feature variations

Preliminary note. The following rules cover details of the arrangement of entries that are the same in all of the essential elements to be regarded, but have some special feature.

(1) **Abridged edition.** When everything else that is to be regarded is the same, file an abridged edition after the unabridged work.

Example.

>Homer
>>The Odyssey of Homer; translated by George Herbert Palmer.　Boston, Houghton, Mifflin ɾc1891ı
>>The Odyssey of Homer; translated by George Herbert Palmer. Abridged school ed.　Boston, Houghton, Mifflin ɾc1891ı

If the imprint dates are different, the abridged edition is arranged in its chronological place by date.

Example:

>Toynbee, Arnold Joseph
>>A study of history.　1934–
>>A study of history.　Abridgement of volumes I–ɾXı by D. C. Somervell.　1947–57.
>>A study of history.　ɾ1948ı–61.

If the title begins with the word "Abridged," file alphabetically by titles.

Example:

>Rider, John Francis
>>Abridged Perpetual trouble shooter's manual.　ɾc1941–
>>How to use meters.
>>Perpetual trouble shooter's manual.　ɾ1931–

(2) **Bound with.** Arrange an entry with a "Bound with . . ." or "With . . ." note after an identical entry without the note.

Example:

Waters, Clara Erskine Clement
    Charlotte Cushman. Boston, Osgood, 1882.

    Charlotte Cushman. Boston, Osgood, 1882.
        Bound with Clarke, A. B. The elder and the younger Booth. Boston, 1882.

(3) **Reprints.** If imprint dates are the same, arrange an entry for a work reprinted as a separate after the entry for the original publication. If a monograph is cataloged both as a volume of a set, with analytical cards, and as a separate, the entry for the analytic precedes the entry for the separate, and both precede the entry for the same work reprinted as a separate.

Examples:

Conger, Arthur Latham   [analytic for original publication]
    President Lincoln as war statesman. [Madison, 1916]
    p. [105]–140. (The State Historical Society of Wisconsin. Separate no. 172)

Conger, Arthur Latham   [reprint published separately]
    President Lincoln as war statesman. [Madison, 1916]
    35p.
        Reprinted from Separate no. 172. State Historical Society of Wisconsin.

Browning, Orville Hickman   [analytic for original publication]
    The diary of Orville Hickman Browning. Springfield, Ill., Trustees of the Illinois State Historical Library, 1925.
    101p. (Collections of the Illinois State Historical Library v. XX, Lincoln series, v. II)

Browning, Orville Hickman   [original publication cataloged as separate]
    The diary of Orville Hickman Browning. Springfield, Ill., Trustees of the Illinois State Historical Library, 1925.
    101p. (Collections of the Illinois State Historical Library v. XX, Lincoln series, v. II)

Browning, Orville Hickman   [reprint published separately]
    The diary of Orville Hickman Browning. Springfield, Ill., Trustees of the Illinois State Historical Library, 1925.
    101p.
        Reprinted from the Collections of the Illinois State Historical Library vol. XX, Lincoln series, vol. II.

(4) **Special edition.** Arrange an entry for a special edition, such as Limited,

124

Large paper, etc., after an identical entry for the trade edition. If imprint dates are different the special edition is arranged in its chronological place by date.

Example:

Beebe, Lucius Morris
> Rio Grande: mainline of the Rockies, by Lucius Beebe & Charles Clegg.   Berkeley, Calif., Howell-North, 1962.

> Rio Grande: mainline of the Rockies, by Lucius Beebe and Charles Clegg.   Berkeley, Calif., Howell-North, 1962.
>> "Of this limited, Timberline edition twelve hundred and fifty copies have been printed and signed by the authors."

(5) **Thesis edition.** When they have the same dates of publication, arrange a thesis edition before other editions.

Example:

Shoup, Carl Sumner
> The sales tax in France.   New York, Columbia University Press, 1930. Thesis (PH.D.)–Columbia University, 1930.

> The sales tax in France.   New York, Columbia University Press, 1930. Issued also as thesis (PH.D.) Columbia University.

(6) **Volumes** When everything is the same except number of volumes, arrange numerically by number of volumes, the lesser number of physical volumes first (e. g., 309 p., 2 v., 3 v.; 2 v. in 1, 2 v.; 2 v., 4 v. in 2, 3 v.).

Example:

Thompson, Benjamin Franklin
> History of Long Island, from its discovery and settlement to the present time.   3d ed. rev. and greatly enl. with additions and a biography of the author by Charles J. Werner.   New York, Dodd, 1918.   3 v.

> History of Long Island, from its discovery and settlement to the present time.   3d ed. rev. and greatly enl. with additions and a biography of the author by Charles J. Werner.   New York, Dodd, 1918.   4 v.

10. Author-title added entries. Arrange an author-title added entry by the title in the heading. If there are no main entries for the work in the catalog, file a secondary author-title heading in its alphabetical place, where the author-title main entries would be if there were any. If there are main entries for the work, arrange the author-title added entries after them, subarranged alphabetically by their main entries.

Note. On Library of Congress cards an author-title heading is traced with the title following immediately after the author's name and some libraries type the heading in that form. The filers should be cautioned that such a title is to be treated as a title, not as a subheading of the author's name. Some librarians insert a "slash" (/) between the author and title in the heading as an indication to the filers. In the examples in these rules the title is given on the line below the author, indented, and this form is recommended, as it facilitates the interpretation of the card for both filing and use.

Examples:

Christoflour, Raymond

  Christoforo Armeno
    Peregrinaggio di tre giovani.
Hodges, Elizabeth Jamison
  Serendipity tales.

Christoforo Armeno
  Die Reise der drei Söhne des Königs von Serendippo.

Homer
    The Odyssey. ₁all editions₁

  Homer
    The Odyssey.
Beny, Roloff
    A time of gods; a photographer in the wake of Odysseus. Quotations from Chapman's Homer . . .

  Homer
    The Odyssey.
Kazantzakēs, Nikos
    The odyssey: a modern sequel.   Translation into English verse . . .

Homer
    The story of Odysseus.

For the arrangement of author-title added entries in relation to other kinds of entries for the same work, see also 26B13 below and Comprehensive examples for 26B9–13, p. 129–31.

11. Analytical entries

Note. Author analytics are made in different forms depending on whether the part analyzed is an independent work, whether it has a separate title page, whether it is paged continuously with other matter in the volume, and whether the catalog entry for the work includes a reference to the part. The forms most commonly used are:

  1) a full unit card with a series note or analytical note beginning with the word "In"

  2) a regular author and title entry with or without an imprint for the part, with no collation, followed by an analytical note beginning with the word "In"

3) the author of the analytic added on the top line of a unit card connected by a line to the title of the analytic wherever it appears
4) a simple added entry for the author (used when the catalog entry includes a reference to the part)
5) an author-title added entry (see *Note* under 26B10 above for comment on form)

Forms 4 and 5 will cause some problems in filing. In form 4, unless the title of the part is added in the heading or indicated wherever it appears on the card, the entry will be arranged by the title of the main work, since an added entry is subarranged by the title of the book. Form 5 is indistinguishable from an author-title added entry that is used to show some connection of one work with another. Because the filers cannot be expected to differentiate between author-title added entries that are analytics and those that show relationships between different works, it is recommended that all entries made in that form be interfiled. The result will be that some analytical entries will appear among the separate editions of the work while others will be found following all editions of the work (see 26B13 below).

Arrange an author analytic by the title of the analytic. If there are no main entries for the work in the catalog, file an author analytic in its alphabetical place, where the author-title main entries would be if there were any. If there is more than one such analytic, subarrange the entries chronologically by the imprint dates of the books. If there are main entries for the work, interfile analytics not made in the form of author-title added entries with them, sub-arranged chronologically by the imprint dates of the books. Arrange analytics made in the form of author-title added entries after main entries for the work, the analytics subarranged by their main entries.

Examples:

Jonson, Ben
> Epicoene.

> Every man in his humour; a comedy in five acts; altered from Ben Jonson, by David Garrick.
> (In The London stage. London ₁1824–27₁ v. 3)

> Every man in his humour; a comedy, in five acts . . . London, G. H. Davidson ₁n. d.₁
> 68 p. 15 cm. (In Cumberland's British theatre. London ₁1827–44₁ v. 10)

> Every man in his humour; a comedy, in five acts.
> (In The British drama. Philadelphia, 1850. v. 2)

> Every man out of his humour.

O'Neill, Eugene Gladstone
    The Emperor Jones, Diff'rent, The straw.   New York, Boni and Live-
right ᵣc1921ᵢ

    The Emperor Jones.
    (In Quinn, A. H.   Contemporary American plays.   ᵣc1923ᵢ)

    The Emperor Jones; with eight illus. by Alexander King.   1928.

Shakespeare, William, 1564–1616
    Hamlet.   ᵣall editionsᵢ

    Shakespeare, William, 1564–1616
        Hamlet.
Grebanier, Bernard D   N
    The heart of Hamlet: the play Shakespeare wrote, with the text of
the play as edited by Professor Grebanier.

    Shakespeare, William, 1564–1616
        Hamlet.
Wilson, Marion Leonardine
    The tragedy of Hamlet told by Horatio . . . with the full text of Shake-
speare's Hamlet.
Shapespeare, William, 1564–1616
    Henry IV.

For the arrangement of author analytics in relation to other kinds of entries
for the same work, see also 26B13 below and Comprehensive examples for
26B9–13, p. 129–31.

12. Author-title subject entries. Arrange an author-title subject entry by
the title in the heading. If there are no author entries for the work in the catalog, file an author-title subject entry in its alphabetical place, where the author
entries would be if there were any. If there are author entries for the work,
arrange author-title subject entries after them, subarranged alphabetically by
their main entries.

    Note. See *Note* under 26B10 above for comment on form of these
headings.

Examples:
Melville, Herman, 1819–1891
    The letters of Herman Melville.

    MELVILLE, HERMAN, 1819–1891
        MARDI.
Davis, Merrell R
    Melville's Mardi, a chartless voyage.

Melville, Herman, 1819–1891
    Moby Dick.

Homer
    The Odyssey. ⌞all editions⌟

    HOMER
       THE ODYSSEY.
Harrison, Jane Ellen
    Myths of the Odyssey in art and literature.

    HOMER
       THE ODYSSEY.
Taylor, Charles Henry.
    Essays on the Odyssey, selected modern criticism.
Homer
    The story of Odysseus.

For the arrangement of author-title subject entries in relation to other kinds of entries for the same work, see also 26B13 below and Comprehensive examples for 26B9–13, below.

13. Different kinds of entries for the same title. Arrange different kinds of entries for the same title under an author in groups in the following order:

    1) Main entries for editions of the work as a separate and analytical entries that are not made in the form of an author-title added entry,[31] interfiled and subarranged by imprint dates. If a main entry and an analytical entry for the same work included in another publication have the same imprint date, arrange the main entry first.

    2) Author-title added entries and author analytics made in the form of author-title added entries,[31] interfiled and subarranged alphabetically by their main entries

    3) Author-title subject entries, subarranged alphabetically by their main entries

Comprehensive examples for 26B9–13:[32]
    O'Neill, Eugene Gladstone
       Anna Christie.
       (In his The hairy ape, Anna Christie, The first man. ⌞c1922⌟)

       "Anna Christie"; with twelve illus. by Alexander King. 1930.

       Anna Christie.
       (In Mantle, R. B. A treasury of the theatre. 1935)

       O'Neill, Eugene Gladstone[33]
          Anna Christie.
    Merrill, Bob
       ⌞New girl in town. Libretto. English⌟
       New girl in town; a new musical (based on the play Anna Christie, by Eugene O'Neill) ⌞c1958⌟

31, 32, 33. For footnotes 31–33, see p. 130.

O'Neill, Eugene Gladstone
The Emperor Jones. Cincinnati, Stewart Kidd Co. ₍c1921₎

The Emperor Jones, Diff'rent, The straw. New York, Boni and Live-
right ₍c1921₎

The Emperor Jones.
(In Quinn, A. H. Contemporary American plays. ₍c1923₎)

The Emperor Jones; with eight illus. by Alexander King. 1928.

The Emperor Jones, Anna Christie, The hairy ape. ₍c1937₎

Homer
The Odyssey of Homer. Translated by Alexander Pope. 1771.

Odyssey.
(In Chalmers, Alexander, ed. The works of the English poets. London, 1810)

The Odyssey of Homer. Translated by Alexander Pope. ₍1822₎
Odyssey; translated into English blank verse, by William Cullen
Bryant. 10th ed. ₍c1871₎
Odyssey; done into English prose, by S. H. Butcher and A. Lang.
Boston, Lothrop, 1882.
Odyssey; with introd., notes, etc. by W. W. Merry. 3d ed. Oxford,
Clarendon Press, 1882–88. 2 v.
The Odyssey of Homer, translated by Alexander Pope, with notes and
introd. by Theodore Alois Buckley. ₍189–₎
The Odyssey of Homer; translated by George Herbert Palmer.
₍c1891₎
The Odyssey of Homer; translated by S. H. Butcher and A. Lang;
with introd., notes and illus. New York, Collier ₍c1909₎ (The Harvard
classics, v. 22)   ₍analytic—unit card₎
The Odyssey of Homer, book XI. Edited with introd., notes, vocabu-
lary, and appendices by J. A. Nairn. 1924.
The Odyssey of Homer, translated by George Herbert Palmer, with
illus. by N. C. Wyeth. Cambridge, Houghton, Mifflin, 1929.
The Odyssey of Homer; translated into English verse by Herbert
Bates. School ed. New York, Harper, 1929.
The Odyssey of Homer, done into English prose by S. H. Butcher
and A. Lang. New York, Modern Library ₍1929₎
The Odyssey ₍by₎ Homer, including also passages from Homer's Iliad,
also Norse legends and American Indian legends. ₍1942₎
The Odyssey of Homer. ₍c1951₎

---

31. See 26B11 *Note* above for the forms in which analytics are made.
32. For additional examples of author analytics and author-title added entries see Shakespeare example, p. 140–48.
33. For the arrangement of this entry when made in the form of an explanatory reference, see Rule 37B11.
Note. References to footnotes 31–33 are on p. 129.

The Odyssey.   Translated by Robert Fitzgerald.   With drawings by
Hans Erni.   [1963]

> Homer
>> The Odyssey.

Beny, Roloff
> A time of gods; a photographer in the wake of Odysseus.   Quotations
> from Chapman's Homer . . .   [1962]

> Homer
>> The Odyssey.

Kazantzakēs, Nikos
> The odyssey: a modern sequel.   Translation into English verse . . .
> by Kimon Friar . . .   1958.

> HOMER
>> THE ODYSSEY.

Harrison, Jane Ellen
> Myths of the Odyssey in art and literature.

> HOMER
>> THE ODYSSEY.

Taylor, Charles Henry
> Essays on the Odyssey, selected modern criticism.

Homer
> The story of Odysseus.
> The toils and travels of Odysseus.

C. Works *about* the author

1. Arrange the subject entries for works *about* the author after all entries
for works *by* the author, in two groups in the following order:

1) Subjects without subdivision, subarranged by their main entries, or
   if an analytic, by the entry for the analytic
   Exception: An author-title subject entry files in the author file in its
   alphabetical place by the title in the heading, immediately after the
   author entries for the same title if there are any (see Rule 26B12).

2) Subjects with subdivisions, arranged alphabetically by the subdivisions

Example:

Shakespeare, William, 1564–1616
> The winter's tale.

> SHAKESPEARE, WILLIAM, 1564–1616

Alexander, Peter
> Shakespeare.

> SHAKESPEARE, WILLIAM, 1564–1616

Brandes, Georg Morris Cohen
> William Shakespeare, a critical study.

SHAKESPEARE, WILLIAM, 1564–1616—BIBLIOGRAPHY
SHAKESPEARE, WILLIAM, 1564–1616—CHARACTERS
SHAKESPEARE, WILLIAM, 1564–1616—DICTIONARIES, INDEXES,
ETC.

2. Omission of dates and titles from names. Until December 1964 it was
the practice of the Library of Congress to omit dates of birth and death and,
in at least one instance, the title of position following a name in the heading
for some fifty-one well-known persons when the name was followed by a subheading.[34] Entries with such headings are to be arranged as though the dates
were present, interfiled with headings that have dates. If the omission of a title
following a given name (e. g., NAPOLÉON I—CAMPAIGNS OF 1813–1814) would
change the basic position of the entries, the title must be added.

Examples:

Old-form heading interfiled:
SHAKESPEARE, WILLIAM, 1564–1616—NATURAL HISTORY
SHAKESPEARE, WILLIAM—PLOTS   [old form]
SHAKESPEARE, WILLIAM, 1564–1616—QUOTATIONS

Heading changed to new form:
Napoléon, Joseph Charles Paul Bonaparte, Prince
The Napoleon dynasty
Napoléon I, Emperor of the French, 1769–1821
NAPOLÉON I, EMPEROR OF THE FRENCH, 1769–1821
NAPOLÉON I, EMPEROR OF THE FRENCH, 1769–1821—CAM-
PAIGNS OF 1813–1814
NAPOLÉON I, EMPEROR OF THE FRENCH, 1769–1821—DEATH
AND BURIAL
NAPOLÉON I, EMPEROR OF THE FRENCH, 1769–1821–EGYP-
TIAN CAMPAIGN, 1798–1799
Napoleon, for and against

3. Phrase IN FICTION, DRAMA, POETRY, ETC. When a subject heading consists
of a surname and forename followed by the phrase IN FICTION, DRAMA, POETRY,
ETC., with or without dates after the name, alphabet by the word "IN"
among the other subject subdivisions. Interfile entries with and without
dates.

---

34. American Library Association. Division of Cataloging and Classification. *A. L. A.
Cataloging Rules for Author and Title Entries.* 2d ed. Chicago, American Library Associa-
tion, 1949. Rule 42.
U. S. Library of Congress. Processing Dept. *Cataloging Service.* Washington, D. C.
Bulletin 68, Dec. 1964, p. 1.

Example:

> BURNS, ROBERT, 1759–1796—CHARACTERS
> BURNS, ROBERT, 1759–1796—DRAMA

Interfile ⎰ BURNS, ROBERT, IN FICTION, DRAMA,   ⌊old form⌋
        ⎱   POETRY, ETC.
         ⎰ BURNS, ROBERT, 1759–1796, IN FICTION,   ⌊new form⌋
            DRAMA, POETRY, ETC.
> BURNS, ROBERT, 1759–1796—MUSEUMS, RELICS, ETC.

A subject heading in the form of a phrase consisting of only the surname followed by IN FICTION, DRAMA, POETRY, ETC. must be arranged in the group of titles, etc. following the surname entries. This form is no longer used.

Example:

SHAKESPEARE, WILLIAM, 1564–1616—VERSIFICATION
Shakespeare in America
SHAKESPEARE IN FICTION, DRAMA, POETRY, ETC.   ⌊old form⌋
Shakespeare in his time

27. Organized author arrangement

For music uniform titles, see Rule 37B.

Preliminary notes This rule covers all situations where the uniform title[35] system is applied in order to secure a special organized arrangement of titles, editions, and translations under an author. In the past, each library has had to work out its own system of uniform titles. Now, general guidelines for the establishment of uniform titles are provided, on a permissive basis, in *Anglo-American Cataloging Rules* (Chapter 4). These are summarized for each of the different situations in the filing rules below. The actual method of indicating the uniform title has varied—it may be (1) indicated in the body of the entry by the use of a device such as angle brackets around part of the title that is to be disregarded in filing, (2) written as a corner mark in the upper right corner of the catalog card, or (3) interposed, in brackets, between the heading and the transcription of the title page. The examples given herein follow the form used in the cataloging rules (i. e., uniform title in brackets on line below author), even though such titles will not appear on most Library of Congress cards.[36]

---

35. For definition of uniform title, see Glossary, p. 239. For degree of application of uniform titles, see *Introductory notes* to Rules 26-27, p. 113, Different methods of arrangement.

36. "Uniform titles on Library of Congress cards will be largely confined . . . to editions of laws and of music, and to recordings of music." *Anglo-American Cataloging Rules*, p. 145.

Because methods of arrangement of entries under uniform titles may vary, the cataloging rules do not provide for the inclusion of the complete filing medium in uniform titles under authors (this is done only in the case of the uniform heading Bible, for which see Rule 29). If a library prefers to subarrange editions under a uniform title by date or by editor, translator, etc., rather than by title page title, it may add the date or the key name after the title, in order to facilitate filing. Some libraries add the name of the original language (contrary to the cataloging rules); this has certain advantages for keeping entries for the original language together, which is not otherwise possible in straight alphabetical filing.

Guide cards and explanatory notes should be used generously in the files under authors where special arrangements have been introduced.

A. Basic rules

1. Arrangement of uniform titles. Arrange uniform titles in their alphabetical places among other titles under an author entry.

2. Arrangement of entries under the same uniform title. Under a uniform title arrange the entries alphabetically by title page titles. When there are two or more editions with the same title page title, subarrange them by imprint dates, according to Rule 26B9. For the order of different kinds of entries under a uniform title follow Rule 26B13.

3. References. Arrange author-title references alphabetically by their titles, interfiled with other titles and uniform titles.

B. Editions published under different titles

Note. When the editions (other than revised editions) of a work appear under various titles, one title is selected as the uniform title. The uniform title is included in the entry only when the publication appears under a title different from that chosen for the uniform title.

1. General rule. Under their uniform title arrange editions according to the basic rule, 27A2 above.

2. References. Make author-title references from variants of the title to the uniform title.

Examples for 27B:

Maugham, W. Somerset
    The circle.

    Fools and their folly
    see his Then and now

    The moon and sixpence.

    ʟThen and nowɟ
    Fools and their folly; originally titled "Then and now." New York, Avon Pub. Co. ʟ1949ɟ

Then and now, a novel.   Garden City, N. Y., Doubleday, 1946.

The trembling of a leaf.

Dickens, Charles
    The adventures of Oliver Twist
    see his Oliver Twist

    David Copperfield.

    [Oliver Twist]
    The adventures of Oliver Twist; illustrated by Barnett Freedman.
    [c1939]

    Oliver Twist.
    (In his Works.   [c1911])

    Oliver Twist, containing the twenty-four original illustrations by
    Cruikshank.   [1922]

    Oliver Twist.   [1936]

    Oliver Twist; with illus. from drawings by George Cruikshank, to-
    gether with an introd. by May Lamberton Becker.   1941.

    [Oliver Twist]
    The story of Oliver Twist; retold and illustrated with 178 new pic-
    tures, drawings by Morton H. Cowen.   [c1935]

    Dickens, Charles
        Oliver Twist.
Browne, Muriel
        Oliver Twist, adapted from the novel by Charles Dickens.   c1938.

    DICKENS, CHARLES
        OLIVER TWIST.
Tillotson, Kathleen Mary
        Oliver Twist.

Dickens, Charles
    Pictures from Italy.

    The story of Oliver Twist
    see his Oliver Twist

C. Parts of a work

Note. The uniform title for a separately published part of a work consists of the uniform title of the whole work followed by the title or designation of the part as a subheading. If the publication consists of three or
more parts of the work or of various extracts from it, the subheading is
"Selections."

135

1. General rule. Arrange subheading for parts, including "Selections," in alphabetical order following entries for the title without subheading, interfiled with language subheadings.[37] Disregard an article at the beginning of the name of a part of a work. For examples, see p. 137–38.

2. Numbered parts. If the parts are numbered, arrange them in numerical order, the larger part beginning with the same number preceding the smaller part. Numbered parts follow all entries for the whole work, including all alphabetical subheadings.

Examples of numbered parts:

Churchill, Sir Winston Spencer
    ⌈The second world war. 1. The gathering storm⌉
    ⌈The second world war. 2. Their finest hour⌉
    ⌈The second world war. 3. The Grand Alliance⌉

Homer
    ⌈The Iliad. Spanish⌉
    ⌈The Iliad. Books 1–6⌉
    ⌈The Iliad. Book 1⌉
    ⌈The Iliad. Book 6⌉

3. References. Make an author-title reference from the title of the part to the uniform title for the part. If the title page title is distinctive and different from the title of the part, make an author-title reference from it to the uniform title.

D. Translations

Note. The uniform title for a translation consists of the uniform title of the work, including an individual part when appropriate, followed by the name of the language as a subheading. If the text appears in two or three languages, all are named; if one of them is the original language it is named last. If the text is given in more than three languages, the term "Polyglot" is used.

The name of the original language is not included in the uniform title for texts in the original language, therefore editions of the whole work in

---

37. Some libraries prefer an organized rather than alphabetical arrangement of a uniform title with subheadings for parts and languages. In the organized arrangement entries are arranged in groups as follows:
    1) Whole work—Original language
    2) Selections—Original language
    3) Translations of the whole work, alphabetically by language, each language followed by Selections in that language
    4) Whole work—Subjects
    5) Parts—By title of part or other designation. Under each part subarrange entries the same as under the whole work, 1-4.

the original language will automatically precede translations of the whole work, and editions of a part in the original language will precede translations of the part. However, the heading for selections in the original language will fall among the headings for parts and other languages.

1. General rule. Arrange language subheadings for translations, including "Polyglot," in alphabetical order following entries for the title without subheading, interfiled with subheadings for parts.[38] For examples, see Examples for 27C–E, below.

2. References. Make an author-title reference from the title of the translation, if significantly different from the original, to the uniform title with appropriate language subheading.

E. Author-title secondary entries in relation to subheadings[39]

1. Arrange author-title added entries and author-title subject entries for a whole work immediately after the author entries for the whole work, before any subheadings, the added entries before the subjects.

2. Arrange author-title added entries and author-title subject entries for a part or translation immediately after the author entries for that part or translation, before any further subheadings, the added entries before the subjects.

For examples for 27E, see Examples for 27C–E, below.

Examples for 27C–E:

Maurois, André

    Magiciens et logiciens.   Rudyard Kipling, H. G. Wells . . .   Paris, Grasset ᵣc1935ₗ

  ᵣMagiciens et logiciens. Englishₗ
  Poets and prophets; translated by Hamish Miles.   London, Cassell ᵣ1936ₗ

    American edition has title: Prophets and poets.

  ᵣMagiciens et logiciens. Englishₗ
  Prophets and poets; translated by Hamish Miles. New York, Harper, 1935.

    English edition has title: Poets and prophets.

  Olympio.

  Poets and prophets
  see his Magiciens et logiciens. English

  Portrait d'une actrice.

  Prophets and poets
  see his Magiciens et logiciens. English

---

38. For an organized arrangement of translations, see footnote 37, p. 136.
39. For position of author secondary entries in an organized arrangement, see footnote 37, p. 136.

Chaucer, Geoffrey
    Canterbury tales
    CANTERBURY TALES
    Canterbury tales.   Clerk's tale
    Canterbury tales.   French
    Canterbury tales.   French.   Selections
    Canterbury tales.   The knight's tale
    CANTERBURY TALES.   THE KNIGHT'S TALE
    Canterbury tales.   The knight's tale.   German
    Canterbury tales.   The knight's tale.   German.   Selections
    Canterbury tales.   The knight's tale.   Selections
    Canterbury tales.   Prologue
    Canterbury tales.   Selections
    Canterbury tales.   Shipman's tale
    Canterbury tales.   Turkish
    Canterbury tales.   The wife of Bath's tale

    Clerk's tale
    see his Canterbury tales.   Clerk's tale

    The knight's tale
    see his Canterbury tales.   The knight's tale

    Parlament of foules

    Shipman's tale
    see his Canterbury tales.   Shipman's tale

    Troilus and Criseyde

    The wife of Bath's tale
    see his Canterbury tales.   The wife of Bath's tale

Dante Alighieri
    La divina commedia
    LA DIVINA COMMEDIA
    La divina commedia.   English
    La divina commedia.   English.   Selections
    La divina commedia.   Il paradiso
    LA DIVINA COMMEDIA.   IL PARADISO
    La divina commedia.   Il paradiso.   English
    La divina commedia.   Il paradiso.   I
    La divina commedia.   Polyglot
    La divina commedia.   Portuguese
    La divina commedia.   Purgatorio
    La divina commedia.   Selections
    La divina commedia.   Spanish

F. Collected editions

Note. Uniform titles for collected editions of an author's works are authorized as follows:[40]

1) Works—for complete works
2) Selected works—for partial collections of whole works

    Partial collections will have this uniform title if the book contains three or more separate works, regardless of whether the title page title is a collective title or begins with the title of a single work.

3) Selections—for publications consisting of parts of various works, extracts, quotations, etc.
4) Appropriate collective titles for collections of three or more works in a single literary form

    Categories commonly encountered are Correspondence, Essays, Plays, Poems, Prose works, Sonnets, Speeches.

Translations of collected works are indicated in a uniform title for collections in the same way as for a single work (see 27D above).

1. General rule. Arrange uniform titles of collected editions in their alphabetical places among the titles for single works and author-title references.[41] Arrange language subheadings for translations in alphabetical order following entries for the title without subheading.

2. Added entries. Arrange an entry for the author as added entry alphabetically by the title of the book unless the entry falls into one of the group categories, in which case it should be arranged as an author-title added entry in that group.

Note. Except for musical works, added entries in the tracing on Library of Congress cards do not include a collective uniform title. If a library wishes to file the added entry in a particular group under an organized author, it should add the uniform title that would be appropriate to its own filing scheme, just as is done for added entries for music.

---

40. The full list would be used only when warranted by the amount and character of the material. Group 4 particularly would be omitted when not applicable. A library desiring a simpler grouped·arrangement might combine groups 2 and 3 in one group.

41. It has been rather common practice to place the groups of collected editions before the titles for single works. In that arrangement the order is as follows:

1) Works
2) Selected works
3) Works in a single literary form
4) Selections
5) Single works
6) Works about the author

In such an arrangement there is no satisfactory location for author-title references from title page titles for other than single works. This makes it more difficult to locate a specific collection by title.

139

3. References. Make an author-title reference from the title page title to the uniform title when the title page title is distinctive or significantly different from the uniform title. Arrange the references alphabetically by their titles in the single alphabet of titles under the author heading.

> *Note to 27F1–3.* The arrangement recommended in rules 27F1–3 combines the advantages of both the alphabetical and the grouped arrangements. The collected editions are grouped but at the same time all titles are in one alphabet. It is possible to provide an entry for each specific title of a book in its alphabetical place; if that entry is a reference to a uniform title, the specific title may then be readily found in its alphabetical place under the uniform title.

4. Explanatory note card. A note card should be placed at the beginning of each author file in which the uniform title system is used for collected editions, explaining the arrangement of that particular file.

G. Spurious and doubtful works. Arrange the title of a single doubtful work in its alphabetical place among the other titles. Arrange the title for a collection of doubtful works in the group with the appropriate uniform title. Disregard the author subheadings "Spurious and doubtful works" and "supposed author" when they appear in old headings (these subheadings will not be used in author headings established according to the *Anglo-American Cataloging Rules*). Arrange subject headings with the subdivision SPURIOUS AND DOUBTFUL WORKS among the subject subdivisions. For examples see Comprehensive example below.

Comprehensive example for Rule 27:[42]

> Shakespeare, William, 1564–1616   ⌈note card⌉
>> Collected editions of the works are grouped under the following uniform titles:
>>> Poems—for collections and selections of the poems
>>> Selected works—for partial collections of whole works
>>> Selections—for parts of works, extracts, quotations, etc.
>>> Works—for complete works, including complete dramatic works
>> These uniform titles are filed in their alphabetical places among the titles for single works. References from the specific titles of books lead to the proper uniform title.
>> Editions of single works are arranged under the best-known title, with references from other forms.
>
>> Aphorisms from Shakespeare
>> *see his* Selections
>
>> As you like it.

---

42. Only a few typical examples of references are included. References would also be made from all of the other title page titles to their corresponding uniform titles.

Comedies, histories, & tragedies
see his Works

Doubtful plays
see his Selected works

Shakespeare, William, 1564–1616
British Museum. Dept. of Manuscripts
 Facsimiles of the Shakespeare deed and a leaf of the Sir Thomas
More play in the British Museum. 1964.

Shakespeare, William, 1564–1616
 <Shakespeare's> Hamlet. The first quarto 1603. Reproduced in
facsimile from the copy in the Henry E. Huntington Library. 1931.

 Hamlet, edited for school use by William Allan Neilson. 1903.

 Hamlet.
 (In Gassner, J. A treasury of the theatre. ₁1951₁)

 Hamlet. Additional notes and exercises by W. F. Langford. ₁c1958₁

 ₁Hamlet₁
 Revealment of Hamlet, by Alfred Stoner. ₁1952₁

 ₁Hamlet₁
 The tragedie of Hamlet, Prince of Denmarke; edited . . . by Charlotte
Porter and Helen A. Clarke. ₁c1905₁

 ₁Hamlet₁
 <Shakespeare's> tragedy of Hamlet, Prince of Denmark, edited,
with notes, by William J. Rolfe. ₁1903₁

Shakespeare, William, 1564–1616   ₁analytic₁
 Hamlet.
Grebanier, Bernard D N
 The heart of Hamlet: the play Shakespeare wrote, with the text of the
play as edited by Professor Grebanier. ₁1960₁

Shakespeare, William, 1564–1616   ₁added entry₁
 Hamlet.
MacKaye, Percy
 The mystery of Hamlet, King of Denmark; or, What we will, a tetral-
ogy, in prologue to The tragical historie of Hamlet, Prince of Denmarke,
by William Shakespeare. 1950.

Shakespeare, William, 1564–1616   ₁added entry₁
 Hamlet.
Morris, James M.
 Ghosts of Hamlet, a radio play based upon the setting and scenes of
Hamlet by William Shakespeare.
 (In his Radio workshop plays. 1940)

Shakespeare, William, 1564–1616   [analytic]
 Hamlet.
Wilson, Marion Leonardine
 The tragedy of Hamlet told by Horatio . . . with the full text of Shake-
speare's Hamlet.   c1956.

SHAKESPEARE, WILLIAM, 1564–1616
 HAMLET.
Leavenworth, Russell E
 Interpreting Hamlet.

SHAKESPEARE, WILLIAM, 1564–1616
 HAMLET—BIBLIOGRAPHY.
Wilson, John Dover
 The manuscript of Shakespeare's Hamlet and the problems of its
transmission.

Shakespeare, William, 1564–1616
 [Hamlet. French]
 La tragique histoire de Hamlet prince de Danemark, tr. par Guy de
Pourtalès . . . 1923.

Shakespeare, William, 1564–1616   [analytic]
 Hamlet. French.
Shakespeare, William, 1564–1616
 Roméo et Juliette; Hamlet.   [1958]

SHAKESPEARE, WILLIAM, 1564–1616
 HAMLET—SOURCES.
Gollancz, Sir Israel
 The sources of Hamlet.

Henry IV   [same for V, VI, VIII]
 see his King Henry IV

Julius Caesar. A midsummer-night's dream.   [1942]

King Henry IV.[43]
King Henry IV.   Part I.
King Henry IV.   Part II.
King Henry V.
King Henry VI.
King Henry VIII.

Locrine
see Locrine (Old play)

[Lucrece]
<Shakespeare's> Rape of Lucrece; with preface, glossary, &c. by
Israel Gollancz.   1904.

Shakespeare, William.   Spurious and doubtful works   [old form]
 The passionate pilgrim.

---

43. Arrange all kings in numerical order.

Shakespeare, William, 1564–1616 ⎡new form⎤
The passionate pilgrim

Plays
see his Selected works
Works

Poëmes et sonnets
see his Poems. French and English

Shakespeare, William, 1564–1616 ⎡note card⎤
Poems.
Included under this title are collections and selections of the poems,
including songs.
For the Sonnets alone, and for single poems, see the specific title,
e. g.,
Sonnets
Lucrece

⎡Poems⎤
The love poems of Shakspere; selected and arranged by Ethel
Harris . . . ⎡c1909⎤

<Shakespeare's> poems: Venus and Adonis, Lucrece, Sonnets, etc.
Edited, with notes, by William J. Rolfe. 1890.

⎡Poems⎤
Songs and sonnets. Edited by F. T. Palgrave. 1879.

⎡Poems⎤
<Shakespeare's> Venus and Adonis, Lucrece, and other poems.
Edited, with notes, by William J. Rolfe. 1883.

Shakespeare, William, 1564–1616 ⎡added entry⎤
Poems.
Arne, Thomas Augustine
⎡Works, vocal. Selections⎤
Nine Shakespeare songs. Edited by Percy Young. ⎡1963⎤

SHAKESPEARE, WILLIAM, 1564–1616
POEMS.[44]
Baldwin, Thomas Whitfield
On the literary genetics of Shakspere's poems & sonnets.

Shakespeare, William, 1564–1616
⎡Poems. French and English⎤
Poëmes et sonnets de William Shakespeare, tr. en vers avec le texte
anglais . . . par Ernest Lafond. 1856.

---

44. This heading as used by the Library of Congress is not a true author-title subject but
is an example of the use of a uniform title based on the special filing arrangement for
voluminous authors. In a catalog in which Poems is not a separate group, POEMS would
be treated as a subdivision and the heading filed among the subject subdivisions (see
p. 148), or the word POEMS might be omitted from the subject heading.

Rape of Lucrece
see his Lucrece

Revealment of Hamlet
see his Hamlet

The riddle of Shakespeare's sonnets
see his Sonnets

Shakespeare, William, 1564–1616   ⌐note card⌐
    Selected works.
       Included under this title are partial collections of whole works.

  ⌐Selected works⌐
  Doubtful plays of William Shakespeare . . .   1869.

  ⌐Selected works⌐
  Hamlet, Prince of Denmark, The tempest, The tragedy of King
Richard the Second.   ⌐c1932⌐

  ⌐Selected works⌐
  The high school Shakespeare, ed. by John B. Opdycke.   1931.
                                             ⌐8 plays⌐

  ⌐Selected works⌐
  Plays of Shakespeare, selected and prepared for use in schools, clubs,
classes, and families . . .   1880.

  ⌐Selected works⌐
  The Shakespeare apocrypha . . .   1918.

  ⌐Selected works⌐
  Three tragedies: Julius Caesar, Hamlet, Macbeth . . .   ⌐1965⌐

  ⌐Selected works⌐
  <Shakespeare's> tragedies.   ⌐1906⌐

Shakespeare, William, 1564–1616   ⌐added entry⌐
    Selected works.
Booth, Edwin
  Plays of Edwin Booth; edited by William Winter.   1899.
      Vols. I–II: The Shakespearean plays of Edwin Booth.

  ⌐Selected works. Spanish⌐
  Tres comedias escogidas de Shakespeare, traducidas al castellano
por Celso García Morán.   1924.

Shakespeare, William, 1564–1616   ⌐note card⌐
    Selections.
       Included under this title are collections consisting of parts of vari-
ous works, extracts, quotations, etc.

  ⌐Selections⌐
  Aphorisms from Shakespeare . . .   1812.

ıSelectionsı
The beauties of Shakespeare. By William Dodd. 1821.

Selections from Shakspeare. By Benjamin Oakley. 1828.

ıSelectionsı
Shakespeare's wit and humour, by William A. Lawson. ı1912ı

ıSelectionsı
The Shakespearian dictionary . . . 1832.

ıSelections. Germanı
Shakespeare-Anthologie . . . hrsg. von F. Kreyssig . . . 1864.

The Shakespeare apocrypha
see his Selected works

Shakespeare, William, 1564–1616
Smith, Charles George
Shakespeare's proverb lore; his use of the Sententiae of Leonard Cul-
man and Publilius Syrus. 1963.

Shakespeare, William, 1564–1616
Shakespeare's wit and humour
see his Selections

The Shakespearian dictionary
see his Selections

Songs
see his Poems

ıSonnetsı
The riddle of Shakespeare's sonnets: the text of the sonnets, with in-
terpretive essays by Edward Hubler . . . ı1962ı

The sonnets of Shakespeare and Milton. 1830:

Sonnets and A lover's complaint, edited by Raymond M. Alden. 1913.

Sonnets. Edited by Douglas Bush & Alfred Harbage. ı1961ı

ıSonnetsı
A time scheme for Shakespeare's Sonnets, with a text and short notes
by J. A. Fort. ı1929ı

Shakespeare, William, 1564–1616   ıanalyticı
    Sonnets.
Eagle, Roderick Lewis
    The secrets of the Shakespeare Sonnets. ı1965ı
        Includes facsim. of the 1609 ed. of the Sonnets.

SHAKESPEARE, WILLIAM, 1564–1616
    SONNETS.
Baldwin, Thomas Whitfield
    On the literary genetics of Shakspere's poems & sonnets.

145

Shakespeare, William, 1564–1616
    ɿSonnets. Germanɿ
    Shakespeare Sonnette, umdichtung von Stefan George.   1909.

    ɿSonnets. Spanishɿ
    Sonetos. Ilustraciones de S. Marco.   ɿ1933ɿ

    Tragedies
    see his Selected works

    Tragedy of Hamlet
    see his Hamlet

    The two noble kinsmen
    see Fletcher, John
        The two noble kinsmen

    Venus and Adonis.
    <Shakespeare's> will . . .   1851.
    The winter's tale.

Shakespeare, William, 1564–1616   ɿnote cardɿ
    Works.
       Included under this title are complete works, including complete dramatic works.

    ɿWorksɿ
    <Mr. William Shakespeare's> Comedies, Histories, and Tragedies faithfully reproduced in facsimile from the edition of 1623.   1910.

    ɿWorksɿ
    <Mr. William Shakespeares> comedies, histories, & tragedies.   A facsimile ed. prepared by Helge Kökeritz . . .   1954. ɿFacsim. of 1623 ed.ɿ

    ɿWorksɿ
    <Mr. William Shakespeare's> comedies, histories, and tragedies, faithfully reproduced in facsimile from the edition of 1685.   1904.

    ɿWorksɿ
    The complete dramatic and poetic works of William Shakespeare; edited from the text of the early quartos and the first folio, by William Allan Neilson. ɿc1910ɿ

    ɿWorksɿ
    Knights cabinet edition of the works of William Shakspere.   1851–

    ɿWorksɿ
    A new variorum edition of Shakespeare, edited by Horace Howard Furness.   1871–19

    ɿWorksɿ
    The Oxford Shakespeare; the complete works of William Shakespeare, edited, with a glossary, by W. J. Craig. ɿ1905?ɿ

146

₍Works₎
The pictorial edition of the works of Shakspere.   Edited by Charles
Knight.   ₍1839₎–43.

₍Works₎
The pictorial edition of the works of Shakspere.   Edited by Charles
Knight.   2d ed. rev.   1867.

₍Works₎
<Shakespeare's> plays; with his life . . .   Ed. by Gulian C. Verplanck
. . . 1847.

The works of William Shakespeare in reduced facsimile from the famous first folio edition of 1623. With an introd. by J. O. Halliwell-
Phillipps.   1876.

The works of Shakespeare, edited by Israel Gollancz.   1899–1900.

₍Works. German₎
<Shakespeare's> dramatische Werke, übers. von August Wilhelm
Schlegel.   1797–1810.

₍Works. German₎
Sämmtliche Werke.   (Dramen und Gedichte)   Deutsche Volksaus-
gabe . . . hrsg. von Max Moltke . . .   ₍1865₎

₍Works. German₎
<William Shakespeare's> Schauspiele.   1798–1806.

₍Works. Spanish₎
Dramas.   ₍1933₎

₍Works. Spanish₎
Obras dramáticas.   1887–99.

SHAKESPEARE, WILLIAM, 1564–1616—BIBLIOGRAPHY
SHAKESPEARE, WILLIAM, 1564–1616—COMEDIES
SHAKESPEARE, WILLIAM, 1564–1616—DICTIONARIES, INDEXES,
    ETC.
SHAKESPEARE, WILLIAM, 1564–1616—HISTORIES

Shakespeare, William, 1564–1616. Paraphrases, tales,
    etc.[45]   ₍old form₎
Carter, Thomas
    Stories from Shakespeare.

SHAKESPEARE, WILLIAM, 1564–1616—PARAPHRASES,
TALES, ETC.[45]   ₍new form₎
Lamb, Charles
    Tales from Shakespeare.

---

45. The subheading "Paraphrases, tales, etc." will no longer be used in main or added
entries. Instead, it will be used as a subject subdivision, preceded by a dash. The two forms
would file together among the subject subdivisions, the old author form preceding the new
subject form.

SHAKESPEARE, WILLIAM, 1564–1616—PARODIES, TRAVESTIES, ETC.

SHAKESPEARE, WILLIAM, 1564–1616. POEMS[46]
Baldwin, Thomas Whitfield
    On the literary genetics of Shakspere's poems & sonnets.

SHAKESPEARE, WILLIAM, 1564–1616—PROSE
SHAKESPEARE, WILLIAM, 1564–1616—QUOTATIONS
SHAKESPEARE, WILLIAM, 1564–1616—SPURIOUS AND DOUBT-
    FUL WORKS[47]   [new form]
SHAKESPEARE, WILLIAM, 1564–1616—TRAGEDIES
(For additional examples of Shakespeare subjects, see p. 131, 132, 133)

28. Corporate entry arrangement

Preliminary note. This rule covers the headings for corporate bodies such as associations, institutions, etc. (e. g., foundations, museums, religious bodies, societies, universities, etc.).

For corporate entries beginning with a geographical name, see Rule 31.

For special forms of corporate entries that begin with a surname, see Rule 23.

A. Filing position. Arrange corporate entries in their alphabetical places like titles.

Example:

American leaders in world affairs	[title]
American Library Association	[corporate heading]
American life in the eighties	[title]

B. Different bodies with same name. Arrange headings for different bodies with the same name alphabetically by the distinguishing designations at the end of the name, interfiled with other headings beginning with the same name, disregarding punctuation. For headings differentiated by numerals or dates, see Rules 36C and 36D.

Example:

Wissenschaftliche Gesellschaft, Bremen
Wissenschaftliche Gesellschaft, Freiburg i. B.
Wissenschaftliche Gesellschaft für Luftfahrt
Wissenschaftliche Gesellschaft, Halle
Wissenschaftliche Gesellschaft in Strassburg

---

46. If the collective uniform title "Poems" is used, this subject heading would file in that group (see p. 143).

47. The subheading "Spurious and doubtful works" will no longer be used in main or added entries. It will still be used as a subject subdivision, but preceded by a dash instead of a period.

Wissenschaftliche Gesellschaft Philomathie in Neisse
Wissenschaftliche Gesellschaft, Wien

C. Different kinds of entries under same name. Arrange different kinds of entries under the same corporate name in groups in the following order:

1) Author (main and/or added entry) without subheading, subarranged by titles according to Rule 26
2) Subject without subdivision, and identical title added entries, interfiled and subarranged alphabetically by their main entries
3) Name with corporate and/or subject subdivisions, the subdivisions interfiled alphabetically with each other and with titles, longer corporate names beginning with the same words, etc., disregarding punctuation; each corporate author heading followed by its own subject entries. Arrange headings for committees, departments, offices, etc. by the first word of the subheading (see Rule 31D).

Examples:

Harvard University
    Addresses at the inauguration of Charles William Eliot . . .

    Harvard University
Annals of mathematics.

Harvard University
    Catalogue.
HARVARD UNIVERSITY
Harvard University. Arnold Arboretum
Harvard University Base Hospital Unit
Harvard University calendar
Harvard University. Class of 1896
Harvard University. Class of 1901
HARVARD UNIVERSITY—DESCRIPTION
Harvard University. Divinity School   [author entry]
HARVARD UNIVERSITY. DIVINITY SCHOOL
HARVARD UNIVERSITY—HISTORY
Harvard University. Library

National Research Council
National Research Council. Building Research Advisory Board
National Research Council. Building Research Institute
National Research Council (Canada)
National Research Council (Canada) Division of Building Research
National Research Council (Canada) Technical Information Service
National Research Council. Committee on Nuclear Science
National Research Council Conference on Glossary of Terms in Nuclear Science and Technology
National Research Council. Disaster Research

149

National Research Council.   Nuclear Science Committee, *see* National
   Research Council.   Committee on Nuclear Science
National Research Council of Canada, *see* National Research Council
   (Canada)
National Research Council of Egypt, *see* . . .
National Research Council of the Philippine Islands
National Research Council.   Office of Critical Tables

United Nations   [author entries]
UNITED NATIONS
United Nations and how it works
UNITED NATIONS—ARMED FORCES
United Nations Association of Great Britain and Northern Ireland
UNITED NATIONS—AUSTRALIA
UNITED NATIONS—BIOGRAPHY
United Nations.   Charter
United Nations Conference on International Organization, San Francisco,
   1945
UNITED NATIONS—CONGO
United Nations.   Economic Commission for Europe
United Nations Educational, Scientific and Cultural Organization
UNITED NATIONS—EGYPT
UNITED NATIONS EMERGENCY FORCE
United Nations forces   [title]
UNITED NATIONS—PALESTINE
United Nations Relief and Rehabilitation Administration
United Nations.   Secretariat
UNITED NATIONS—YEARBOOKS

PRESBYTERIAN CHURCH
PRESBYTERIAN CHURCH AND STATE, *see* . . .
PRESBYTERIAN CHURCH—BIOGRAPHY
Presbyterian Church case   [title]
PRESBYTERIAN CHURCH—CATECHISMS AND CREEDS
PRESBYTERIAN CHURCH—HISTORY
The Presbyterian Church in American politics   [title]
PRESBYTERIAN CHURCH IN DETROIT
PRESBYTERIAN CHURCH IN MARYLAND
PRESBYTERIAN CHURCH IN THE SOUTHERN STATES
Presbyterian Church in the U. S.
PRESBYTERIAN CHURCH IN THE U. S.
Presbyterian Church in the U. S.   American Presbyterian Congo Mission
PRESBYTERIAN CHURCH IN THE U. S.—BIOGRAPHY
Presbyterian Church in the U. S.   Board of Christian Education
PRESBYTERIAN CHURCH IN THE U. S. (GENERAL)
Presbyterian Church in the U. S.   General Assembly

PRESBYTERIAN CHURCH IN THE U. S. (GENERAL)—CLERGY
PRESBYTERIAN CHURCH IN THE U. S. (GENERAL)—HISTORY
PRESBYTERIAN CHURCH IN THE U. S.—GOVERNMENT
PRESBYTERIAN CHURCH IN THE U. S.—HISTORY
Presbyterian Church in the U. S. Presbyteries. Brazos
Presbyterian Church in the U. S. Presbyteries. Kentucky
Presbyterian Church in the U. S. Presbyteries. Lexington
Presbyterian Church in the U. S. Presbytery of Holston
Presbyterian Church in the U. S. Presbytery of Norfolk
Presbyterian Church in the U. S. Synodical of Oklahoma
Presbyterian Church in the U. S. Synods. Appalachia
Presbyterian Church in the U. S. Synods. West Virginia
Presbyterian Church in the U. S. United Synod
Presbyterian Church in the U. S. Young People's Division
Presbyterian Church in the U. S. A.
PRESBYTERIAN CHURCH IN THE U. S. A.
Presbyterian Church in the U. S. A. Associated Presbyteries
PRESBYTERIAN CHURCH IN THE U. S. A.—CATECHISMS AND
    CREEDS
Presbyterian Church in the U. S. A. College Board
PRESBYTERIAN CHURCH IN THE U. S. A.—FORM OF GOVERN-
    MENT
Presbyterian Church in the U. S. A. General Assembly
Presbyterian Church in the U. S. A. Liturgy and ritual
Presbyterian Church in the U. S. A. Liturgy and ritual
    ɪThe book of common worshipɪ   ɪnew formɪ[48]
Presbyterian Church in the U. S. A. Liturgy and ritual. ¶The book
    of common worship   ɪold form, interfiledɪ[48]
PRESBYTERIAN CHURCH IN THE U. S. A. LITURGY AND RIT-
    UAL. ¶THE BOOK OF COMMON WORSHIP
                         ɪold form, interfiledɪ[48]
Presbyterian Church in the U. S. A. Liturgy and ritual
    ɪMarriage serviceɪ   ɪnew formɪ[48]
Presbyterian Church in the U. S. A. (New school)
Presbyterian Church in the U. S. A. North India Mission
Presbyterian Church in the U. S. A. (Old school)
Presbyterian Church in the U. S. A. Presbyteries
Presbyterian Church in the U. S. A. Presbyteries. Chicago

---

48. According to *Anglo-American Cataloging Rules* 119 the title of a particular liturgical work will be used as a uniform title rather than as a subheading. In cases where the
name of the ritual as a subheading would be the same when used as a uniform title, old-
and new-form entries may be interfiled by inserting a paragraph sign (¶) before the subheading, indicating that it is to be filed as a title. If the uniform title would be different
from the subheading, the old entries should be changed, or the old and new forms may be
related by *see also* references.

PRESBYTERIAN CHURCH IN THE U. S. A.   PRESBYTERIES.
  GENEVA
Presbyterian Church in the U. S. A. Presbyteries. Westchester
Presbyterian Church in the U. S. A. Presbytery of Alaska
Presbyterian Church in the U. S. A. Presbytery of Westminster
Presbyterian Church in the U. S. A. Publication Committee
Presbyterian Church in the U. S. A. Synods. Baltimore
Presbyterian Church in the U. S. A. Synods. Wisconsin
Presbyterian Church in the U. S. A. Welsh synods
PRESBYTERIAN CHURCH IN VIRGINIA
Presbyterian Church. Liturgy and ritual
PRESBYTERIAN CHURCH OF AUSTRALIA
PRESBYTERIAN CHURCH OF NOVA SCOTIA
PRESBYTERIAN CHURCH—SERMONS
Presbyterian Church, South, *see* Presbyterian Church in the U. S.
Presbyterian Church throughout the world   [title]

ANONYMOUS CLASSIC ENTRY ARRANGEMENT
(RULES 29–30)

29. Bible

Note. The rules for Bible headings in the *Anglo-American Cataloging Rules* are different in several respects from previous cataloging rules. There will be fewer entries under Bible than formerly, some of the entries under Bible will be simpler, and some of the changes will have a major effect on the arrangement of Bible entries in the catalog. Since the order resulting from the new entry rules is more desirable, it is recommended that the new cataloging rules be adopted and old headings changed, if possible. Following is a brief résumé of areas that will be affected:[49]

  1) *Apocryphal books.* An individual apocryphal book will be entered under its own title, and collections under compiler or title. A form subject heading, unmodified, may be used for collections; with subject subdivisions, for works about the apocryphal books. The only entries under Bible will be explanatory references.
Individual book:
    Old: Bible. N. T. Apocryphal books. Epistle of Barnabas.
        English. 1920
    New: Epistle of Barnabas. English

---

49. The new subject forms have been suggested by the Library of Congress as headings they might establish at such time as they adopt the new entry rules.

Collection:

Old: Bible. N. T. Apocryphal books. English. 1926. James
The apocryphal New Testament . . . translated by
Montague Rhodes James.

New: James, Montague Rhodes
The apocryphal New Testament.
APOCRYPHAL BOOKS (NEW TESTAMENT)

Books about:

Old: BIBLE. N. T. APOCRYPHAL BOOKS—CRITICISM,
INTERPRETATION, ETC.

New: APOCRYPHAL BOOKS (NEW TESTAMENT)—
CRITICISM, INTERPRETATION, ETC.

2) *Compound headings.* Headings combining more than one part of
the Bible in a single heading will no longer be used. The new headings will be simpler, easier to file, and result in better arrangement.

Old: Bible. O. T. Apocrypha and apocryphal books. English.
1913

New: Bible. O. T. Apocrypha. English. 1913
APOCRYPHAL BOOKS (OLD TESTAMENT)

Old: Bible. N. T. Acts, Epistles, and Revelation. Russian.
1862

New: Bible. N. T. Russian. Selections. 1962

3) *Harmonies.* "Harmonies" will not be used as a form subdivision in
the main heading for a harmony. Instead, harmonies will be
taken care of by a subject heading.

Old: Bible. N. T. Gospels. English. Harmonies. 1955.
Confraternity version

New: Bible. N. T. Gospels. English. Confraternity version.
1955
BIBLE—HARMONIES

4) *Liturgical works.* The heading "Bible. N. T. Epistles and Gospels, Liturgical" will no longer be used. Books of readings from
the Bible that are intended for use as part of a worship service
will be entered under the denominational church. There will probably be a collective subject heading but the form is uncertain at
the time of this writing; it may not be under Bible.

Old: Bible. N. T. Epistles and Gospels, Liturgical. English.
1959. Authorized
Epistles and Gospels . . . from the Service book and
hymnal of the Lutheran Church in America.

New: Lutheran Church. Liturgy and ritual

5) *Manuscripts.* Manuscripts of the Bible will no longer be entered under uniform headings beginning "Bible. Manuscripts . . ." Instead, they will be treated like any other version of the Bible. A collective subject heading may be used, subdivided by language.

> Old: Bible. Manuscripts, Anglo-Saxon. N. T. Gospels
> (Lindisfarne Gospels)
> New: Bible. N. T. Gospels. Anglo-Saxon. Lindisfarne
> Gospels
> BIBLE—MANUSCRIPTS, ANGLO-SAXON

6) *Paraphrases.* Paraphrases will be entered under the person who did the adapting or rewriting, with a form subject heading under Bible.

> Old: Bible. English. Paraphrases. 1943
> Greater poems of the Bible; metrical versions, Biblical forms and original poems, by Wilson MacDonald.
> New: MacDonald, Wilson
> Greater poems of the Bible . . .
> BIBLE—PARAPHRASES, ENGLISH

7) *Selections.* The form division "Selections" has been moved progressively from the first subdivision position to the second (following language), and in the 1967 rules, to the third (following language and version). Thus, the tendency is to give it less and less importance as an assembling element in the heading and to scatter the selections more and more.

> Old: Bible. English. Selections. 1958. Revised standard
> New: Bible. English. Revised standard. Selections. 1958

8) *Versions.* A change in entry rules that will result in a major change in filing arrangement is the reversal of the former order of date followed by version in the heading. Placing version before date will bring all editions of a particular version together, which in most libraries will be considered a more useful arrangement. The headings for selections from a particular version will follow the headings for the version itself. More headings will include a name in the "version" position, since names of translators and special names or phrases that identify a particular publication will be used whenever such a useful identification is available. With the new form of heading the heading for the version may be used as a subject; however, the Library of Congress will retain the old-form subject heading BIBLE. ENGLISH—VERSIONS—[NAME OF VERSION].

> Old: Bible. English. 1956. Revised standard
> New: Bible. English. Revised standard. 1956

A. Filing position. Entries for Bible, the sacred book, follow entries for the single surname Bible.

B. Basic order. Arrange Bible entries in straight alphabetical order word by word, disregarding kind of entry, form of heading, and punctuation.[50] Under the same author heading subarrange alphabetically by titles.

C. Dates in headings. Arrange headings which include a date alphabetically up to the date, then arrange the same headings with different dates chronologically by date, earliest date first. For details of date arrangement follow Rule 26B9a(2).

If desired, old- and new-form headings that are the same except for order of the elements may be interfiled and arranged in the position of the new headings, with the key word in the old-form headings indicated in some way.

> *Note.* Because imprint date is included in Bible headings, arrangement of editions of the Bible under the same basic heading will be chronological, whereas editions of literary, musical, and other works under authors that are cataloged with uniform titles without dates will be alphabetical by title page titles.

Example:

Bible. English. 1875
Bible. English. 1912
Bible. English. Authorized. 1854
Bible. English. 1943. Authorized   [old-form]
Bible. English. Authorized. 1962
Bible. English. ∧ Selections. 1941. Authorized   [old form]
Bible. English. Authorized. Selections. 1958

D. Different kinds of entries under the same heading. Arrange different kinds of entries under the same heading in groups in the following order:

1) Author (main and/or added entry), subarranged alphabetically by titles according to Rule 26
2) Subject, subarranged alphabetically by main entries

E. Parts of books. Arrange entries for chapters and verses after all entries for the whole book, in numerical order. The larger part beginning with the same chapter precedes the smaller part. Verses under the same chapter are arranged numerically by the first number.

---

50. Libraries that prefer grouped arrangements for the Bible and its parts may find rules for such arrangements in American Library Association. *A. L. A. Rules for Filing Catalog Cards.* Chicago, 1942, and U. S. Library of Congress. Processing Dept. *Filing Rules for the Dictionary Catalogs of the Library of Congress.* Washington, 1956. For an example of a highly organized arrangement, with the books of the Bible in canonical order, plus a general alphabetical index to all the Bible entries, see *A Catalog of Books Represented by Library of Congress Printed Cards Issued to July 31, 1942.* Ann Arbor, Mich., Edwards Brothers, 1943. v. 14.

Example:

Bible. N. T. Luke. English. 1960
Bible. N. T. Luke I–LI
                      I–VIII
                      I–II
                      I, 5–II, 40
                      I, 26–38, II, 1–20
                      I, 39–48
                      II, 1–20
                      XI

F. Numbered books. Numbered books of the Bible follow in numerical order the same name used collectively without number. Arrange in the following order:

1) Headings for the whole, with all its author and subject subdivisions alphabetically
2) Headings for numbered books, in numerical order, each arranged in two groups as follows:
   a) alphabetical—for author and subject subdivisions
   b) numerical—for chapters and verses

Example:

BIBLE. N. T. CORINTHIANS—COMMENTARIES
Bible. N. T. Corinthians. English. 1961
BIBLE. N. T. 1 CORINTHIANS—COMMENTARIES
Bible. N. T. 1 Corinthians. English. 1958
BIBLE. N. T. 1 CORINTHIANS X–XI—COMMENTARIES
BIBLE. N. T. 2 CORINTHIANS—COMMENTARIES

G. Abbreviations. Arrange the abbreviations "N. T." and "O. T.," used when followed by a subheading, as "New Testament" and "Old Testament."

Comprehensive example for Rule 29:[51]

Bible, Dana Xenophon
Bible   ᵣauthor entriesₗ
BIBLE
Bible. Acts, *see* Bible. N. T. Acts
BIBLE—ADDRESSES, ESSAYS, LECTURES
BIBLE AND SCIENCE
BIBLE—ANTIQUITIES
Bible. Apocrypha, *see* Bible. O. T. Apocrypha
Bible. Apocryphal books ᵣexplanatory referenceₗ

---

51. All examples are shown in the new form according to the *Anglo-American Cataloging Rules,* with corresponding new subject forms as suggested by the Library of Congress. Headings no longer authorized are not included.

Bible. Aramaic. 1959
BIBLE AS LITERATURE
Bible biographies
BIBLE—BIOGRAPHY
BIBLE—COMMENTARIES
The Bible companion
Bible. English. 1875
Bible. English. 1912
BIBLE. ENGLISH. AUTHORIZED   ɪpossible new subjectɪ
Bible. English. Authorized. 1854
Bible. English. Authorized. 193–?
    The Holy Bible containing the Old and New Testaments . . .
Bible. English. Authorized. 193–?
    The Oxford self-pronouncing Bible.
Bible. English. Authorized. 1930
Bible. English. Authorized. 1943?
    The Holy Bible, containing the Hebrew and Greek Scriptures . . .
Bible. English. Authorized. 1943
    The Holy Bible, containing the Old and New Testaments. Author-
ized (King James) version . . .
Bible. English. Authorized. 1943
    The Holy Bible, containing the Old and New Testaments, translated
out of the original tongues and with the former translations diligently
compared and revised by His Majesty's special command . . .
Bible. English. Authorized. 1949
BIBLE. ENGLISH. AUTHORIZED. 1949   ɪpossible new subjectɪ
Bible. English. Authorized. Selections. 1941
Bible. English. Authorized. Selections. 1958
Bible. English (Basic English) 1949
BIBLE. ENGLISH—BIBLIOGRAPHY
Bible. English. Confraternity version. 1955
BIBLE. ENGLISH—HISTORY
Bible. English (Middle English) Wycliffe. 1850
Bible. English. Revised. 1923
Bible. English. Revised standard. 1956
Bible. English. Selections. 1925
BIBLE. ENGLISH—VERSIONS
BIBLE. ENGLISH—VERSIONS—AUTHORIZED
BIBLE. ENGLISH—VERSIONS, CATHOLIC
BIBLE. ENGLISH—VERSIONS—CONFRATERNITY
BIBLE. ENGLISH—VERSIONS—DRAMA
Bible. Epistle of Barnabas, *see* Epistle of Barnabas
Bible. 1 Esdras (Apocrypha) *see* Bible. O. T. Apocrypha. 1 Esdras
Bible. 1 Esdras (Vulgate) *see* Bible. O. T. Ezra
Bible. 3 Esdras, *see* Bible. O. T. Apocrypha. 1 Esdras
BIBLE—GEOGRAPHY

Bible. Greek. Codex Sinaiticus
Bible. Hebrew. 1957
BIBLE. HEBREW—HISTORY
BIBLE—HISTORY
BIBLE—HISTORY OF BIBLICAL EVENTS
The Bible in art
BIBLE IN LITERATURE
The Bible in our day
Bible. Latin. Mainz. Gutenberg (42 lines) ca. 1454–55
Bible. Latin. Old Latin. 1647   [version]
Bible. Latin. Old Latin. 1957   [version]
Bible. Latin. Vulgate. 1956
Bible lessons for youth
BIBLE—MANUSCRIPTS
BIBLE—MANUSCRIPTS, ANGLO-SAXON
BIBLE—MANUSCRIPTS—CATALOGS
BIBLE. N. T. ACTS—BIOGRAPHY
Bible. N. T. Acts. Czech. Petrů. 1954
Bible. N. T. Acts. English. Authorized. 1959
Bible. N. T. Acts. English. Barclay. 1957
BIBLE. N. T.—ANTIQUITIES
Bible. N. T. Apocryphal books [explanatory reference]
Bible. N. T. Catholic Epistles. French. Leconte. 1953
BIBLE. N. T.—COMMENTARIES
Bible. N. T. English. American revised. 1959
Bible. N. T. English. Authorized. 1924
Bible. N. T. English. Authorized. Selections. 1961
Bible. N. T. English. Selections. 1895
Bible. N. T. Epistle of Barnabas, *see* Epistle of Barnabas
Bible. N. T. Epistles. English. Phillips. 1957
Bible. N. T. Epistles of John. English. Barclay. 1960
BIBLE. N. T.—MANUSCRIPTS, *see* BIBLE—MANUSCRIPTS
Bible. N. T. Pastoral epistles. English. Barclay. 1960
Bible. N. T. Philippians
The Bible of the world
Bible. O. T. Apocrypha. Baruch. German. Schneider. 1954
Bible. O. T. Apocrypha. English. Authorized. 1953
BIBLE. O. T. APOCRYPHA—INTRODUCTIONS
Bible. O. T. Apocrypha. Judith. Hebrew. 1957
Bible. O. T. Apocryphal books [explanatory reference]
Bible. O. T. Genesis
BIBLE. O. T.—MANUSCRIPTS, *see* BIBLE—MANUSCRIPTS
Bible. O. T. Pentateuch. Aramaic. Targum Onḳelos. 1561
Bible. O. T. Pentateuch. Aramaic. Targum Yerushalmi. 1899
BIBLE—PARAPHRASES
BIBLE—PARAPHRASES, ENGLISH

BIBLE—PARAPHRASES—HISTORY AND CRITICISM
Bible. Philippians, *see* Bible. N. T. Philippians
Bible. Polyglot. 1901
Bible. Polyglot. 1957
BIBLE STORIES
Bible stories in pictures
BIBLE STORIES, WELSH
Bible. Welsh . . .

30. Other anonymous classics and sacred books

Note. Uniform title headings for other anonymous works are not as detailed as those for the Bible. Imprint dates and names of versions, editors, translators, etc. are not included in the heading. If a library has an extensive file under any such heading and wishes to arrange its entries by date, editor, etc. rather than by title page title, it may add its full filing medium in the heading.

A. General rule. Arrange sacred scriptures other than the Bible in the same manner as Bible entries, in straight alphabetical order word by word (see Rule 29).

Under the same heading arrange all entries according to the regular rules for author arrangement (Rule 26).

Example:

Talmud, Éra Davidovna
Talmud
TALMUD
Talmud. Appendices, *see* Talmud. Minor tractates
Talmud. Baba batra
TALMUD. BABA BATRA—COMMENTARIES
Talmud. Baba batra. Hebrew
Talmud. Baba batra. Selections
Talmud. Berakot
Talmud. Berakot. Selections
TALMUD—COMMENTARIES
Der Talmud der Wirtschaft
Talmud. English
Talmud. English. Selections
Talmud. German
TALMUD—INTRODUCTIONS
Talmud, Jerusalem, *see* Talmud Yerushalmi
Talmud. Manuscripts
Talmud. Minor tractates
Talmud. Minor tractates. English
Talmud. Minor tractates. Gerim
Talmud. Minor tractates. Semaḥot

Talmud. Minor tractates. Semaḥot. German
Talmud. Nazir
Talmud. Selections
TALMUD—STUDY AND TEACHING
Talmud. Ta'anit
Talmud. Ta'anit. English
TALMUD TORAHS—CURRICULA
The Talmud unmasked
Talmud Yerushalmi
Talmud Yerushalmi. Berakot
TALMUD YERUSHALMI—COMMENTARIES
Talmud Yerushalmi. English
Talmud Yerushalmi. English. Selections
Talmud Yerushalmi. French
Talmud Yerushalmi. Selections
Talmud. Yiddish
Talmud. Yiddish. Selections

Note. According to *Anglo-American Cataloging Rules* 115D the main
entry for an anonymous midrash will be under its vernacular title.[52]
Formerly, the heading consisted of the uniform title "Midrash" with the
name of the particular midrash as a subheading, a period being used even
when the word "Midrash" was an integral part of the name of the particular midrash. Headings for those in which "Midrash" is the first word of
the name need not be changed, because when punctuation in the heading
is disregarded those with a period after "Midrash" may be interfiled with
the same heading without a period.

Example:

Midrash Bene Zion, Jerusalem
Midrash ha-gadol. Exodus
Midrash ha-gadol. Genesis
Midrash ha-ne'elam, *see* Zohar. Midrash ha-ne'elam
Midrash Mekilta, *see* Mekilta ꜀formerly a heading: Midrash. Mekilta꜀
Midrash rabbah
Midrash rabbah. English
Midrash rabbah. Ruth
Midrash. Tanḥuma   ꜀old heading꜀ ⎫
Midrash Tanḥuma   ꜀new heading꜀ ⎬Interfile, disregarding period
Midrash Tanḥuma. Yiddish   ⎭

---

52. Library of Congress announced its adoption of this rule in June 1965. (U. S. Library
of Congress. Processing Dept. *Cataloging Service.* Washington, D. C. Bulletin 70, June
1965, p. 1)

B. Anonymous classic with explanatory designation in parentheses. Arrange an anonymous classic heading that consists of one or more words or a personal name followed by an explanatory designation in parentheses in its alphabetical place with other kinds of entries. Disregard the parentheses and alphabet by the word or words enclosed therein.

Examples:

Genesis	ɾtitle of a bookɿ
Genesis and birth of the Federal Constitution	
Genesis and Exodus (Middle English poem)	
Genesis and modern science	
Genesis (Anglo-Saxon poem)	
Genesis (Book of the Old Testament) *see* . . .	
Genesis Down	ɾfiction titleɿ
Genesis (Middle English poem)	
Genesis (Middle High German poem)	
The genesis of the diamond	
Genesis (Old Saxon poem)	
Genesis printed in colors	
Genesis rabbah, *see* . . .	

Judith, Julie Bernat, called Mlle.	
Judith	ɾtitle of a bookɿ
Judith and Claudia	
Judith (Anglo-Saxon poem)	
Judith (Book of Apocrypha) *see* . . .	
Judith, Countess of Flanders, *see* . . .	
JUDITH (JEWISH HEROINE)	
Judith (Middle High German poem)	
Judith Montefiore College, Ramsgate, Eng.	
Judith of Flanders, Duchess of Bavaria	

Phoenix, Stephen Whitney
The phoenix and turtle
Phoenix (Anglo-Saxon poem)
Phoenix, Ariz.
PHOENIX (FABULOUS BIRD)
Phoenix (Firm)
The phoenix flame
PHOENIX (FRIGATE)
Phoenix Insurance Company, Hartford, Conn.
PHOENIX (STEAMER)

Richard, Walter Littauer	
Richard	ɾtitle of a bookɿ
Richard Carvel	

Richard Coeur de Lion, *see* Richard I, King of England
Richard Coeur de Lion (Romance)
Richard (Firm)
Richard I, King of England, 1157–1199
Richard II, King of England, 1367–1400
RICHARD II, KING OF ENGLAND, 1367–1400—DRAMA
Richard III, King of England, 1452–1485
Richard Lavalle, Enrique
Richard of Bordeaux ꞏ ꞏ ꞏ ꞏ [title]
Richard the rhymer ꞏ ꞏ ꞏ ꞏ [title]

    Richard II ꞏ ꞏ ꞏ ꞏ [the second]
Shakespeare, William

    Richard II (Drama) ꞏ ꞏ ꞏ ꞏ [the second]

    Richard III ꞏ ꞏ ꞏ ꞏ [the third]
Shakespeare, William

Richard W. Thompson memorial

C. Romances, etc.

Note. In the *Anglo-American Cataloging Rules* the subheading "(Romances, etc.)" will not be used with the name of a person to form an anonymous classic entry. [PERSON]—ROMANCES will probably be used instead as a form subject heading.[53]

The following examples illustrate the arrangement of both the old- and the new-form headings.

Examples:

Alexander, William Marvin
Alexander and some other cats
Alexander I, Emperor of Russia
Alexander, Me.
Alexander of Aphrodisias
Alexander VI, Pope
Alexander (Ship)
Alexander Süsskind ben Moses
Alexander the god
ALEXANDER THE GREAT, 356–323 B. C.
ALEXANDER THE GREAT, 356–323 B. C.—DRAMA
ALEXANDER THE GREAT, 356–323 B. C.—RELIGION
ALEXANDER THE GREAT, 356–323 B. C.—ROMANCES[53] [new form]
Alexander the Great (Romances, etc.) ꞏ ꞏ ꞏ ꞏ [old form]

---

53. The new subject forms for romances and legends (30C and D) have been suggested by the Library of Congress as headings they might establish at such time as they adopt the new entry rules.

Alexander, the magician, *see* . . .
Alexander Trallianus

Arthur, William Reed
Arthur de Richemont, *see* . . .
Arthur I, Duke of Brittany
Arthur Frankland; or, The experiences of a tragic poet
ARTHUR, KING
ARTHUR, KING—BIBLIOGRAPHY
ARTHUR, KING—JUVENILE LITERATURE
ARTHUR, KING—POETRY
ARTHUR, KING—ROMANCES[54]   [new form]
Arthur, King (Romances, etc.)   [old form]
Arthur Pendragon of Britain
Arthur William Patrick Albert, Prince of Great Britain, *see* . . .

Charlemagne headings in old form:

Charlemagne, Georges
Charlemagne, 742–814
CHARLEMAGNE, 742–814
CHARLEMAGNE, 742–814—CANONIZATION
CHARLEMAGNE, 742–814—DRAMA
CHARLEMAGNE, 742–814—POETRY
Charlemagne   [title of a book]
Charlemagne and his knights
Charlemagne (Drama)
Charlemagne et ses pairs
Charlemagne. Gesta Karoli Magni ad Carcassonam et Narbonam
Charlemagne; or, The church delivered
Charlemagne (Romances, etc.)
CHARLEMAGNE (ROMANCES, ETC.)
Charlemagne. Vita Karoli Magni sec. XII
Charlemagne. Voyage à Jérusalem et à Constantinople
Charlemagne. Ystorya de Carolo Magno

Charlemagne headings in new form:

Charlemagne, Georges
Charlemagne   [title of a book]
Charlemagne and his knights
Charlemagne, Emperor, 742–814[55]
CHARLEMAGNE, EMPEROR, 742–814

---

54. This may appear only as a *see* reference to a possible new heading, ARTHURIAN
LEGENDS or ARTHURIAN ROMANCES.
55. "Emperor" has been added after the name to make it conform to the rule to add
the title after the name of a monarch.

CHARLEMAGNE, EMPEROR, 742–814—CANONIZATION
CHARLEMAGNE, EMPEROR, 742–814—DRAMA
CHARLEMAGNE, EMPEROR, 742–814—POETRY
CHARLEMAGNE, EMPEROR, 742–814—ROMANCES[56]
Charlemagne et ses pairs
Charlemagne; or, The church delivered
Charlemagne (Play)

D. Legends

Note. There were a few cases where the name of a person or thing was followed by the subheading "Legend." This type of heading is not authorized in the *Anglo-American Cataloging Rules*. A suitable collective form subject heading (e. g., GRAIL—LEGENDS) will be used instead.[57]

The following examples illustrate the arrangement of both the old- and the new-form headings.

Examples:

Grail, Stephen
GRAIL
GRAIL—BIBLIOGRAPHY
Grail fire
Grail. Legend   [old form]
GRAIL—LEGENDS[57]   [new form]
The grail of spring

Francesco d'Assisi headings in old form:

Francesco d'Assisi e il suo secolo
Francesco d'Assisi, Saint, 1182–1226
FRANCESCO D'ASSISI, SAINT, 1182–1226—DRAMA
Francesco d'Assisi, Saint. Legend
Francesco d'Assisi, Saint. Legend. Fioretti
Francesco d'Assisi, Saint. Legend. Speculum perfectionis
FRANCESCO D'ASSISI, SAINT, 1182–1226—POETRY
Francesco und Beatrice

Francesco d'Assisi headings in new form:

Francesco d'Assisi e il suo secolo
Francesco und Beatrice
Francis of Assisi, Saint, 1182–1226
FRANCIS OF ASSISI, SAINT, 1182–1226—DRAMA
FRANCIS OF ASSISI, SAINT, 1182–1226—LEGENDS[57]
FRANCIS OF ASSISI, SAINT, 1182–1226—POETRY

---

56. See footnote 53, p. 162.
57. See footnote 53, p. 162.

E. Manuscripts without names. Arrange entries for manuscripts without names that are entered under the heading for the repository followed by "MSS." and the repository's designation for the manuscript among the other subdivisions under the heading for the repository. Alphabetize MSS. as the word Manuscripts, then alphabet by the designation, then arrange numerically by the number.

Example:

> British Museum. Dept. of Manuscripts
> British Museum. Dept. of Prints and Drawings
> British Museum. Hirsch Library, *see* British Museum. Dept. of Printed
>   Books. Hirsch Library
> British Museum. MSS. (Additional 17376)
> British Museum. MSS. (Additional 27879)
> British Museum. MSS. (Additional 29704)
> British Museum. MSS. (Arundel 384)
> British Museum. MSS. (Cottonian Nero D. IV)
> British Museum. Manuscripts Dept., *see* British Museum. Dept. of Man-
>   uscripts
> British Museum. MSS. (Egerton 2615)
> British Museum. MSS. (Royal A.I)
> British Museum (Natural History)
> British Museum. Printed Books, Dept. of, *see* British Museum. Dept.
>   of Printed Books
> British Museum. Thomason Collection, *see* British Museum. Dept. of
>   Printed Books. Thomason Collection

31. Place arrangement

A. Filing position. Entries beginning with a geographical name follow the same name used as a single surname.

Example:

> France, Anatole
> France, Wesley George
> France   [the country]

B. Basic order. Arrange all entries beginning with the same geographical name in one straight alphabetical file, word by word, disregarding punctuation.

For details of arrangement of subject subdivisions under place, see Rule 32.

For arrangement of numbered military units, congresses, etc., see Rule 36.

Note. Headings established according to the *Anglo-American Cataloging Rules* will vary in several respects from those established according to previous cataloging rules. Some of the changes are as follows:

1) Some form divisions under jurisdictions will be different, e. g.,

165

Old	New
Old	*New*
Charters	Charter
Ordinances, etc.	Ordinances, local laws, etc.
In British Commonwealth	Laws, by-laws, etc.

2) When the first word of the name of an institution is the name of a place, entry will be directly under the name, omitting period after the place. In straight alphabetical filing according to the rule above, in cases where the place name has no geographical designation the headings will file in the same position, therefore old headings with a period after the place and new headings without the period may be interfiled without changing the old headings.

3) Some corporate bodies formerly entered under place or jurisdiction will be entered directly under their names. However, in most cases a cross reference from the geographical name with the body as a subheading will still be needed and this will correspond to the heading in the old rules as far as filing position is concerned.

C. Different kinds of entries under the same heading. Arrange different kinds of entries under the same geographical name heading in groups in the following order:

1) Author (main and/or added entry) without subheading, subarranged by titles according to Rule 26. Disregard terms such as "appellant," "defendant," etc., which show the relationship of the place to one particular work, and alphabet by the title.

2) Subject without subdivision, and identical title added entries, interfiled and subarranged alphabetically by their main entries

3) Heading with corporate and/or subject subdivisions, the subdivisions interfiled alphabetically with each other and with titles, etc., disregarding punctuation; each corporate author heading followed by its own subject entries

D. Official governmental divisions. Arrange headings for the official governmental divisions of a place (i. e., bureaus, committees, departments, etc.) by the first word of the subheading, e. g.,

U. S.   Bureau of Education
U. S.   Dept. of Agriculture

with a reference from the distinctive word in the subheading, e. g.,

U. S.   Agriculture, Dept. of, *see* U. S.   Dept. of Agriculture

Note. This arrangement is preferable to arrangement by the topical word because it is unequivocal. The structure of many subheadings is such that they are difficult to invert and a uniform system of inversion is almost impossible to establish and maintain. Thorough cross references will take care of all parts of the name not used as the primary filing medium.

E. Different places of the same name. Different places, jurisdictions, and governments of the same name are alphabeted by the geographical or parenthetical designations following the names. Arrangement is first by the complete designation, then under each different heading according to the general rules 31B–D above.

Note. Distinguishing designations are omitted in the headings for chief cities and the better known jurisdictions. The result in straight alphabetical filing is that all entries for the lesser known places are kept together by the designation, while entries for the place with no designation are scattered throughout the file under that name. Washington and New York are exceptions—for these every place and jurisdiction, even state, is designated.

Former headings on Library of Congress cards did not include "(City)" or "(State)" after New York when it was followed by the name of an institution. It is recommended that the appropriate designation be added to the headings without them, or at least that the entries be interfiled in the appropriate group.

Designations for governments will no longer begin with dates (e. g., the heading will be "Russia (U. S. S. R.)," not "Russia (1923– U. S. S. R.)"), and will contain dates only in the case of occupying or insurgent governments (e. g., Germany (Territory under Allied occupation, 1945–1955)). Headings with a designation that begins with a date would file after the last alphabetical entry for the same place. Headings in which the designation begins with a word file alphabetically by the word. Therefore, the position of the "Russia (U. S. S. R.)" entries will be changed.

F. Abbreviations. Arrange the abbreviations "U. S." and "Gt. Brit.," used at the beginning of a heading when followed by a subheading, as "United States" and "Great Britain"; abbreviations for states, provinces, countries, etc., used as designations following a place name, as if written in full (see Rule 6B).

Examples for Rule 31:

      United States, petitioner
Burroughs Corporation et al., defendants
    (United States, petitioner)
      Action brought under the Sherman antitrust law . . .

United States
    Application by the Government of the United States of America . . .

   -    United States, complainant
Sullivan and Cromwell, New York
    Issuer summaries . . .

United States
    Mutual security program budget estimates.

United States, appellant
U. S. Court of Appeals (6th Circuit)
Opinion by Taft . . .

United States
U. S. Dept. of State
Papers relating to Behring Sea fisheries . . .

United States, defendant
Swift & Company, plaintiff, v. the United States . . .

United States
The United States economy and the mutual security program . . .

United States, plaintiff
United States v. the Sugar Institute, inc. . . . .

UNITED STATES
U. S. Adjutant-General's Office
U. S. ADJUTANT-GENERAL'S OFFICE
U. S. Agricultural Adjustment Administration
United States Agricultural Society
U. S.—AGRICULTURE, *see* AGRICULTURE—U. S.
U. S. Agriculture, Dept. of, *see* U. S. Dept. of Agriculture
U. S.—ALTITUDES
The United States among the nations   ɩtitleɩ
U. S. Bureau of Education
U. S. Bureau of Standards, *see* U. S. National Bureau of Standards
U. S. camera
U. S. Constitution
U. S. CONSTITUTION
U. S.—CONSTITUTIONAL HISTORY
U. S. Education, Bureau of, *see* U. S. Bureau of Education
U. S. Education, Office of, *see* U. S. Office of Education
UNITED STATES (FRIGATE)
U. S. Government research reports   ɩtitleɩ
U. S. National Bureau of Standards
U. S. Office of Education
U. S. School of Music, New York
U. S. Standards, Bureau of, *see* U. S. National Bureau of Standards
United States Steel Corporation
U. S.—TERRITORIAL EXPANSION

(For additional examples of U. S. entries see p. 25–26)

Each city with geographical designation:
Lincoln, William Sever
Lincoln and Ann Rutledge   ɩtitleɩ
Lincoln, Argentine Republic

LINCOLN, BATTLE OF, 1217
Lincoln County coast directory   [title]
LINCOLN CO., KY.
LINCOLN CO., WIS.—BIOGRAPHY
Lincoln Co., Wis.   Board of Supervisors
Lincoln, Eng.
Lincoln, Eng.   City Surveyor's Office
Lincoln, Eng. (Diocese)
LINCOLN, ENG.—HISTORY
Lincoln, Eng.   Public Library
LINCOLN HIGHWAY
Lincoln, Ill.
LINCOLN, MOUNT, COLO.
LINCOLN, MOUNT, N. H.
Lincoln, Neb.
LINCOLN, NEB.—BIOGRAPHY
Lincoln, Neb.   Charter
Lincoln, Neb.   City Library
LINCOLN, NEB.—LIBRARIES
Lincoln, Neb.   Ordinances, local laws, etc.
Lincoln plays   [title]
LINCOLN TUNNEL

Each jurisdiction with designation:

New York Academy of Medicine
New York and the Seabury investigation   [title]
New York (Archdiocese)
NEW YORK (BATTLESHIP)
New York Business Development Corporation
New York (City)
New York (City)   Aqueduct Commission
New York (City)   Board of Education
New York (City)   Botanical Garden
NEW YORK (CITY)—CHARITIES
New York (City)   Conference on Asian Affairs, *see* . . .
New York City Council of Political Reform
New York (City)   Dept. of Parks
NEW YORK (CITY)—DESCRIPTION
New York City folklore   [title]
New York (City)   Public Library, *see* New York Public Library
New York (City)   St. James Episcopal Church, Bronx
New York (City)   Stock Exchange
New York (City)   World's Fair, 1939–1940
New York (Colony)
New York cookbook   [title]
New York (County)

169

New York (Cruiser)
New York holiday   ɩtitleɩ
NEW YORK METROPOLITAN AREA
New York Public Library
New York School of Social Work
New York (State)
New York (State)   Agricultural Experiment Station, Ithaca
New York State Bar Association
NEW YORK (STATE)—BOUNDARIES
New York (State)   Bureau of Adult Education
New York State Historical Association
NEW YORK (STATE)—HISTORY
New York State legislative annual   ɩtitleɩ
New York (State)   State College for Teachers, Albany
New York (State)   State Commission on Pensions
NEW YORK (STATE)—STATISTICS, MEDICAL
New York (State)   University
New York Surgical Society
New York times   ɩtitleɩ
New York University
New Yorker

Chief city without geographical designation:

London, Jack
London   ɩplace as authorɩ

   LONDON
Harrison, Frederic

   London   ɩtitleɩ
Johnson, Samuel

   LONDON
Loftie, William John

London and Londoners   ɩtitleɩ
London.   Central Criminal Court
LONDON, DECLARATION OF, 1909
LONDON—DESCRIPTION
London (Diocese)
LONDON (DIOCESE)
London (Diocese)   Courts
LONDON (DOG)
LONDON (GATWICK)   AIRPORT
LONDON IN LITERATURE
London, Ky.
London.   Laws, by-laws, etc.
London.   National Gallery

London, Ohio
London Old Boy's Association
London, Ont. Council
LONDON, ONT.—HISTORY
London, Ont. University of Western Ontario
London scene   [title]
London. School Board
London Shakespeare League
LONDON, TREATY OF, 1915
London. University
LONDON—WHARVES

State, without designation; including cities of same name and institution with subdivisions:

California
California. Adjutant General's Office
California. Agricultural Experiment Station, Berkeley
CALIFORNIA—ANTIQUITIES
California as I saw it   [title]
California, Baja, *see* Baja California
CALIFORNIA, GULF OF
California Institute of Technology, Pasadena
California   Legislature
California, Lower, *see* Baja California
California, Mo.
California. Office of State Controller
California, Pa.
CALIFORNIA—POLITICS AND GOVERNMENT
California (Province)
California. Secretary of State
CALIFORNIA, SOUTHERN
CALIFORNIA, SOUTHERN—CLIMATE
CALIFORNIA, SOUTHERN—HISTORY
California. State Board of Equalization
California State Chamber of Commerce
California. State College, Fresno
California. State College of Applied Arts and Sciences, Los Angeles
California. State College, San Diego
California. State Dept. of Employment
California the wonderful   [title]
California (U. S. cruiser)
California. University
California. University. Art Dept.
California. University at Los Angeles, *see* California. University. University at Los Angeles
California. University. Bancroft Library

171

CALIFORNIA. UNIVERSITY—BIOGRAPHY
California. University, Davis
California. University, Davis. College of Agriculture
California. University, Davis. Conference on Quality of Water for Irrigation, 1958, *see* . . .
California. University, Davis. Dept. of Irrigation
California. University. Library
CALIFORNIA. UNIVERSITY. LIBRARY
CALIFORNIA. UNIVERSITY. LIBRARY—HISTORY
California. University. Library. Rare Books Dept.
California. University, Los Angeles, *see* California. University. University at Los Angeles
California. University, Santa Barbara
California. University. School of Law
California. University. University at Los Angeles
CALIFORNIA. UNIVERSITY. UNIVERSITY AT LOS ANGELES—BIBLIOGRAPHY
California. University. University at Los Angeles. Bureau of Governmental Research
California. University. University at Los Angeles. Dept. of Engineering
CALIFORNIA. UNIVERSITY. UNIVERSITY AT LOS ANGELES—HISTORY
California University. University at Los Angeles. Western Data Processing Center
California. University. University Extension
California. University. Water Resources Center
California. Vocational Rehabilitation Service

Country with parenthetical designations denoting both administrative units and changes in government:
Mexico
Mexico and the war in the Pacific   [title]
Mexico (Archdiocese)
Mexico. Archivo general de la nación
Mexico (City)
Mexico. Congresso
Mexico (Ecclesiastical province)
MEXICO—ECONOMIC CONDITIONS
Mexico (Empire, 1821–1823)
Mexico (Empire, 1864–1867)
Mexico. Establecimiento de minería
Mexico (Federal District)
MEXICO—HISTORY
Mexico, Me.
Mexico. Ministerio de . . .
Mexico, Mo.

Mexico (Republic, 1823–1864) *see* Mexico
Mexico. Secretaría de . . .
Mexico (State)
Mexico this week   ɪtitleɪ
Mexico (Viceroyalty)

*Country with parenthetical designations denoting both different govern-
ments and the governments of occupying powers:*

Germany
Germany. Auswärtiges Amt
GERMANY—BIBLIOGRAPHY
Germany. Constitution
Germany (Democratic Republic)
GERMANY (DEMOCRATIC REPUBLIC)
Germany (Democratic Republic) Amt für Information
GERMANY (DEMOCRATIC REPUBLIC)—ARMED FORCES
Germany (Democratic Republic) Constitution
GERMANY (DEMOCRATIC REPUBLIC)—ECONOMIC CONDI-
    TIONS
Germany (Democratic Republic) Zentralinstitut für Bibliothekswesen
GERMANY—DESCRIPTION AND TRAVEL
Germany divided   ɪtitleɪ
GERMANY, EASTERN—DESCRIPTION AND TRAVEL
GERMANY, EASTERN—HISTORY
Germany (Federal Republic)
Germany (Federal Republic) Auswärtiges Amt
GERMANY (FEDERAL REPUBLIC)—DESCRIPTION AND TRAVEL
Germany (Federal Republic) Laws, statutes, etc.
Germany. Heer
GERMANY, NORTHERN
Germany plots with the Kremlin   ɪtitleɪ
Germany (Territory under Allied occupation, 1945–1955)
Germany (Territory under Allied occupation, 1945–1955) Control Author-
    ity. Fuel Committee
GERMANY (TERRITORY UNDER ALLIED OCCUPATION, 1945–
    1955)—POLITICS AND GOVERNMENT
Germany (Territory under Allied occupation, 1945–1955. British Zone)
Germany (Territory under Allied occupation, 1945–1955. British Zone)
    Control Commission
Germany (Territory under Allied occupation, 1945–1955. French Zone)
GERMANY (TERRITORY UNDER ALLIED OCCUPATION, 1945–
    1955. U. S. ZONE)
Germany (Territory under Allied occupation, 1945–1955. U. S. Zone)
    Laws, statutes, etc.
Germany (Territory under Allied occupation, 1945–1955. U. S. Zone)
    Office of Military Government

173

> Germany (Territory under Allied occupation, 1945–1955. Vereinigtes
> Wirtschaftsgebiet)
> Germany. Wehrmacht

32. Subject arrangement

A. Filing position. Subject entries follow the same word used as a single surname.

Example:

> Stone, Thomas
> STONE

B. Identical subject entries—Subarrangement. Arrange entries with the same subject heading alphabetically by the main entries of the books; or, if the entry is a subject analytic for a part of a book and the analytic has an author or title main entry of its own different from the main entry for the whole book, arrange by the entry for the analytic. Arrange different titles by the same author alphabetically by title; different editions of the same title, according to the rules for editions (26B9). Subarrange analytics with the same subject, author entry, and title according to the rules for analytics (26B11).

Example:

> BISON, AMERICAN
> Allen, Joel Asaph
> The American bisons, living and extinct.
>
> BISON, AMERICAN
> The American buffalo and its relatives.
> (In Prose and poetry of the live stock industry of the United States)
>
> BISON, AMERICAN
> Anderson, George S
> A buffalo story.
> (In Roosevelt, Theodore. American big-game hunting)
>
> BISON, AMERICAN
> Garretson, Martin S
> The American bison.
>
> BISON, AMERICAN
> Garretson, Martin S
> A short history of the American bison.
>
> BISON, AMERICAN
> The Westerners. Chicago Corral
> From buffalo to beef—the saga of cattle.
> (In The Westerners brand book [monthly publication of the Chicago Corral])

C. Basic order. Arrange a subject, its subdivisions, etc. in groups in the following order:

1) Subject without subdivision, interfiled with identical title added entries alphabetically by their main entries
2) Period divisions, arranged chronologically (for detailed rules see 32G below)
3) Alphabetical extensions of the main subject heading: form, subject, and geographical subdivisions, inverted subject headings, subject followed by a parenthetical term, and phrase subject headings, interfiled word by word in one alphabet with titles and other headings beginning with the same word, disregarding punctuation

Note. In the framework of the basic principles on which these rules are based it seems more logical for the chronological group to precede the alphabetical group, because (1) alphabetically, dates are "nothing," therefore come before "something" (words filed alphabetically), (2) with subject subdivisions interfiled with phrase subjects, titles, corporate entries, etc., dates at the end of the whole alphabetical file would be too far separated from the basic heading, and (3) dates are being used more and more simply to show when the book was published. Dates that designate a different thing are different from dates that designate periods of the same thing and so should be arranged after the alphabetical group of entries (see example on p. 185 for RECONSTRUCTION; RECONSTRUCTION (1014–1909); RECONSTRUCTION (1939–1951)).

In straight alphabetical filing there is no need for cross references that are made simply to refer from a heading in one group to the same heading in a different form in another group, as PETROLEUM GEOLOGY, *see* PETROLEUM—GEOLOGY. Also, only one form of a *see* reference is needed (see Rule 35B4).

D. Further subdivisions. Arrange the further subdivisions of subheadings in the same order as the subheadings themselves are arranged (according to 32C above).

E. Abbreviations. If form and subject subdivisions are abbreviated in headings, arrange them as if written in full. For a list of these abbreviations, see Rule 6G.

F. Special cases. In straight alphabetical filing disregarding punctuation there are a few problem cases of different headings consisting of the same words but punctuated differently. When this occurs, arrange the heading with punctuation and a subheading before the longer heading.

Examples:

COLORADO—SPRINGS, *see* ...
Colorado Springs   ɾthe placeɿ

MARBLE—COLORADO
Marble, Colo.   ɾthe placeɿ

G. Period divisions

1. Arrange period divisions chronologically by the first date in the heading.[58]

Periods of time beginning with the same year but extending to different years are arranged so as to bring the longest period first. If a period subdivision is open (e. g., 1865–   ), it precedes all other period subdivisions beginning with the same or later years. Period subdivisions consisting of the name of a century (e. g., 19TH CENTURY) precede all subdivisions beginning with years within that century, including the first year bearing the numerals of that century (e. g., 1800–1837).

The earliest period frequently is in the form of a phrase without a beginning date (e. g., TO 1485; ANCIENT TO 640 A. D.; EARLY TO 1643). This type precedes subdivisions that start with a date. Care must be taken when dates are in the B. C. period because those dates run in reverse order from A. D. dates (e. g., 510 B. C. is earlier than 265 B. C., and 510–30 B. C. is a longer period than 510–265 B. C.).

2. Period divisions in the form of phrases (e. g., U. S.—HISTORY—COLONIAL PERIOD; U. S.—HISTORY—CIVIL WAR), and those consisting of a distinctive word, name, or phrase followed by dates (e. g., GT. BRIT.—HISTORY—RESTORATION, 1660–1668; GT. BRIT.—HISTORY—VICTORIA, 1837–1901) are arranged chronologically, not alphabetically. When there is a guide card for a heading with a period division expressed only in words it would be helpful to both filers and users if the corresponding dates were added on the guide card. A cross reference from the heading in its alphabetical position in the alphabetical group to its chronological position would also be useful and would forestall misfilings. See examples of such references in the filing examples below.

Geological time periods under the subjects GEOLOGY, STRATIGRAPHIC; PALEOBOTANY, and PALEONTOLOGY, which never contain dates, are arranged alphabetically.

3. Under language and literature subjects, such subdivisions as OLD FRENCH; EARLY MODERN (TO 1700); 18TH CENTURY, etc., are regarded as period subdivisions.

4. The divisions ANCIENT, PRIMITIVE, MEDIEVAL, RENAISSANCE, BAROQUE, MODERN, etc. are arranged alphabetically, not chronologically, even when followed by a date (e. g., HISTORY, MODERN—20TH CENTURY), except when used as further divisions of the subdivisions HISTORY or HISTORY AND CRITICISM (e. g., MUSIC—HISTORY AND CRITICISM—ANCIENT).

5. Phrase subdivisions used to segregate early writings on a subject (e. g., EARLY WORKS TO 1800; TO 1800; PRE-LINNEAN WORKS) are arranged alphabetically, unless definitely part of a sequence of similar subdivisions.

---

58. For the proper chronological order, and to ascertain whether a subdivision is to be considered a period division, consult U. S. Library of Congress. Subject Cataloging Division. *Subject Headings Used in the Dictionary Catalogs of the Library of Congress.*

Examples for Rule 32:

COOKERY
COOKERY, AMERICAN
COOKERY, AMERICAN—ALASKA
COOKERY, AMERICAN—BIBLIOGRAPHY
COOKERY, AMERICAN—CALIFORNIA
COOKERY (APPLES)
COOKERY, CHINESE
COOKERY—DICTIONARIES
COOKERY—EARLY WORKS TO 1800
COOKERY (EGGS)
COOKERY FOR DIABETICS
Cookery for girls   [title]
COOKERY, FRENCH
COOKERY—HISTORY
COOKERY IN LITERATURE
COOKERY, INTERNATIONAL
COOKERY, JAPANESE
COOKERY ON SHIPS, *see* ...
COOKERY, OUTDOOR, *see* ...
Cookery Teachers Association of New South Wales
COOKERY—YEARBOOKS

Parenthetical term, limiting the subject to a particular field, used with each heading:

Composition and properties of Soviet gas turbine steels   [title]
COMPOSITION (ART)
Composition for photographers   [title]
COMPOSITION (LAW)
COMPOSITION (LAW)—AUSTRIA
COMPOSITION (LAW)—MEXICO
COMPOSITION (MUSIC)
COMPOSITION (MUSIC)—HISTORY
COMPOSITION (MUSIC)—MECHANICAL AIDS
Composition of Shakespeare's plays   [title]
COMPOSITION (PHOTOGRAPHY)
COMPOSITION (RHETORIC) *see* ...
Composition through pictures   [title]

Parenthetical term indicating different aspects and/or different subjects, not used with one of the headings:

MASS
MASS—ADDRESSES, ESSAYS, LECTURES
Mass and Lord's prayer   [title]
MASS (CANON LAW)

MASS—CELEBRATION
MASS (CHEMISTRY) *see* . . .
Mass, class, and bureaucracy   ɿtitleɿ
MASS COMMUNICATION
Mass media and education   ɿtitleɿ
MASS—MEDITATIONS
MASS (MUSIC)
Mass of the Roman rite   ɿtitleɿ
MASS (PHYSICS)
Mass spectrometry   ɿtitleɿ
MASS, STANDARDS OF, *see* . . .
MASS—STUDY AND TEACHING

GENERAL EXAMPLES OF ORDER—
WITH PERIOD SUBDIVISIONS

EDUCATION
EDUCATION—1945–
EDUCATION—1945–   ADDRESSES, ESSAYS, LECTURES
EDUCATION—1945–   CONGRESSES
EDUCATION—AFRICA
EDUCATION—AIMS AND OBJECTIVES
EDUCATION, ANCIENT
Education and American civilization   ɿtitleɿ
EDUCATION—COLLECTED WORKS
EDUCATION—COLLECTIONS
EDUCATION—EARLY WORKS TO 1800
EDUCATION, ELEMENTARY
EDUCATION, ELEMENTARY—1945–
EDUCATION, ELEMENTARY—BIBLIOGRAPHY
EDUCATION, MEDIEVAL
EDUCATION OF CHILDREN
EDUCATION, PRIMITIVE
Education through art   ɿtitleɿ
EDUCATION—U. S.
EDUCATION—U. S.—1945–
EDUCATION—U. S.—1945–   ADDRESSES, ESSAYS, LECTURES
EDUCATION—U. S.—ADDRESSES, ESSAYS, LECTURES
EDUCATION—U. S.—BIBLIOGRAPHY
EDUCATION—U. S.—HISTORY
EDUCATION—YEARBOOKS

GEOGRAPHY
GEOGRAPHY—15TH–16TH CENTURIES
GEOGRAPHY—17TH–18TH CENTURIES
GEOGRAPHY—ABSTRACTS
GEOGRAPHY, AERIAL

GEOGRAPHY, ANCIENT
GEOGRAPHY—COLLECTIONS
GEOGRAPHY, COMMERCIAL
GEOGRAPHY, MATHEMATICAL
GEOGRAPHY, MEDIEVAL
GEOGRAPHY—METHODOLOGY
GEOGRAPHY, POLITICAL

Details of period divisions:

U. S.—HISTORY

  —COLONIAL PERIOD   ᵗchronological groupᴵ
  —KING WILLIAM'S WAR, 1689–1697
  —QUEEN ANNE'S WAR, 1702–1713
  —FRENCH AND INDIAN WAR, 1755–1763
  —REVOLUTION
  —REVOLUTION—CAMPAIGNS AND BATTLES
  —REVOLUTION—CAUSES
  —REVOLUTION—SOURCES
  —1783–1865
  —CONFEDERATION, 1783–1789
  —CONSTITUTIONAL PERIOD, 1789–1809
  —1801–1809
  —WAR OF 1812
  —1815–1861
  —WAR WITH ALGERIA, 1815
  —1849–1877
  —CIVIL WAR
  —1865–
  —1865–1898
  —1898–
  —WAR OF 1898
  —20TH CENTURY
  —1933–1945

U. S.—HISTORY—BIBLIOGRAPHY   ᴵalphabetical groupᴵ
U. S. history bonus book   ᵗtitleᴵ
U. S.—HISTORY—CIVIL WAR
 Cards with this heading are filed in the group of chronological sub-
divisions, preceding this alphabetical group.
U. S.—HISTORY—COLONIAL PERIOD
 Cards with this heading are filed in the group of chronological sub-
divisions, preceding this alphabetical group.
U. S.—HISTORY—DRAMA
United States history in rhyme   ᵗtitleᴵ
U. S.—HISTORY, LOCAL
U. S.—HISTORY, MILITARY
U. S.—HISTORY—SOURCES

179

FRANCE—HISTORY—1789–
     —1789–1900
     —1789–1815
     —REVOLUTION
     —REVOLUTION, 1789–1799
     —REVOLUTION, 1789–1797
     —REVOLUTION, 1789–1796
     —REVOLUTION, 1789–1795
     —REVOLUTION, 1789–1791
     —REVOLUTION, 1789–1790
     —REVOLUTION, 1789
     —REVOLUTION, 1790–1794

GT. BRIT.—FOREIGN RELATIONS—1789–1820
         —19TH CENTURY
         —1800–1837
         —1820–1830
         —1837–1901
         —20TH CENTURY
         —1901–1910
         —1910–1936

GT. BRIT.—HISTORY—TO 1485
     —TO 1066
     —TO 449
     —TO 55 B. C.
     —ROMAN PERIOD 55 B. C.–449 A. D.
     —ANGLO-SAXON PERIOD, 449–1066

ROME—HISTORY—ABORIGINAL AND EARLY PERIOD
     —KINGS, 753–510 B. C.
     —REPUBLIC, 510–30 B. C.
     —REPUBLIC, 510–265 B. C.
     —REPUBLIC, 265–30 B. C.
     —CIVIL WAR, 49–48 B. C.
     —EMPIRE, 30 B. C.–476 A. D.
     —EMPIRE, 30 B. C.–284 A. D.
     —THE FIVE JULII, 30 B. C.–68 A. D.
     —AUGUSTUS, 30 B. C.–14 A. D.
     —TIBERIUS, 14–37
     —CLAUDIUS, 41–54

U. S.—FOREIGN RELATIONS
       —REVOLUTION [chronological group]
       —1783–1865
       —CONSTITUTIONAL PERIOD,
        1789–1809

—1789–1797
—1893–1897
—20TH CENTURY
—1945–1953
—1961–1963
—1961–1963—ADDRESSES, ESSAYS,
LECTURES
—1961–1963—SOURCES

U. S.—FOREIGN RELATIONS—ADDRESSES, ESSAYS,
LECTURES   [alphabetical group]
U. S.—FOREIGN RELATIONS ADMINISTRATION
U. S.—FOREIGN RELATIONS—ARABIA
U. S.—FOREIGN RELATIONS—BIBLIOGRAPHY
U. S.—FOREIGN RELATIONS—CANADA
U. S.—FOREIGN RELATIONS—CATHOLIC CHURCH
U. S.—FOREIGN RELATIONS—COLLECTIONS
U. S.—FOREIGN RELATIONS—COMMUNIST COUNTRIES
U. S.—FOREIGN RELATIONS—GERMANY
U. S.—FOREIGN RELATIONS—GERMANY (FEDERAL REPUBLIC)
U. S.—FOREIGN RELATIONS—PERIODICALS
U. S.—FOREIGN RELATIONS—REVOLUTION
    Cards with this heading are filed in the group of chronological sub-
divisions, preceding this alphabetical group.
U. S.—FOREIGN RELATIONS—RUSSIA
U. S.—FOREIGN RELATIONS—TREATIES

CHURCH HISTORY
                —PRIMITIVE AND EARLY   [chronological
                    CHURCH   group]
                —4TH CENTURY
                —MIDDLE AGES
                —13TH CENTURY
                —MODERN PERIOD
                —REFORMATION, *see* . . .
                —17TH CENTURY
                —20TH CENTURY
                —1945–
CHURCH HISTORY—ADDRESSES, ESSAYS,   [alphabetical
    LECTURES   group]
CHURCH HISTORY—MIDDLE AGES
    Cards with this heading are filed in the group of chronological sub-
divisions, preceding this alphabetical group.
CHURCH HISTORY—MODERN PERIOD
    [Same explanatory reference]
Church history of the first three centuries   [title]
CHURCH HISTORY—PERIODICALS

181

CHURCH HISTORY—PRIMITIVE AND EARLY CHURCH
        ﹝Same explanatory reference﹞
CHURCH HISTORY—SOURCES

Geological periods:
PALEONTOLOGY
                —AFRICA
                —BIBLIOGRAPHY
                , BOTANICAL, *see* . . .
                —CAMBRIAN
                —CANADA
                —COLLECTED WORKS
                —COLLECTING OF SPECIMENS
                —DEVONIAN
                —EARLY WORKS TO 1800
                —EOCENE
                —GERMANY
                —MESOZOIC
                —NEBRASKA
                , STRATIGRAPHIC
                —TECHNIQUE
                —TERTIARY

Literature headings:
ENGLISH LITERATURE
                    —OLD ENGLISH, *see* ANGLO-SAXON
                        LITERATURE   ﹝chronological group﹞
                    —MIDDLE ENGLISH (1100–1500)
                    —MIDDLE ENGLISH (1100–1500)—
                        HISTORY AND CRITICISM
                    —EARLY MODERN (TO 1700)
                    —EARLY MODERN (TO 1700)—
                        BIBLIOGRAPHY
                    —18TH CENTURY
                    —20TH CENTURY
ENGLISH LITERATURE—ADDRESSES, ESSAYS,   ﹝alphabetical
    LECTURES   group﹞
English literature and the Hebrew renaissance   ﹝title﹞
ENGLISH LITERATURE—AUSTRALIA, *see* AUSTRALIAN LITERA-
    TURE
ENGLISH LITERATURE—CATHOLIC AUTHORS
ENGLISH LITERATURE—CEYLON
ENGLISH LITERATURE (COLLECTIONS)
ENGLISH LITERATURE—EARLY MODERN (TO 1700)
        Cards with this heading are filed in the group of chronological sub-
    divisions, preceding this alphabetical group.

ENGLISH LITERATURE—HISTORY AND CRITICISM
English literature in Germany   [title]
ENGLISH LITERATURE—IRISH AUTHORS
ENGLISH LITERATURE—LANCASHIRE
ENGLISH LITERATURE—MIDDLE ENGLISH (1100–1500)
     [Same explanatory reference]
ENGLISH LITERATURE—OLD ENGLISH, *see* ANGLO-SAXON
    LITERATURE
ENGLISH LITERATURE (SELECTIONS: EXTRACTS, ETC.)
ENGLISH LITERATURE—TRANSLATIONS FROM ARABIC

GREEK DRAMA
GREEK DRAMA—ADDRESSES, ESSAYS, LECTURES
GREEK DRAMA (COMEDY)—HISTORY AND CRITICISM
GREEK DRAMA—HISTORY AND CRITICISM
GREEK DRAMA, MODERN
GREEK DRAMA (SATYR PLAY)
GREEK DRAMA—TECHNIQUE
GREEK DRAMA (TRAGEDY)—HISTORY AND CRITICISM
GREEK DRAMA—TRANSLATIONS INTO ENGLISH
GREEK DRAMA—TRANSLATIONS INTO FRENCH

Ancient, Medieval, Modern, etc.:
HISTORY
HISTORY, ANCIENT
History and evolution of Freemasonry   [title]
HISTORY—DICTIONARIES
HISTORY, MEDIEVAL, *see* . . .
HISTORY—METHODOLOGY
HISTORY, MODERN
HISTORY, MODERN—16TH CENTURY
HISTORY, MODERN—20TH CENTURY
HISTORY—MODERN—1945–
History of American journalism   [title]
HISTORY—PHILOSOPHY

MUSIC—HISTORY AND CRITICISM
                —ANCIENT   [chronological
                —MEDIEVAL   group]
                —16TH CENTURY
                —17TH CENTURY
                —20TH CENTURY
MUSIC—HISTORY AND CRITICISM—ANCIENT   [alphabetical
                                         group]
      Cards with this heading are filed in the group of chronological sub-
divisions, preceding this alphabetical group.

MUSIC—HISTORY AND CRITICISM—MEDIEVAL
    [Same explanatory reference]
MUSIC—HISTORY AND CRITICISM—METHODS, *see* . . .
MUSIC—HISTORY AND CRITICISM—OUTLINES, SYLLABI, ETC.
MUSIC—HISTORY AND CRITICISM—SOURCES

Period of early writings:
ASTRONOMY
ASTRONOMY, ANCIENT
ASTRONOMY—DICTIONARIES
ASTRONOMY—EARLY WORKS TO 1800
ASTRONOMY—HISTORY
ASTRONOMY, MEDIEVAL

NATURAL HISTORY—PICTORIAL WORKS
NATURAL HISTORY—PRE-LINNEAN WORKS
NATURAL HISTORY—PUERTO RICO

RELIGION AND SCIENCE
RELIGION AND SCIENCE—EARLY WORKS TO 1800
RELIGION AND SCIENCE—1800–1859
RELIGION AND SCIENCE—1860–1899
RELIGION AND SCIENCE—1900–1925
RELIGION AND SCIENCE—1926–1945
RELIGION AND SCIENCE—1946–
RELIGION AND SCIENCE—HISTORY OF CONTROVERSY

ARITHMETIC
ARITHMETIC—BEFORE 1846
ARITHMETIC—1846–1880
ARITHMETIC—1881–1900
ARITHMETIC—1901–
ARITHMETIC—BIBLIOGRAPHY

Music scores:
PIANO MUSIC
PIANO MUSIC—ANALYTIC GUIDES
PIANO MUSIC, ARRANGED
PIANO MUSIC—BIBLIOGRAPHY
PIANO MUSIC (BOOGIE WOOGIE)
PIANO MUSIC (3 HANDS)
PIANO MUSIC (4 HANDS)
PIANO MUSIC (4 HANDS), ARRANGED
PIANO MUSIC (4 HANDS)—TO 1800
PIANO MUSIC (6 HANDS)
PIANO MUSIC—HISTORY AND CRITICISM
PIANO MUSIC (JAZZ)
PIANO MUSIC, JUVENILE

PIANO MUSIC, JUVENILE (4 HANDS)
PIANO MUSIC, JUVENILE (2 PIANOS)
PIANO MUSIC (2 PIANOS)
PIANO MUSIC (2 PIANOS), ARRANGED
PIANO MUSIC (2 PIANOS, 8 HANDS)
PIANO MUSIC (3 PIANOS)
PIANO MUSIC—TO 1800

Dates denoting different things:
RECONSTRUCTION
RECONSTRUCTION—ARKANSAS
RECONSTRUCTION—BIBLIOGRAPHY
Reconstruction Finance Corporation
RECONSTRUCTION—MISSISSIPPI
Reconstruction of Berlin
RECONSTRUCTION—TEXAS
RECONSTRUCTION (1914–1939)
RECONSTRUCTION (1914–1939)—EUROPE
RECONSTRUCTION (1914–1939)—GERMANY
RECONSTRUCTION (1939–1951)
RECONSTRUCTION (1939–1951)—AUSTRIA
RECONSTRUCTION (1939–1951)—BIBLIOGRAPHY
RECONSTRUCTION (1939–1951)—EUROPE
RECONSTRUCTIONIST JUDAISM

33. Title entry arrangement

Preliminary note. This rule covers title added entries and title main entries.

For arrangement of titles under authors, see Rules 26–27; for series titles, see Rule 34; for music uniform titles and other special non-book material title headings, see Rule 37.

A. Filing position. Arrange title entries in their alphabetical places with other kinds of entries, after surname entries under the same word. Follow the basic rules for alphabetical arrangement as they may apply (e. g., disregard initial articles).

B. Identical title added entries—Subarrangement

1. Arrange identical title added entries alphabetically by the main entries of the books; or, if the entry is a title analytic for a part of a book written by an author other than the author of the whole work, arrange by the author of the analytic. Subarrange analytics with the same title and author chronologically by the imprint dates of the books in which they appear (according to Rule 26B11).

Example:

    Electra
  Euripides

    Electra
Giraudoux, Jean
    (In Bentley, E. R.   The modern theatre.   1955.   v. 1)
    Electra
Sophocles

  2. Arrange different editions of the same title chronologically by their imprint dates, following the same rules as those for arrangement under author (Rule 26B9).

  3. If different editions of the same title are by different authors, subarrange alphabetically by authors, even though this may place the editions out of order.

Example:

    Advanced electrical measurements
Michels, Walter Christian
    Advanced electrical measurements, by Walter C. Michels.   2d ed.
    ₜ1941ₜ
        First edition, 1932 ₜbyₜ William R. Smythe and Walter C. Michels.

    Advanced electrical measurements
Smythe, William Ralph
    Advanced electrical measurements, by William R. Smythe and Walter C. Michels.   1932.

  4. When a title and a partial title are identical and have the same main entry, subarrange alphabetically by the full title of the work, even though this may place the partial title first.

Example:

    Practical sign painting
Owen, Robert E
    New Practical sign painting.   ₜ1958ₜ
    Practical sign painting
Owen, Robert E
    Practical sign painting.   ₜ1948ₜ

  C. Order of title main entries, title added entries, and other kinds of entries under the same word or words. Arrange title main and added entries and other kinds of entries under the same word or words in groups in the following order (all examples follow 33D below):
    1) Personal name or pseudonym; corporate name, place name, or uniform title heading (for examples see American, The house that Jack built, Life, New Zealand, Time, and United Nations); *see* reference from initials that are identical with a serial title (for examples see Rule 5F, Initials, and Rule 35B2, Cross reference arrangement)

2) Subject *see* reference (for example see Economic geology)
3) Title entries for periodicals and newspapers (for details of subarrangement see 33D below)
4) Title *main* entries for separate works and serials other than periodicals and newspapers, subarranged in groups in the following order:
   a) Those with nothing following the title, subarranged by place of publication
   b) Those with subtitles or other phrases following the title, subarranged alphabetically by the subtitles or phrases
   In relation to other entries in the catalog consider only the title proper. Regard a subtitle only when there is more than one entry with the same main title, to distinguish between them. Subarrange different kinds of entries under the title of the same publication in the same order as that for periodicals and newspapers, according to 33D2 below. (For examples see Abraham Lincoln, Encyclopaedia Britannica, Japan year book, Life, New Zealand, The Times, United Nations, and Who's who)
5) Title *added* entries (titles with authors) and identical subject entries, interfiled and subarranged alphabetically by their main entries
6) Longer entries beginning with the same word or words
   Note. Title main entries precede identical title added entries and subjects because basically they are shorter entries, i. e., only a title need be considered in filing as compared to both title and main entry for added entries and subjects. All title main entries follow *see* references because a cross reference is shorter than an actual entry under the same word or words.

D. Title main entries for periodicals and newspapers—Details of subarrangement

1. In title main entries for periodicals and newspapers disregard subtitles and alternative titles. In relation to other entries in the catalog consider only the title proper. Subarrange identical titles first by place of publication and then by date, with earliest date first.

    Note. It is recommended that subtitles and alternative titles be disregarded because they are not generally known and tend to change frequently. Also, the placement of entries for a periodical or newspaper title as author in correct relationship to the title main entry for the same publication is facilitated (cf. 33D3 below).

2. Arrange different kinds of entries under the title of the same publication in groups in the following order:
   1) Title main entry for the publication
   2) Author entries (main and/or added entries) for the publication, subarranged alphabetically by titles according to Rule 26B2

Note. Periodical and newspaper titles will no longer be used as author main entries; they will be used as added entries instead (*Anglo-American Cataloging Rules*). If added entries are subarranged by their titles (according to Rule 26B2) the filing order will be the same whether the heading is a main entry or an added entry and old entries under the periodical or newspaper as author need not be changed.

3) Subject entries for the publication, subarranged by their main entries
4) Special editions of the publication (for examples see Life and Radio and television news)
5) Indexes, sections, supplements, etc. which appear as subheadings of the title (for example see The Times)

3. In author and subject headings for a periodical or newspaper disregard a place of publication following the title in relation to other entries in the catalog. Regard it only when there are entries for more than one serial with the same title, to distinguish between them. Likewise, disregard a subtitle in the rare instances where it is part of the heading. If desired, special marks may be used to indicate this to the filer (e. g., Time, <the weekly newsmagazine>).

Note. When there is more than one serial with the same title, the author and subject headings are usually identified by the city of publication, and, when necessary, by the years of publication in addition. In June 1949 the Library of Congress changed the punctuation of such modifiers after periodical titles from a period to parentheses, e.g., "Life. Chicago" to "Life (Chicago)."[59] The latter form is now applicable to newspapers also (*Anglo-American Cataloging Rules*, 6A). The headings file in the same position regardless of form.

Arrange the author and subject headings for each different publication following the corresponding title main entry, even though the title main entry may have a subtitle while the author and subject headings have only a place of publication. If there is no main entry for a publication in the catalog, file an author or subject heading where the main entry for that publication would be if there were one. (For examples see The American, Horizon, Life, The Times.)

Note. The designation "(Periodical)" is sometimes added after a periodical title to distinguish it from the same heading used with a different meaning. Never alphabet by "(Periodical)"; regard it only as a means of determining the correct position of the title as a periodical in relation to other entries in the catalog. (For example see United Nations.)

---

59. U. S. Library of Congress. Processing Dept. *Cataloging Service*. Washington, D. C. Bulletin 20, June 1949, p. 6.

Examples for 33C–D:

Abraham Lincoln. Boston, Educational Pub. Co. ₁1895₁
Abraham Lincoln. New York, Gilbertson Co., 1958.
Abraham Lincoln. ₁South Pasadena, Calif., W. A. Abbott, c1919₁
Abraham Lincoln. A study. Liverpool, McKowen & Finglass, 1865.
Abraham Lincoln; an appreciation. New York, Francis D. Tandy Co. ₁1906₁
Abraham Lincoln; articles from the magazines. ₁v. p.₁ 1909.
Abraham Lincoln. By an Oxford M. A. Portsmouth ₁Eng.₁ Holbrook & Son ₁1920?₁
Abraham Lincoln, by some men who knew him. Bloomington, Ill., Pantagraph Printing & Stationery Co. ₁c1910₁
Abraham Lincoln, 10 magazine articles. ₁v. p., 1880–1902₁
Abraham Lincoln: the story of his life . . . ₁Boston, Boston Sunday Globe, 1909₁

    Abraham Lincoln
Drinkwater, John

    Abraham Lincoln
₁Howison, George Holmes₁

Abraham Lincoln Association, Springfield, Ill.

    Abraham Lincoln; farmer's boy and president
₁Smith, George Barnett₁

Abraham Lincoln Fraternal League of America
Abraham Lincoln, late president of the United States, demonstrated to be the Gog of the Bible. ₁Memphis, Public ledger office₁ 1868.
Abraham Lincoln quarterly
Abraham Lincoln's religion

American
    A journal of a tour in Italy, in the year 1821
    see Dwight, Theodore

    An American
Oppression, a poem by an American.

An American
    The rationale of the China question
    see Nye, Gideon

The American; a national journal. v. 1–33; Oct. 16, 1880–Dec. 8, 1900. Philadelphia.
The American (Philadelphia)
    The administration and the Indians.
The American. v. 1–38; 1888–1925. Pittsburgh, Pa.
The American. v. 1, no. 1; May 1904. Saint Louis.

The American
James, Henry

An American ABC
AMERICAN (ARTIFICIAL LANGUAGE)
American Bridge Company

ECONOMIC GEOLOGY, *see* . . .
Economic geology.   v. 1–   Oct. 1905–   Lancaster, Pa. ɪetc.ɪ
Economic geology
 Fiftieth anniversary volume, 1905–1955.
Economic geology
 Monograph.
The economic geology of the Fife coalfields

Encyclopaedia Britannica, a new survey of universal
 knowledge   ɪtitle main entryɪ
Encyclopaedia Britannica
 Contemporary American painting.

 Encyclopaedia Britannica
Gateway to the great books.

Encyclopaedia Britannica
 Graphic arts.
ENCYCLOPAEDIA BRITANNICA

Horizon.   v. 1–2; Sept./Oct. 1936–Apr./May 1937.   Brooklyn, N. Y.
Horizon; a review of literature and art.   v. 1–20; Jan. 1940–Dec. 1949/
 Jan. 1950.   London.
Horizon (London)
 The golden Horizon.
Horizon; revue des lettres.   année 1–   1945–   Nantes.
Horizon; health, beauty, vitality.   v. 1–2, no. 2; 1936–38.   New York.
Horizon.   v. 1–3; 1937–40.   New York.
Horizon.   v. 1–   Sept. 1958–   ɪNew Yorkɪ

 Horizon (New York, 1958–   )
Mercer, Charles E
 Alexander the Great.

 Horizon (New York, 1958–   )
Isenberg, Irwin
 Caesar.

 Horizon
MacInnes, Helen

The Horizon book of ancient Greece

The house that Jack built   ɪuniform title headingɪ
 The house that Jack built; a Mother goose rhyme.

The house that jack built; a new game of questions   [title main entry]
    & commands.

    The house that Jack built
Caldecott, Randolph

The Japan year book. 1933–
The Japan year book; complete cyclopaedia of general information . . .
    1905–31.

Life, Cora Smith
Life; or, Religion & politics. no. 1–16; Apr. 3–July 17,1834. Birmingham.
Life. v. 1–   Nov. 23, 1936–   Chicago.
Life (Chicago)
    America's arts and skills.

    Life (Chicago)
Boswell, Peyton
    Modern American painting.

Life (Chicago)
    The world's great religions.
LIFE (CHICAGO)
Life. International ed. v. 1–   July 22, 1946–   Chicago.
Life; a record for busy folk. v. 1–   Jan. 1904–   Melbourne.
Life. v. 1 100, 1883–Nov. 1936. New York.
Life. New York   [old form]
    Auto fun.

    Life (New York)
The Spice of Life.

Life (New York)
    War as viewed by Life.
Life; digest of outstanding reading. v. 1–   Apr. 1, 1938–   West
    Melbourne.
The life. Boston, Colby & Rich [187–?]   [title main entry]

    LIFE
Mayer, Charles Leopold

    Life
Rutherford, Joseph Franklin

    LIFE
St. John-Stevas, Norman

Life à la Henri
LIFE (BIOLOGY)
LIFE-BOATS
Life can begin again
LIFE, FUTURE, *see . . .*

The life of reason
LIFE—ORIGIN

New Zealand, George Augustus Selwyn, bp. of, 1841–1867, *see* Selwyn,
    George Augustus, bp. of Lichfield, 1809–1878
New Zealand
    Official handbook of New Zealand.
New Zealand
    Trade discussions between the government of New Zealand and the
    government of the United Kingdom . . .
New Zealand.   Prepared under the direction of Frederick
    M. Rea.   ɪtitle main entryɪ
NEW ZEALAND
New Zealand.   Board of Health
NEW ZEALAND—DESCRIPTION AND TRAVEL
New Zealand forestry research notes

Radio and television news
Radio and television news.   Radio-electronic engineering edition

    Radio and television news
Brown, Donald E

Time, Mark, pseud.
Time, a monthly magazine. v. 1–24; Apr. 1879–91. London.
Time. v. 1–10; Aug. 23, 1884–Feb. 22, 1890. New York.
Time, the weekly news-magazine. v. 1–   Mar. 3, 1923–   New York.
Time, the weekly news-magazine
    December 7, the first thirty hours.

    Time, the weekly news-magazine
Havemann, Ernest
    They went to college.

Time, the weekly news-magazine
    Three hundred years of American painting.
TIME, THE WEEKLY NEWS-MAGAZINE

    TIME
Asimov, Isaac

    Time
Bates, Herbert Ernest
    (In his The woman who had imagination, and other stories)

    TIME
Bell, Thelma Harrington

Time and its mysteries
TIME, COGNITION OF, *see* . . .
Time, inc.

Time magazine, *see* Time, the weekly news-magazine
Time remembered

The Times.   v. 1 (no. 1–45); Dec. 12, 1807–Oct. 15, 1808.   Boston.
Times; a shorthand literary magazine.   v. 1; 1884.   Chicago.
The Times (Hartford) *see* The Hartford times
The Times (London)
    American railway number, Friday, June 28, 1912.

    The Times (London)
Robinson, W   Kay
    The course of nature.

The Times (London)
    St. Paul's in war and peace.
The Times (London)
    Special number on the Royal Society tercentenary.
THE TIMES (LONDON)
The Times (London) (Indexes)
    Index to the Times.   Jan./June 1914–
The Times (London)   Literary supplement.   1st–   year; Jan. 17, 1902–
The Times (London)   Literary supplement
    The American imagination.
The Times (London)   Russian section
The Times.   v. 1, no. 1; Jan. 15, 1848.   Washington.
The times.   By a young Bostonian.   1820.   ɾtitle main entryɪ
The times; or, A fig for invasion.   1797.   ɾtitle main entryɪ

    The times
Pinero, Sir Arthur Wing

Times and places
Times Bookshop, London
Times-Herald (Washington, D. C.)
The Times Literary supplement, *see* The Times (London)   Literary sup-
    plement
The Times of India (Bombay)
Times of trial

United Nations   ɾauthor entryɪ
The United Nations (Periodical) *see* . . .
United Nations; a fully illustrated album for the stamps and postal station-
    ery of United Nations.   v.   New York, Minkus
    Publications.   ɾloose-leaf—no dateɪ
The United Nations; a handbook of the U. N.   1946–
    ɾNew Yorkɪ C. E. Merrill Co.   ɾserialɪ
The United Nations; what you should know about it.
    New York.   ɾserial—no dateɪ
UNITED NATIONS

United Nations and how it works
UNITED NATIONS—ARMED FORCES
United Nations.   Charter
United Nations.   Secretariat
UNITED NATIONS—YEARBOOKS

"Who's who," a directory of Stratford.   [1st–   1937–
Who's who?   A society register containing the names of Cincinnati fam-
    ilies . . .   1892–
Who's who . . . an annual biographical dictionary . . .   18   –
Who's who; the official who's who among students in American universities
    and colleges.   v. 1–   1935–

    Who's who
Columbus, Ohio.   Chamber of Commerce

   , Who's who
Massachusetts.   State Normal School, Bridgewater

Who's who among association executives
Who's who in America; a biographical dictionary of notable living men and
    women.   v. [1]–   1899–1900—
Who's who in America
    The memorial everlasting.
WHO'S WHO IN AMERICA

E. Inverted titles

Note. It is recommended that inverted titles not be used. The Library
of Congress discontinued the use of inverted titles as of December 31,
1940. If such entries are used, arrange them according to the following
rule.

Interfile an inverted title alphabetically with other titles and entries beginning with the same word, disregarding both the punctuation and an initial
article following the comma.

Example:

Antiques
Antiques A to Z
Antiques, The book of
Antiques for profit
Antiques, Furnishing with
Antiques in their periods, 1600–1830
Antiques, A treasury of
The Antiques treasury of furniture and other decorative arts

34. Series entry arrangement

A. Series entries under title. Arrange series entries and series references under title in their alphabetical places with other titles, etc. Arrange a series
entry after an identical *see* reference.

1. Unnumbered series. Subarrange unnumbered series entries alphabetically by their main entries.

If there is an identical title added entry (title with an author) its position in relation to the series entries will depend on the form of the series entries. If the series entries are unit cards, interfile the series and title added entries, subarranging them by their main entries.

Example:

      Our debt to Greece and Rome   ɪseriesɪ
Abbott, Frank Frost
      Roman politics.

      Our debt to Greece and Rome   ɪseriesɪ
Campbell, James Marshall
      The Greek fathers.

      Our debt to Greece and Rome   ɪseriesɪ
Nixon, Paul
      Martial and the modern epigram.

      Our debt to Greece and Rome   ɪtitle added entryɪ
Osborn, Edward Bolland

      Our debt to Greece and Rome   ɪɑorioɑɪ
Roberts, William Rhys
      Greek rhetoric and literary criticism.

If, however, the series entries are combined, arrange the series entries first, then the title added entries.

Example:

Our debt to Greece and Rome
      Abbott, F. F.   Roman politics.
      Campbell, J. M.   The Greek fathers.
      Nixon, P.   Martial and the modern epigram.
      Roberts, W. R.   Greek rhetoric and literary criticism.

      Our debt to Greece and Rome   ɪtitleɪ
Osborn, Edward Bolland

2. Numbered series. Subarrange numbered series numerically. This order should be followed in the listing on combined cards as well as for unit cards. In either case, title added entries under the same title as the series follow the series entries.

Examples:

      The Reference shelf, v. 35, no. 6
Steel, Ronald
      Italy.

The Reference shelf, v. 36, no. 1
Colby, Vineta
        American culture in the sixties.

The Reference shelf, v. 36, no. 2
Madow, Pauline
        The Peace Corps.

The Reference shelf, v. 36, no. 3
Debate index.   1964.

The Reference shelf, v. 37, no. 1
Isenberg, Irwin
        Ferment in Eastern Europe.

AMERICAN STATESMEN, *see . . .*

American statesmen, v. 1
Morse, John Torrey
        Benjamin Franklin.

American statesmen, v. 2
Hosmer, James Kendall
        Samuel Adams.

American statesmen, v. 31
McCall, Samuel Walker
        Thaddeus Stevens.

American statesmen.   Second series, v. 2
Burton, Theodore Elijah
        John Sherman.

American statesmen   ［title added entry］
Griggs, Edward Howard

If the series is cataloged both as a set and as separates, the title main entry
for the set precedes the series entries for the separates.

Example:

The American nation: a history from original sources by
        associated scholars.   28v.   ［title main entry］

The American nation, v. 1
Cheyney, Edward Potts
        European background of American history.

The American nation, v. 2
Farrand, Livingston
        Basis of American history.

The American nation, v. 8
Howard, George Elliott
        Preliminaries of the Revolution.

The American nation   ɪtitle added entryɪ
Hicks, John Donald

3. Dated series. Subarrange dated series chronologically. This order should be followed in the listing on combined cards as well as for unit cards.

Example:

The Charles Eliot Norton lectures, 1937–1938
Tinker, Chauncey Brewster
   Painter and poet.

The Charles Eliot Norton lectures, 1953–1954
Read, Sir Herbert Edward
   Icon and idea.

The Charles Eliot Norton lectures, 1958–1959
Chávez, Carlos
   Musical thought.

B. Series entries under author and title

1. Arrange author-title series entries and series references alphabetically the same as any author-title entry, interfiling the series titles with other titles that have the same author entry.

   Note. If author-title series entries on unit cards are typed as "double headings," i. e., with the title on a separate line below the author, filing of the entries in the author and title file will be much easier.

2. Subarrange author-title series the same as series under title, i. e., alphabetically by main entry, numerically, or chronologically, depending on the form of the heading.

Examples for 34B:

New Mexico.   University
   The alumni directory.
New Mexico.   University
   Biological series
   see its Bulletin.   Biological series
New Mexico.   University
   Bulletin.   Bibliographical series.

New Mexico.   University
   Bulletin.   Biological series, v. 4, no. 1.
Castetter, Edward Franklin
   Uncultivated native plants used as sources of food.

New Mexico.   University
   Bulletin.   Biological series, v. 4, no. 5.
Castetter, Edward Franklin
   The ethnobiology of the Chiricahua and Mescalero Apache.

197

New Mexico.   University
   Bulletin.   English literature and language series, v. 1, no. 1.
Pearce, Thomas Matthew
   Christopher Marlowe, figure of the renaissance.

New Mexico.   University
   Bulletin.   English literature and language series, v. 1, no. 2.
St. Clair, George
   Dante viewed through his imagery.

New Mexico.   University
   Bulletin.   Political science series.
New Mexico.   University
   Catalogue.
New Mexico.   University
   English literature and language series
   see its Bulletin.   English literature and language series
New Mexico.   University
   Ethnobiological studies in the American Southwest.

American Management Association
   Reporting sales data effectively.

American Management Association
   Research report, no. 6.
Dale, Ernest
   The unionization of foremen.

American Management Association
   Research report, no. 18.
Cutter, Walter Airey
   Organization and functions of the safety department.

American Management Association
   Research report, no. 30.
Evans, Chester E
   Supervisory responsibility and authority.

American Management Association
   Research report.
      Continued, with no. 31, as:
   American Management Association
      Research study.

American Management Association
   Research study.
      Continuation, with no. 31, of:
   American Management Association
      Research report.

American Management Association
Research study, no. 31.
Floyd, Elizabeth R
Compensating American managers abroad.

American Management Association
Research study, no. 32.
Thompson, Stewart
Management creeds and philosophies.

American Management Association
The sales supervisor and his place in management.

American Management Association   [added entry]
Dooker, M   Joseph
Selection of management personnel.

American Management Association
Special report, no. 1.
American Management Association
Tested approaches to capital equipment replacement.

American Management Association
Special report, no. 27.
American Management Association.   Marketing Division
Materials and methods of sales forecasting.

American Management Association
Successful production planning and control.

C. Series only partly numbered. When part of a series is numbered and part is not, the method of arrangement of the entries will have to be determined individually for each series. If the numbering started after some volumes had been published without numbers, the unnumbered volumes may be arranged first, alphabetically, followed by the numbered volumes in numerical order. If volume numbers are supplied later for the earlier volumes in a series, they should be added to the series notes and series entries for them.

35. Cross reference arrangement

A. Filing position. A reference or explanatory note precedes all other entries under the same word or words. In relation to other entries in the catalog consider only the heading on a cross reference or explanatory note; disregard the words "see" and "see also," the heading or headings referred to, and the note. If there are references to more than one heading, subarrange the references alphabetically by the headings referred to (it is preferable, however, to combine all such headings alphabetically in one reference).

Note. A reference precedes an entry for a work because basically a reference is shorter than an actual entry.

B. "See" references

Note. Whenever the intent is to interfile variant forms under the form referred to, an explanatory reference should be used rather than a straight *see* reference (see Rules 10–11 and 13B).

1. File *see* references in their alphabetical places. *See* references from subject subdivisions, inverted subjects, etc. are arranged according to the regular rules for subject arrangement. For the position of a *see* reference in relation to an explanatory note card under the same heading, see 35E below.

Examples:

Henry, Norman Fordyce McKerron
Henry, O., *see* Porter, William Sydney
Henry, Omer

COUNTY CHARTERS
The county fair
COUNTY FINANCE, *see* . . .
COUNTY GOVERNMENT

HYGIENE
HYGIENE, DENTAL, *see* . . .
Hygiene for students
HYGIENE—HISTORY
HYGIENE, INDUSTRIAL, *see* . . .
HYGIENE, JEWISH

MOVING-PICTURES
MOVING-PICTURES—CENSORSHIP
MOVING-PICTURES—COPYRIGHT, *see* . . .
MOVING-PICTURES, DOCUMENTARY
MOVING-PICTURES—EDITING
MOVING-PICTURES—FESTIVALS, *see* . . .
MOVING-PICTURES IN EDUCATION
MOVING-PICTURES—LAW

2. If a *see* reference is the same as an actual entry, arrange the *see* reference first, except that a surname entry always precedes a reference.

Examples:

Corea, Lois Fleming
    New marine mollusks.
COREA, *see* KOREA

DOCTORS, *see* PHYSICIANS

    The doctors   ₍fiction title₎
Soubiran, André

Siddhārtha, *see* Gautama Buddha

Siddhartha   [fiction title]
Hesse, Hermann

AIR NAVIGATION, *see* . . .
Air navigation . . . Pub. under the supervision of the Training
    Division, Bureau of Aeronautics, U. S. Navy   [title main entry]
AIR NAVIGATION AIDS, *see* . . .

3. If two different kinds of *see* references are identical in wording, arrange
them alphabetically by the headings referred to (do not combine such references).

Example:

HIGH TEMPERATURE MATERIALS, *see* MATERIALS AT HIGH
    TEMPERATURES
High-temperature materials, *see* Plenum Press handbooks of
    high-temperature materials   [series]

4. If, due to disregarding punctuation, two different forms of the same *see*
reference would be filed in the same place, only one need be retained. The
following examples show the form suggested for retention.

Examples:

BIRDS—NESTS, *see* . . .
BIRDS' NESTS, *see* . . .   [keep]

ENGINEERING—MATERIALS, *see* . . .
ENGINEERING MATERIALS, *see* . . .   [keep]

GASES—IONIZATION, *see* . . .
GASES, IONIZATION OF, *see* . . .   [keep]

C. "See also" references. File a *see also* reference before the first entry
under the same word or words. If *see also* references are made for headings
under which there are no entries in the catalog, file the reference where the
heading itself would be filed. For the position of a *see also* reference in relation to an explanatory note card under the same heading when both are used,
see 35E below.

Examples:

CHILDREN, *see also* . . .
CHILDREN
CHILDREN, ADOPTED
CHILDREN—CARE AND HYGIENE, *see also* . . .
CHILDREN—CARE AND HYGIENE
CHILDREN—CARE AND HYGIENE—BIBLIOGRAPHY

TREASON, *see also* . . .

    Treason   [fiction title]
Gessner, Robert

    TREASON
Thérive, André

Treason at the point
TREASON—CANADA
Treason of the people
TREASON—U. S.

Pennsylvania.   Adjutant-General's Office
Pennsylvania.   Agricultural College
    see also Pennsylvania State College
                Pennsylvania State University
Pennsylvania angler

D. Author-title references. Arrange author-title references (which may be used for certain pseudonyms, series, legal headings, uniform titles, etc.) in their alphabetical places as if they were author and title entries.

Examples:

An American gentleman
    The patriot muse
    see Prime, Benjamin Young
American gentleman . . . The leading men's fashion journal of the world
                                           [periodical title]

United States
    Chamizal arbitration.
United States
    Constitution
    see U. S.   Constitution
United States
    The counter case of the United States of America . . .

Beethoven, Ludwig van
    [Minuets, orchestra, K. 12]
Beethoven, Ludwig van
    Moonlight sonata
    see his Sonata, piano, no. 14, op. 27, no. 2, C♯ minor
Beethoven, Ludwig van
    [Overtures.   Selections]

E. Explanatory cards. File explanatory notes and references before the first entry under the same heading. An explanatory note precedes a *see* or *see also* reference under the same heading. For an example of an explanatory note in relation to a *see* reference and actual entries, see "M" in Examples on p. 17.

1. History cards

Examples:

American Federation of Labor
>The Federation of Organized Trades and Labor Unions of the United States and Canada was organized in 1881. At its 6th annual session in 1886 the American Federation of Labor was organized and absorbed the older organization. On Dec. 5, 1955 the American Federation of Labor merged with the Congress of Industrial Organizations to form the American Federation of Labor and Congress of Industrial Organizations.

American Federation of Labor, *see also* American Federation of Labor and Congress of Industrial Organizations

American Federation of Labor
>American Federation of Labor; history, encyclopedia, reference book.

AMERICAN FEDERATION OF LABOR
American Federation of Labor and Congress of Industrial Organizations
>Formed Dec. 5, 1955, by the merger of the American Federation of Labor with the Congress of Industrial Organizations.

American Federation of Labor and Congress of Industrial Organizations
>*see also* American Federation of Labor
>>Congress of Industrial Organizations

American Federation of Labor and Congress of Industrial Organizations
>Proceedings of the . . . convention.

AMERICAN FEDERATION OF LABOR AND CONGRESS OF INDUSTRIAL ORGANIZATIONS
American Federation of Labor and Congress of Industrial Organizations. Committee on Political Education
American Federation of Labor. Dept. of Education

2. Information cards

Example:

Epstein, Beryl Williams
>Works by Beryl Williams Epstein in collaboration with Samuel Epstein, published under the names Adam Allen and Douglas Coe, are entered in this catalog under Allen, Adam and Coe, Douglas, respectively.

Epstein, Beryl Williams
>Fashion is our business.

3. Scope notes

Example:

INTERPLANETARY VOYAGES
> Here are entered the early, imaginary, and descriptive accounts of travel beyond the earth.
> Works on the physics and technical details of flight beyond the atmosphere of the earth are entered under the heading SPACE FLIGHT.

INTERPLANETARY VOYAGES, *see also* . . .

INTERPLANETARY VOYAGES
Coggins, Jack
> By space ship to the moon.

In a subject note that has further examples in brackets at the end of the heading, e. g., CORPORATIONS, AMERICAN, [FRENCH, ETC.], disregard the words in brackets and alphabet under the part of the heading that precedes the brackets, e. g., CORPORATIONS, AMERICAN.

Example:

CORPORATIONS
CORPORATIONS—ACCOUNTING
CORPORATIONS, AMERICAN, [FRENCH, ETC.]
> Here are entered works on foreign corporations chartered by nationals of individual countries.
> Works on foreign corporations in general are entered under the heading CORPORATIONS, FOREIGN.

CORPORATIONS, AMERICAN
Bryson, George D
> American management abroad.

4. Miscellaneous note cards

Examples:

Church of . . .
> Local churches are entered under the name of the city or other community in which they are located.

The church of Christ [title]
Church of Christ of Latter-Day Saints
Church of Christ, Scientist
Church of England
The church of the Fathers [title]

INTERNATIONAL LAW
> Books cataloged before Dec. 1, 1944 will be found under the heading INTERNATIONAL LAW AND RELATIONS.

INTERNATIONAL LAW, *see also* . . .

INTERNATIONAL LAW
Americano, Jorge
 The new foundation of international law.   1947.

INTERNATIONAL LAW AND RELATIONS
  Books cataloged after Dec. 1, 1944 will be found under the head-
ings
 INTERNATIONAL LAW
 INTERNATIONAL RELATIONS

INTERNATIONAL LAW AND RELATIONS
Alguy, Jeremiah S
 Permanent world peace.   1943.

Arabian nights
  For separately published stories from this work see:
 Ali Baba
 Sindbad, the sailor
Arabian nights
 Arabian nights.
Arabian nights
 Tales from the Arabian nights.

5. Authority cards. If authority cards are included in the same file with
actual entries they should precede all entries for the same heading.

36. Numerical and chronological arrangement

See also Rule 9, Numerals; Rule 20, Surname entries; Rule 25, Given name
entries; Rule 29, Bible; Rule 32, Subject arrangement; Rule 34, Series entry
arrangement.

A. General rule. A numerical or a chronological arrangement, rather than
an alphabetical, should be followed when numbers or dates distinguish between entries, or headings, otherwise identical, with lowest number or earliest
date first.

In relation to other entries in the catalog disregard a numeral or date that
indicates a sequence. Regard it only for the purpose of arranging a sequence.
If the number precedes the item it modifies it must be mentally transposed to
follow the item (i. e., file "U. S. Army. 1st Cavalry" as "U. S. Army. Cavalry,
1st").

B. Titles

**1. Numerical designations following or at end of titles that are otherwise
identical up to that point**

Examples:

More, Paul Elmer
 Aristocracy and justice; Shelburne essays, ninth series.

More, Paul Elmer
   Benjamin Franklin.
More, Paul Elmer
   The drift of romanticism; Shelburne essays, eighth series.
More, Paul Elmer
   Pages from an Oxford diary.
More, Paul Elmer
   Shelburne essays.   1st series.
More, Paul Elmer
   Shelburne essays.   Second series.
More, Paul Elmer
   Shelburne essays.   Fourth series.
More, Paul Elmer
   Shelburne essays.   Seventh series.
More, Paul Elmer
   Shelburne essays.   Eighth series
   see his The drift of romanticism
More, Paul Elmer
   Shelburne essays.   Ninth series
   see his Aristocracy and justice
More, Paul Elmer
   Shelburne essays.   Tenth series
   see his With the wits
More, Paul Elmer
   With the wits; Shelburne essays, tenth series.

Venezuela.   Laws, statutes, etc.
   Reglamento de aduanas n° 1 sobre . . .
   Reglamento de aduanas n° 2 relativo a . . .
   Reglamento de aduanas n° 3 relativo a . . .
   Reglamento de aduanas n° 4 referente al . . .

Bolles, Albert
   The financial history of the United States, from 1774 to 1789.
   The financial history of the United States, from 1789 to 1860.
   The financial history of the United States, from 1861 to 1885.

Long, Augustus White
   American poems, 1776–1900.
   American poems, 1776–1922.   Rev.

Titles that can be arranged in a numerical sequence under author cannot always be so arranged as title added entries because as added entries they must take their place with other titles beginning with the same words. For an example of titles like "Europe since 1815" see p. 44.

2. Numerical designations preceding otherwise identical titles

a. Alphabetize by the word following the number, then subarrange numerically, under the author entry.

Example:

California.   Dept. of Education
    Legal calendar for public school officials.
    1935 legislative proposals.
    1937 legislative proposals.
    1939 legislative proposals.
    1941 legislative proposals.
    Lessons in English for intermediate students.

b. Titles such as "Report" preceded by a series of numbers are subarranged numerically under the author entry whether the numbers are written as numerals or as words.

Example:

By-laws
Final report
General report
Proceedings
First report
Second report
Third report
Fourth report

c. Other cases in which the same title is preceded by a series of numbers, especially those by personal authors and those in which the numbers are written as words, are arranged alphabetically by the first word of the titles under the author.

Example:

Reinfeld, Fred
    The complete chessplayer.
    Eighth book of chess.
    Fifth book of chess.
    Fourth book of chess.
    The great chess masters and their games.
    Second book of chess.
    Seventh book of chess.

C. Corporate headings—General examples
1. Dates only

Examples:

Massachusetts.   Constitutional Convention, 1779–1780
Massachusetts.   Constitutional Convention, 1853
Massachusetts.   Constitutional Convention, 1917–1919

Scientific Society of San Antonio (1892–1894)
Scientific Society of San Antonio (Founded 1904)

Yale University.   Class of 1797
Yale University.   Class of 1802
Yale University.   Class of 1816

2. Number only

Examples:

Lexington (U. S. aircraft carrier, 1st of the name)
Lexington (U. S. aircraft carrier, 2d of the name)

U. S.   Circuit Court (1st Circuit)
U. S.   Circuit Court (2d Circuit)
U. S.   Circuit Court (5th Circuit)

3. Number and date

Example:

Hague.   International Peace Conference, 1899
Hague.   International Peace Conference, 2d, 1907

Disregard a place name when it follows a number.

Example:

American Peace Congress, 1st, New York, 1907
American Peace Congress, 3d, Baltimore, 1911
American Peace Congress, 4th, St. Louis, 1913

4. Place and date. If there is no numeral to indicate a sequence, the heading being followed only by a place and date in that order, arrange alphabetically by the place, disregarding the date at end.

Examples:

Conference on Religious Education, London, 1945–1947
Conference on Religious Education, University of Illinois, 1905

OLYMPIC GAMES
Olympic games, Athens, 1896
Olympic games, London, 1948
Olympic games, Los Angeles, 1932
Olympic games 1964*   [title]
OLYMPIC GAMES—REVIVAL, 1896–
Olympic games, Rome, 1960
Olympic games, Stockholm, 1912
Olympic games, Tokyo, 1964
Olympic games (Winter) Garmisch-Partenkirchen, 1936
Olympic games (Winter) Innsbruck, 1964

Olympic games (Winter) Lake Placid, 1932
Olympic games (Winter) Squaw Valley, 1960

*In this title the date is filed as if it were spelled out ɩnineteen sixty-fourɩ because it is not part of a sequence.

D. Same heading with and without distinguishing numerals or dates
See also Rule 9D, Names of things that include a numeral.

When the same name is used for more than one different thing (as a ship, balloon, etc.) or organization (as Ku Klux Klan) and one of them has no distinguishing numerals in its heading, arrange them in groups in the following order:

1) The heading with no numerals, without subheadings
2) The heading with no numerals, with all its corporate and subject subdivisions and longer entries beginning with the same name, interfiled
3) The heading with numerals, without subheadings
4) The heading with numerals, with all its corporate and subject subdivisions

Examples:

Explorer   ɩtitleɩ
EXPLORER (ARTIFICIAL SATELLITE)
EXPLORER (BALLOON)
EXPLORER II (BALLOON)
An explorer comes home
EXPLORER (SCHOONER)

KU KLUX KLAN
KU KLUX KLAN—FICTION
Ku Klux Klan in American politics
KU KLUX KLAN (1915–   )
KU KLUX KLAN (1915–   )—BIBLIOGRAPHY

United Nations
UNITED NATIONS—AFRICA
United Nations agreements
UNITED NATIONS—BUILDINGS
United Nations Conference on Trade and Employment . . .
United Nations. Economic Affairs Dept.
UNITED NATIONS—ITALY
United Nations studies   ɩseries titleɩ
UNITED NATIONS—YEARBOOKS
United Nations (1942–1945)
United Nations (1942–1945) International Military Tribunal
UNITED NATIONS (1942–1945)—SONGS AND MUSIC
United Nations (1942–1945) Treaties, etc.

209

E. **Numerals or dates designating parts of a whole or inclusive heading.** When a series of numerals or dates designates parts of a whole and there are also alphabetical extensions of the inclusive heading, arrange the alphabetical group before the numerical group.

The following are typical examples of headings with entries for the whole and also for numbered or dated parts. For treaties, see 36F below.

1. **Chiefs of state.** Disregard the name in parentheses that follows the dates.

Examples:

New York (State) Governor
New York (State) Governor, 1933–1942 (Lehman)
New York (State) Governor, 1942 (Poletti)
New York (State) Governor, 1943–1954 (Dewey)

U. S. President
U. S. President, Executive Office of the, *see . . .*
U. S. President, 1789–1797 (Washington)
U. S. President, 1801–1809 (Jefferson)
U. S. President, 1953–1961 (Eisenhower)

2. **Constitutions, charters, etc.**

Examples:

France. Constitution
FRANCE. CONSTITUTION—AMENDMENTS
France. Constitution, 1791
France. Constitution, 1795
France. Constitution, 1814
FRANCE—CONSTITUTIONAL HISTORY

New York (City) Charter
New York (City) Charter, 1901
New York (City) Charter, 1938

U. S. Constitution
U. S. CONSTITUTION—AMENDMENTS
U. S. CONSTITUTION—AMENDMENTS—FILMSTRIPS
U. S. Constitution. 1st–10th amendments
U. S. Constitution. 1st amendment
U. S. Constitution. 4th amendment
U. S. Constitution. 13th–15th amendments
U. S. Constitution. 14th amendment
U. S. Constitution. 15th amendment
U. S. CONSTITUTION—ANNIVERSARIES
U. S. CONSTITUTION—SIGNERS

3. Laws, statutes, etc.

Note. Earlier cataloging rules allowed for the addition to the subheading "Laws, statutes, etc." of the inclusive dates of the reign, administration, or legislative period and in parentheses the name of the incumbent executive or the designation of the legislative period for acts enacted during that period. The *Anglo-American Cataloging Rules* do not have this provision. Older entries with dates may be left in the catalog, arranged after the heading without dates, as in the following example.

Example:

> Gt. Brit.   Laws, statutes, etc.
> Gt. Brit.   Laws, statutes, etc., 449–1066
> Gt. Brit.   Laws, statutes, etc., 871–901 (Alfred the Great)
> Gt. Brit.   Laws, statutes, etc., 1066–1087 (William I)
> Gt. Brit.   Laws, statutes, etc., 1837–1901 (Victoria)

4. Legislatures

Examples:

> Gt. Brit.   Parliament
> Gt. Brit.   Parliament.   All-Party Delegation to Hungary
> GT. BRIT.   PARLIAMENT—HISTORY
> Gt. Brit.   Parliament.   House of Commons
> Gt. Brit.   Parliament.   House of Commons.   Standing Committee on . . .
> Gt. Brit.   Parliament.   House of Lords
> Gt. Brit.   Parliament.   House of Lords.   Select Committee . . .
> Gt. Brit.   Parliament.   Joint Committee on . . .
> GT. BRIT.   PARLIAMENT—REFORM
> Gt. Brit.   Parliament.   Select Joint Committee to . . .
> Gt. Brit.   Parliament, 1305
> Gt. Brit.   Parliament, 1642
> Gt. Brit.   Parliament, 1648.   House of Commons
> Gt. Brit.   Parliament, 1766.   House of Lords
> Gt. Brit.   Parliament, 1776.   House of Commons
> Gt. Brit.   Parliament, 1911

> U. S.   Congress   ⌜main and/or added entries⌝
> U. S.   CONGRESS
> U. S.   Congress.   Aviation Policy Board
> U. S.   CONGRESS—BIOGRAPHY
> U. S.   Congress.   Committee on . . .
> U. S.   Congress.   Conference Committees, 1905–1906
> U. S.   Congress.   Conference Committees, 1942
> U. S.   Congress.   Conference Committees, 1962
> U. S.   CONGRESS—HISTORY

U. S.   Congress.   House   [main and/or added entries]
U. S.   CONGRESS.   HOUSE
U. S.   Congress.   House.   Committee on . . .
U. S.   CONGRESS.   HOUSE—HISTORY
U. S.   Congress.   House.   Special Committee to . . .
U. S.   Congress.   Joint Committee on the Library
U. S.   Congress.   Joint Select Committee on Retrenchment
U. S.   CONGRESS—RULES AND PRACTICE
U. S.   Congress.   Senate   [main and/or added entries]
U. S.   CONGRESS.   SENATE
U. S.   Congress.   Senate.   Committee on . . .
U. S.   CONGRESS.   SENATE—ELECTIONS
U. S.   Congress.   Senate.   Select Committee on . . .
U. S.   Congress.   Special Committee on . . .
U. S.   Congress.   Yorktown Centennial Commission, *see* . . .
U. S.   1st–2d Congress, 1789–1793
U. S.   1st Congress, 1789–1791
U. S.   1ST CONGRESS, 1789–1791
U. S.   1st Congress, 1789–1791.   House
U. S.   1st Congress, 1789–1791.   Senate
U. S.   1ST CONGRESS, 1789–1791.   SENATE
U. S.   1st Congress, 1st session, 1789
U. S.   1st Congress, 1st session, 1789.   House
U. S.   1st Congress, 2d session, 1790.   House
U. S.   40th Congress, 1867–1869
U. S.   63d Congress, 1913–1915
U. S.   63d Congress, 1913–1915.   House
U. S.   63d Congress, 1913–1915.   Senate
U. S.   63d Congress, Special session, 1913.   Senate   [held before 1st sess.]
U. S.   63d Congress, 1st session, 1913
U. S.   63d Congress, 1st session, 1913.   House
U. S.   63D CONGRESS, 1ST SESSION, 1913.   HOUSE
U. S.   63d Congress, 1st session, 1913.   Senate
U. S.   63D CONGRESS, 1ST SESSION, 1913.   SENATE
U. S.   63d Congress, 2d session, 1913–1914
U. S.   63d Congress, 2d session, 1913–1914.   House
U. S.   63d Congress, 2d session, 1913–1914.   Senate
U. S.   63d Congress, 3d session, 1914–1915
U. S.   63D CONGRESS, 3D SESSION, 1914–1915
U. S.   63d Congress, 3d session, 1914–1915.   House
U. S.   63d Congress, 3d session, 1914–1915.   Senate
U. S.   86th Congress, 1st session, 1959

5. Military units. Military units with distinctive names are arranged alphabetically by their names. Units beginning with a number (whether an Arabic or Roman numeral or spelled out) are arranged alphabetically by the word following the number, then numerically by the number. Regard the full name of the unit but disregard subdivisions or modifications of a unit except in relation to other headings under the same unit (i. e., "U. S. Army Air Forces. 305th Bombardment Group (Heavy)" precedes "U. S. Army Air Forces. 386th Bombardment Group").

Examples:

Connecticut Infantry
Connecticut Infantry. Connecticut Battalion, 1764
Connecticut Infantry. Lyman's Regiment, 1757
Connecticut Infantry. Mott's Regiment, 1776
Connecticut Infantry. New Haven Grays, 1816–
Connecticut Infantry. Putnam Phalanx
Connecticut Infantry. 1st Regt., 1762–1763
Connecticut Infantry. 1st Regt., Co. K, 1898
Connecticut Infantry. 1st Regt. (Militia)
Connecticut Infantry. 2d Regt., 1776, *see also* . . .
Connecticut Infantry. 2d Regt., 1861
Connecticut Infantry. 6th Regt., 1775
Connecticut Infantry. 6th Regt., 1861–1865, *see also* . . .
Connecticut Infantry. 6th Regt., 5th Co.
Connecticut Infantry. 21st Regt., 1862–1865
Connecticut Infantry. 29th Regt., 1864 1865
Connecticut Infantry. Ward's Regiment, 1776–1777
Connecticut Infantry. Waterbury's Regiment, 1776

U. S. Army
U. S. Army. A. E. F., 1917–1920
U. S. Army. A. E. F., 1917–1920. Air Service
U. S. Army. A. E. F., 1917–1920. 1st Army
U. S. Army. A. E. F., 1917–1920. 1st Division
U. S. Army. A. E. F., 1917–1920. 2d Division
U. S. Army. A. E. F., 1917–1920. 82d Division
U. S. Army. A. E. F., 1917–1920. General Staff
U. S. ARMY. A. E. F., 1917–1920—REGIMENTAL HISTORIES
U. S. Army. A. E. F., 1917–1920. Services of Supply
U. S. Army Air Forces
U. S. Army Air Forces. 7th Air Force
U. S. Army Air Forces. 8th Air Force
U. S. Army Air Forces. 8th Air Force. 34th Bombardment Group,
    see . . .
U. S. Army Air Forces. 8th Air Force. 401st Bombardment Group,
    see . . .
U. S. Army Air Forces. 8th Air Force. 65th Fighter Wing, *see* . . .
U. S. Army Air Forces. Air Service Command

U. S. Army Air Forces. 9th Bombardment Division
U. S. Army Air Forces. 34th Bombardment Group
U. S. Army Air Forces. 303d Bombardment Group
U. S. Army Air Forces. 305th Bombardment Group (Heavy)
U. S. Army Air Forces. 386th Bombardment Group
U. S. Army Air Forces. 11th Bombardment Squadron
U. S. Army Air Forces. 513th Bombardment Squadron
U. S. Army Air Forces. 3d Bombardment Wing. WAC Detachment,
      see . . .
U. S. Army Air Forces. 308th Bombardment Wing (Heavy)
U. S. ARMY AIR FORCES—DRAMA
U. S. Army Air Forces. Flying Training Command
U. S. ARMY AIR FORCES—HISTORY
U. S. Army Air Forces. 82d Interceptor Control Squadron, *see* . . .
U. S. Army. American Expeditionary Force, 1917–1920, *see* U. S.
      Army. A. E. F., 1917–1920
U. S. Army and Navy Munitions Board
U. S. Army. 555th Antiaircraft Artillery Battalion
U. S. ARMY—APPOINTMENTS AND RETIREMENTS
U. S. Army. 1st Armored Division
U. S. Army. 3d Armored Division
U. S. Army. Armored Force
U. S. Army. First Army
U. S. Army. Second Army
U. S. Army. Third Army
U. S. Army. Fourth Army
U. S. Army. Fifth Army
U. S. Army. Army Nurse Corps, *see* . . .
U. S. Army. Army of the Shenandoah
U. S. ARMY—BIOGRAPHY
U. S. Army. Cavalry
U. S. ARMY. CAVALRY—DRILL AND TACTICS
U. S. Army. 1st Cavalry
U. S. Army. 1st Cavalry (Colored)
U. S. Army. 1st Cavalry (Volunteer)
U. S. Army. 3d Cavalry
U. S. Army. 1st Cavalry Division
U. S. Army. Continental Army
U. S. Army. II Corps
U. S. Army. IV Corps
U. S. Army. Corps of Engineers
U. S. Army. Counter Intelligence Corps

U. S. Army. Dept. of Texas
U. S. Army. 10th Division
U. S. Army. 24th Division
U. S. Army. 101st Division
U. S. Army. Division of Military Aeronautics
U. S. Army. Division of the Philippines
U. S. Army. Engineer Amphibian Command
U. S. Army. 148th Field Artillery
U. S. Army. 148th Field Artillery. Battery C
U. S. Army. 305th Field Artillery
U. S. Army. 110th Field Artillery Battalion
U. S. Army. 66th Field Artillery Brigade

F. Treaties, etc.

Note. Application of the *Anglo-American Cataloging Rules* results in headings different from those established according to earlier cataloging rules. Both prescribe the form subheading "Treaties, etc." after the name of a country, but whereas formerly the name of a second party to a treaty never appeared in the heading, according to the new rules that name will be the first element after the subheading "Treaties, etc." when applicable. Also, instead of the dates of reign or administration and the name of the executive incumbent in the year of signing, the exact date of signing will be added. The heading for a treaty between the United States and Burma signed June 24, 1959 would vary as follows:

> Old: U. S. Treaties, etc., 1953–1961 (Eisenhower)
> New: U. S. Treaties, etc. Burma, June 24, 1959

The problem of arranging long files of similar titles under the same heading will be greatly alleviated because the former all-inclusive heading for administrations will be broken down into very specific headings with few titles under each.

1. Old headings. Arrange old-form entries for treaties chronologically by the dates following the subheading "Treaties, etc."

Example (Old headings):

U. S. Treaties, etc.
U. S. Treaties, etc., 1845–1849 (Polk)
U. S. Treaties, etc., 1853–1857 (Pierce)
U. S. Treaties, etc., 1923–1929 (Coolidge)
U. S. Treaties, etc., 1945–1953 (Truman)
U. S. Treaties, etc., 1953–1961 (Eisenhower)
U. S. Treaties, etc., 1961–1963 (Kennedy)
U. S. Treaties, etc., 1963–   (Lyndon B. Johnson)

215

2. New headings

Note. Since in the new method of forming the headings there are two distinct sets of subdivisions rather than a whole with a chronological sequence of parts, arrangement is according to the rule for Subject arrangement (32C).

Arrange new-form entries with the subheading "Treaties, etc." in groups in the following order:

1) The subheading without further subdivisions
2) The subheading followed by a date, subarranged chronologically by dates, first by year, then by month and day
3) The subheading followed by the name of a country or other body that is a party to the treaty, subarranged alphabetically by the names in the sub-subheadings; each name further subdivided chronologically by dates, first by year, then by month and day

Examples (New headings):

Italy. Treaties, etc.
Italy. Treaties, etc. Australia, Feb. 12, 1959
Italy. Treaties, etc. Catholic Church, Feb. 11, 1929
Italy. Treaties, etc. Gt. Brit., July 12, 1917

U. S. Treaties, etc.
U. S. Treaties, etc. Feb. 20, 1928
U. S. Treaties, etc. Apr. 11, 1946
U. S. Treaties, etc. Sept. 6, 1952
U. S. Treaties, etc. Sept. 18, 1952
U. S. Treaties, etc. Burma
U. S. Treaties, etc. Burma, Feb. 6, 1952
U. S. Treaties, etc. Burma, Oct. 24, 1952
U. S. Treaties, etc. Burma, June 24, 1959
U. S. Treaties, etc. European Coal and Steel Community, Apr. 23, 1954
U. S. Treaties, etc. Mexico
U. S. Treaties, etc. Mexico, Jan. 31, 1952
U. S. Treaties, etc. Mexico, May 6, 1952
U. S. Treaties, etc. Mexico, May 19, 1952
U. S. Treaties, etc. Mexico, July 15, 1952
U. S. Treaties, etc. Mexico, Aug. 26, 1952
U. S. Treaties, etc. Mexico, Jan. 7, 1953

3. Interfiling of old and new headings. The new-form entries may be interfiled with the old by arranging the headings with specific dates chronologically following the appropriate inclusive administration dates in the old-form headings, with sub-subheadings for names following all dates.

The following example shows the order that would result from using the new headings for all books *cataloged* after a certain date.

Example:

U. S. Treaties, etc.
U. S. Treaties, etc., 1923–1929 (Coolidge)
U. S. Treaties, etc. Feb. 20, 1928
U. S. Treaties, etc., 1945–1953 (Truman)
U. S. Treaties, etc. Apr. 11, 1946
U. S. Treaties, etc. Sept. 6, 1952
U. S. Treaties, etc. Sept. 18, 1952
U. S. Treaties, etc., 1963–   (Lyndon B. Johnson)
U. S. Treaties, etc. Jan. 3, 1967
U. S. Treaties, etc. Burma
U. S. Treaties, etc. Burma, Feb. 6, 1952
U. S. Treaties, etc. European Coal and Steel Community, Apr. 23, 1954
U. S. Treaties, etc. Mexico
U. S. Treaties, etc. Mexico, Jan. 31, 1952

It may be preferable to adopt the new headings only for treaties *signed* after a certain date. Under this method the headings for administrations could be depended on to display the entries for all treaties signed during each administration (except the one in which the change of entry occurs), but the files under country and other subdivisions would not be all-inclusive.

The following example shows the order that would result from using the new headings only for treaties *signed* after a certain date, e. g., Jan. 1, 1968. An explanatory note should be inserted in the file where the change occurs.

Example:

U. S. Treaties, etc.
U. S. Treaties, etc., 1953–1961 (Eisenhower)
U. S. Treaties, etc., 1961–1963 (Kennedy)
U. S. Treaties, etc., 1963–   (Lyndon B. Johnson)
U. S. Treaties, etc. Jan. 3, 1967
U. S. Treaties, etc. Jan. 20, 1967
U. S. Treaties, etc. Feb. 1, 1967
U. S. Treaties, etc. Feb. 6, 1967
U. S. Treaties, etc. Burma
U. S. Treaties, etc. Burma, Mar. 2, 1967
U. S. Treaties, etc. Burma, June 21, 1967
U. S. Treaties, etc. Mexico
U. S. Treaties, etc. Mexico, Feb. 13, 1967
U. S. Treaties, etc. Mexico, Aug. 11, 1967

37. Non-book material arrangement

Preliminary note. This rule provides for the arrangement of entries for non-book materials and for their integration with entries for books and book-like materials.

Many libraries maintain separate catalogs for non-book materials such as music, phonorecords, motion pictures, etc. Filing is easier if each category is kept separate. However, the cataloging rules for such materials are so designed that the resulting entries may be integrated with those for books.

A. General rule. Interfile entries for non-book materials in their alphabetical places with other entries. If the same heading occurs for both book and non-book materials, arrange entries for the non-book materials after those for the books. In relation to longer entries beginning with the same words consider only the part preceding the designation of physical medium in the non-book entry; do not alphabet by the designation. When there is more than one special category with the same heading, arrange the categories alphabetically by the designations of physical medium.

B. Music

For arrangement of added entries when the main entry has a uniform title see Rule 26B2; for an example of music score subjects, see p. 184.

Note. Uniform titles[60] are frequently used in the cataloging of music. They appear on Library of Congress cards between the heading and the transcription of the title page, in brackets (they have been used on Library of Congress cards since about 1943). Like other uniform titles, they serve as a means of organizing the entries in a systematic manner. The special arrangement, however, can be achieved only with the application of the filing rules which are given below.

Make composer-title cross references from forms of the title not used as the uniform title, as may be advisable.

1. Basic rule. Arrange all titles under a composer entry alphabetically (with minor exceptions for certain uniform titles as specified below), interfiling uniform titles with other titles and composer-title cross references. File titles for complete works and selections in their alphabetical places with other titles.[61]

Note. On some older entries the word "works" appears as the second word of the uniform title. File such entries as though the uniform title were inverted and "works" were the first word, e. g.,

---

60. For definition of uniform title see Glossary, p. 239.

61. Uniform titles beginning with the word "Works" may be filed before all other titles if it is the library's regular policy to file entries for collected editions first (see footnote 41, p. 139).

ɪWorksɪ
ɪWorks. Selectionsɪ
ɪOrgan worksɪ = ɪWorks, organɪ
ɪPiano worksɪ = ɪWorks, pianoɪ
ɪWorks, Violinɪ

2. Singular and plural forms. Interfile singular and plural forms of the names of musical forms, regardless of language, (e. g., Sonata, Sonatas; Concerti, Concerto, Concertos) in the filing position of the singular.

Example:

ɪTrios, piano & stringsɪ
ɪTrio, piano & strings, no. 1, G majorɪ
ɪTrio-sonatasɪ

3. Numerals. File numerals that designate sequences of compositions numerically.

Examples:

ɪSymphony, no. 1, op. 21, C majorɪ
ɪSymphony, no. 2, op. 36, D majorɪ
ɪSymphony, no. 5, op. 67, C minorɪ

ɪSymphony, K. 128, C majorɪ
ɪSymphony, K. 129, G majorɪ
ɪSymphony, K. 134, A majorɪ

A numeral preceding a noun is to be considered as though it followed the noun. Arrange the entries numerically.

Example:

ɪDivertimento, flute, oboe & stringsɪ
ɪDivertimento, 2 flutes, clarinet & bassoonɪ
ɪDivertimento, 3 flutesɪ

Arrange compositions that are differentiated by dates chronologically, earliest date first.

Example:

ɪConcerto, violin (1907–08)ɪ
ɪConcerto, violin (1938)ɪ

4. Punctuation. Regard marks of punctuation in uniform titles that are identical up to the different punctuation mark. The filing sequence of these marks of punctuation is as follows:

1) Closing bracket
2) Semicolon
3) Period
4) Parentheses
5) Comma
6) No punctuation (longer titles)

Examples:

⌊Concertos, organ, op. 7⌋
⌊Concertos, organ, op. 7; arr.⌋
⌊Concertos, organ, op. 7. Selections⌋
⌊Concerto, organ, op. 7, no. 1, B♭ major⌋
⌊Concerti grossi, op. 6⌋   ⌊longer title⌋
⌊Concerto grosso, op. 6, no. 1, G major⌋

⌊Carmen. Suite⌋
⌊Carmen (Carmen Jones) Selections⌋
⌊Carmen (Passion flower) Piano-vocal score. English⌋

When the medium of performance element in a uniform title contains an ampersand (&), arrange it after a statement of a shorter medium beginning with the same word, i. e., treat the ampersand as a comma, do not alphabetize it as "and."

Examples:

⌊Concerto, violoncello, D major⌋
⌊Concerto, violoncello & string orchestra, D major⌋

⌊Concertos, harpsichord solo⌋   ⌊formerly "unacc."⌋
⌊Concerto, harpsichord & string orchestra⌋

On the other hand, when there are other entries with a longer medium of performance phrase, treat the ampersand as "and."

Example:

⌊Divertimento, 2 horns & strings, K. 320ᵇ (334) D major⌋
⌊Divertimento, 2 horns, bassoon & strings, K. 173ᵃ (205) D major⌋

5. Elements following a period. Interfile in one alphabetical file all elements that follow a period in a uniform title (e. g., Libretto, Piano-vocal score, Selections, etc.) including names of excerpts.[62] For examples see Comprehensive examples for music following 37B10 below, p. 224–27.

Disregard articles at the beginning of the name of an excerpt.

---

62. The entries for excerpts may be filed in a separate group following the special terms if it is the library's regular policy to file entries for parts after entries for the whole work (see footnote 37, p. 136).

Example:

[Der Ring des Nibelungen.   Götterdämmerung]
[Der Ring des Nibelungen.   Das Rheingold]
[Der Ring des Nibelungen.   Siegfried]

If the parts are numbered the alphabetical elements precede the numbered parts.

Example:

[Album für die Jugend]
[Album für die Jugend.   Selections; arr.]
[Album für die Jugend.   No. 9]
[Album für die Jugend.   No. 10]

6. Adaptations. Disregard an article at the beginning of the title of an adaptation in parentheses following the uniform title of the original work. For examples see Strauss in the Comprehensive examples for music following 37B10 below, p. 224–27.

7. Entries without uniform titles. In entries without uniform titles and composer-title cross references, regard first only the title proper, whether it is followed by a mark of punctuation or not. Interfile such titles with uniform titles beginning with the same title, subarranging by the words following the title proper. Even though such entries are not subject to the strict punctuation filing rules for uniform titles, this regard for the title proper will place them in the proper group of titles and thus maintain the filing pattern achieved by the use of uniform titles.

> *Note.* Punctuation has not been consistent in the titles in composer-title cross references; such titles have often appeared in the normal title page transcription form. So that these titles may be filed in their proper position, it is recommended that a comma be inserted, when needed, at the right place in the title. The Library of Congress will do this henceforth in the references it prepares. In older entries, it must be done mentally (some such entries are included in the example to illustrate the interfiling).

Example:

Bach, Johann Sebastian
  Concerto, A minor, for piano, *see his* . . .
  Concerto en ré mineur . . . *see his* . . .
  [Concerto, flute, violin, harpsichord & string orchestra]
  Concerto, for three harpsichords . . . *see his* . . .
  Concertos for two pianos, *see his* . . .
  [Concertos, harpsichord]

Concerto in A major ... *see his* ...
Concerto no. 2, in A minor ... *see his* ...
Concerto, no. 2, in E ɾfor violinɿ *see his* ...
ɾConcerto, organ, S. 596, D minorɿ
ɾConcerti grossiɿ
Concerto grosso, for piano, arr. by Ray Lev, *see his* ...
ɾConcerti grossi, no. 1–2ɿ
ɾConcerto grosso, no. 1ɿ
Concerto italien, *see his* ...
ɾConcerto nach italienischen Gusto, harpsichord solo, F majorɿ

8. Arrangement of entries under the same uniform title. ⌈Arrange entries
that are identical up to the end of the uniform title alphabetically by title page
titles.⌉ When there are two or more editions with the same title, subarrange
them by imprint dates, according to Rule 26B9. When all items to be considered in filing are identical on two or more entries for scores, arrange in
the following order: (1) Score; (2) Miniature score; (3) Parts only. For examples see Beethoven in the Comprehensive examples for music following 37B10
below, p. 224–27.

9. Different kinds of entries for the same title. Regard the title portion of
composer-title added entries, analytical entries made in the form of composer-
title added entries, and composer-title subject entries as a uniform title (except that the brackets are omitted). For the order of different kinds of entries
under the same uniform title follow Rule 26B13. For examples see Beethoven
in the Comprehensive examples for music following 37B10 below, p. 224–27.

10. Phonorecords—Music with uniform titles

> *Note.* Uniform titles are formulated for musical works on phonorecords
> on the same basis as they are for music and the germane term for the
> physical medium of the work (Phonodisc, Phonotape, Phonowire, etc.) is
> added, after the closing bracket of the uniform title.

a. General rule. When uniform titles are otherwise identical, arrange an
entry for a phonorecord after the corresponding entry without a statement of
physical medium. Do not alphabet by the word "Phonodisc," etc. in relation
to words within the brackets of uniform titles.

Example:

ɾLa traviataɿ
ɾLa traviataɿ Phonodisc
ɾLa traviata. Libretto. English and Italianɿ
ɾLa traviata. Selectionsɿ
ɾLa traviata. Selectionsɿ Phonodisc
ɾLa traviata. Selections; arr.ɿ
ɾLa traviata. Selections; arr.ɿ Phonodisc

b. Arrangement of entries under the same uniform title. Arrange entries that are identical up to the end of the uniform title and term following the closing bracket alphabetically by transcribed titles. When there are two or more entries with the same title, subarrange alphabetically by the name of the record publisher, then alphabetically by the letter prefix and numerically by the record number.

> *Note.* It is recommended that subarrangement under the same title be by publisher rather than date because imprint dates do not appear on phonorecords, may not be supplied in local cataloging, and are not generally known.

Example:

Verdi, Giuseppe
[Operas. Selections] Phonodisc.
Arias. Columbia ML 5654. [1961]

[Operas. Selections] Phonodisc.
Arias. Columbia MS 6254. [1961]

[Operas. Selections] Phonodisc.
Baritone arias. RCA Victor LM 1932. [1955]

[Operas. Selections] Phonodisc.
Great baritone arias. RCA Victor ERA-65.

[Operas. Selections] Phonodisc.
Opera overtures. Cetra A-50, 151. [195–]

[Operas. Selections] Phonodisc.
Overtures. Angel Records ANG. 35676. [1960]

[Operas. Selections] Phonodisc.
Overtures. Columbia SL 123 (ML 4662)

[Operas. Selections] Phonodisc.
Overtures. Mercury MG 50156. [1958]

c. Different kinds of entries for the same title. Arrange composer-title added entries for phonorecords and analytical entries made in the form of composer-title added entries in the group of phonorecords following the same title as a score. For the order of different kinds of entries under the same uniform title follow Rule 26B13.

> *Note.* The terms for designation of medium, as "Phonodisc," have not been used in the tracing for composer-title added entries on Library of Congress cards, but they will be in the future. These entries may be more easily filed in the proper group if the designation is added to the heading.

Comprehensive examples for music, 37B1–10:

Rossini, Gioacchino Antonio
[Il barbiere di Siviglia]
[Il barbiere di Siviglia]   Phonodisc.
[Il barbiere di Siviglia; arr.]
[Il barbiere di Siviglia.   Ecco ridente in cielo]
[Il barbiere di Siviglia.   Largo al factotum]
[Il barbiere di Siviglia.   Largo al factotum; arr.]
[Il barbiere di Siviglia.   Libretto.   English & Italian]
[Il barbiere di Siviglia.   Overture]
[Il barbiere di Siviglia.   Overture; arr.]
[Il barbiere di Siviglia.   Piano-vocal score.   English & Italian]
[Il barbiere di Siviglia.   Piano-vocal score.   Italian]
[Il barbiere di Siviglia.   Piano-vocal score.   Russian]
[Il barbiere di Siviglia.   Selections]   Phonodisc.
[Il barbiere di Siviglia.   Selections; arr.]
[Il barbiere di Siviglia.   Selections; arr.]   Phonodisc.
[Il barbiere di Siviglia.   Una voce poco fa]
[Il barbiere di Siviglia.   Una voce poco fa; arr.]
[Il barbiere di Siviglia.   Zitti, zitti; arr.]

Strauss, Johann
[Die Fledermaus]
[Die Fledermaus.   English]   Phonodisc.
[Die Fledermaus.   Libretto.   English & German]
[Die Fledermaus.   Overture]
[Die Fledermaus.   Overture]   Phonodisc.
[Die Fledermaus.   Piano-vocal score.   English]
[Die Fledermaus.   Piano-vocal score.   English & German]
[Die Fledermaus.   Selections]   Phonodisc.
[Die Fledermaus.   Waltzes; arr.]   Phonodisc.
[Die Fledermaus (The bat: Park)   Piano-vocal score.   English]
[Die Fledermaus (Golden Butterfly)   Piano-vocal score.   English]
[Die Fledermaus (Masquerade in Vienna)   Piano-vocal score.   English]

Beethoven, Ludwig van, 1770–1827
Artur Schnabel plays Beethoven, *see his . . .*
Beethoven for the young musician, *see his . . .*
Beethoven, the man and the artist, as revealed in his own words.
The celebrated Clara waltz, composed for the piano forte.
Letters.
Rondo, for violin and piano, *see his . . .*
[Rondo, piano, op. 51, no. 1, C major]
[Rondo, violin & piano, G major; arr.]
[Rondo à capriccio, piano]
Sonatas, for 'cello and piano (complete)   Seven variations . . . , *see his . . .*

ɾSonatas, pianoɿ

BEETHOVEN, LUDWIG VAN, 1770–1827
  SONATAS, PIANO.
Fischer, Edwin
  Ludwig van Beethovens Klaviersonaten.

Beethoven, Ludwig van, 1770–1827
  ɾSonatas, piano. Selectionsɿ
  ɾSonatas, piano. Selectionsɿ Phonodisc.
  ɾSonata, piano, no. 1, op. 2, no. 1, F minorɿ Phonodisc.
  ɾSonatas, piano, no. 5–7, op. 10ɿ Phonodisc.
  ɾSonata, piano, no. 7, op. 10, no. 3, D majorɿ Phonodisc.

  ɾSonata, piano, no. 23, op. 57, F minorɿ
  Sonata, F minor. Op. 57.
  (In Century library of music. 1900–02. v. 7 (1901))

  ɾSonata, piano, no. 23, op. 57, F minorɿ
  Sonata. F moll. Op. 57. (Appassionata) Leipzig, Forberg ɾc1902ɿ

  ɾSonata, piano, no. 23, op. 57, F minorɿ Phonodisc.
  Sonata in F minor, op. 57 (Appassionata) Sonata in C major, op. 2,
no. 3. RCA Victor LSC 2812. ɾ1965ɿ

  ɾSonata, piano, no. 23, op. 57, F minorɿ Phonodisc.
  Sonata, no. 23, in F minor, op. 57 (Appassionata) Sonata, no. 8, in C
minor, op. 13 (Pathétique) RCA Victor LM 1908. ɾ1955ɿ

  ɾSonata, piano, no. 23, op. 57, F minorɿ Phonodisc.
  Sonata, no. 23, in F minor, op. 57 (Appassionata) Sonata, no. 21, in
C major, op. 53 (Waldstein) Angel Records ANG. 35024. ɾ1953ɿ

    Beethoven, Ludwig van, 1770–1827
      Sonata, piano, no. 23, op. 57, F minor. Phonodisc.
Beethoven, Ludwig van, 1770–1827
  ɾSonata, piano, no. 17, op. 31, no. 2, D minorɿ Phonodisc.
  Sonata no. 17, in D minor, op. 31, no. 2 ("Tempest") Sonata no. 23,
in F minor, op. 57 ("Appassionata") RCA Victor LM 1964. ɾ1956ɿ

Beethoven, Ludwig van, 1770–1827
  ɾSonatas, violin & piano. Selectionsɿ Phonodisc.
  ɾSonata, violin & piano, no. 5, op. 24, F majorɿ
  ɾSonata, violin & piano, no. 9, op. 47, A majorɿ Phonodisc.

  ɾSonatas, violoncello & pianoɿ Phonodisc.
  Sonatas for cello and piano. Musical Heritage Society MHS 596–597.
ɾ1965ɿ

  ɾSonatas, violoncello & pianoɿ Phonodisc.
  Sonatas for cello and piano. Musical Heritage Society MHS 596S–
597S. ɾ1965ɿ

BEETHOVEN, LUDWIG VAN, 1770–1827
SONATA, VIOLONCELLO & PIANO, NO. 3, OP. 69, A MAJOR.

Beethoven, Ludwig van, 1770–1827
Ein Skizzenbuch zur Pastoralsymphonie, op. 68, und zu den Trios, op. 70, 1 und 2.
Edited from the holograph . . . which contains . . . sketches for the Sonata for violoncello and piano, op. 69.

Beethoven, Ludwig van, 1770–1827
Sonata pastorale, *see his* . . .

Beethoven, Ludwig van, 1770–1827
ʟSymphoniesʝ

BEETHOVEN, LUDWIG VAN, 1770–1827
SYMPHONIES.

Grove, Sir George
Beethoven and his nine symphonies.

Beethoven, Ludwig van, 1770–1827
ʟSymphonies; arr.ʝ

Beethoven, Ludwig van, 1770–1827, supposed composer[63]
Symphony, C major (Jena)
see Witt, Friedrich
Symphony, C major (ca. 1822)

Beethoven, Ludwig van, 1770–1827
ʟSymphony, no. 6, op. 68, F majorʝ

BEETHOVEN, LUDWIG VAN, 1770–1827
SYMPHONY, NO. 6, OP. 68, F MAJOR.

Beethoven, Ludwig van, 1770–1827
Ein Skizzenbuch zur Pastoralsymphonie, op. 68, und zu den Trios, op. 70, 1 und 2.

Beethoven, Ludwig van, 1770–1827
ʟSymphony, no. 6, op. 68, F majorʝ   Phonodisc.

ʟSymphony, no. 9, op. 125, D minorʝ

The symphony of life, letters by Ludwig van Beethoven.
ʟWorksʝ
ʟWorks. Selections; arr.ʝ
ʟWorks, chamber music. Selectionsʝ
ʟWorks, piano. Selectionsʝ

ʟWorks, piano. Selectionsʝ Phonodisc.
Artur Schnabel plays Beethoven. RCA Victor LCT 1155. ʟ19

---

63. "supposed composer" will no longer be used. Since the term is disregarded in filing, this entry made without it will file in the same place as the entry with it.

ɪWorks, piano. Selectionsɪ Phonodisc.
Bagatelles. Deutsche Grammophon Gesellschaft LPM 18934. ɪ1964ɪ

ɪWorks, piano. Selectionsɪ Phonodisc.
Bagatelles. Deutsche Grammophon Gesellschaft SLPM 138,934.
ɪ1964ɪ

ɪWorks, piano. Selectionsɪ Phonodisc.
Piano music. Angel COLH 65. ɪ1965ɪ

ɪWorks, piano. Selections; arr.ɪ

Die Wuth über den verlorenen Groschen ausgetobt in einer Kaprize,
see his Rondo à capriccio, piano

BEETHOVEN, LUDWIG VAN, 1770–1827—BIBLIOGRAPHY
BEETHOVEN, LUDWIG VAN, 1770–1827—THEMATIC CATALOGS

11. Explanatory reference from literary work

Note. If the non-musical part of a musical work such as an opera,
musical comedy, etc. is based on another work, according to the old
cataloging rules an author-title added entry was made for the original
work. *Anglo-American Cataloging Rules* 230A specifies that an explanatory reference be made from the author and title of the other work to the
composer and title of the musical work.

Arrange an explanatory reference from the author and title on which a
musical work is based before all other entries for that author and title.

Example:

O'Neill, Eugene Gladstone[64]
    Anna Christie.
      For a musical composition based on this work see:
    Merrill, Bob
      New girl in town.
O'Neill, Eugene Gladstone
    "Anna Christie"; with twelve illus. by Alexander King. 1930.

C. Manuscripts. Manuscripts are generally entered under a personal or
corporate name or title the same as books; these entries should present no
problems of interfiling with entries for books. Following are two special types
of entries for manuscripts:

1) A name followed by the designation "collector." Disregard the designation and interfile with other titles under the author.

Example:

Thacher, John Boyd, 1847–1909
    The continent of America.

---

64. For the arrangement of this entry when made in the form of an author-title added
entry see example on p. 129.

    Thacher, John Boyd, 1847–1909, collector   [manuscript]
        John Boyd Thacher collection of autographs of European notables, 1374–1895.

    Thacher, John Boyd, 1847–1909
        Little speeches by John Boyd Thacher.

2) Entry under name of a family. Arrange the author entries before the subject entries for the same family name.

Example:

    Adams family   [manuscript]
        Papers, 1639–1889.

    Adams family   [manuscript]
        Papers, 1759–1892.

        ADAMS FAMILY
    Adams, James Truslow
        The Adams family.

D. Motion pictures and filmstrips

    Note. Motion pictures and filmstrips are entered under their titles, followed by the designation "(Motion picture)" or "(Filmstrip)."

1. General rule. Interfile entries for motion pictures and filmstrips in their alphabetical places with other entries. If there is an identical entry for a book, arrange the entry for a motion picture or filmstrip after it. When there are entries with different designations arrange alphabetically by the designations.

Examples:

    Toward spiritual security
    Fallow, Wesner

    Toward statehood (Filmstrip)

    Toward the automatic factory
    Walker, Charles Rumford

    Alice in Wonderland
    Dodgson, Charles Lutwidge

    Alice in Wonderland
    Le Gallienne, Eva

    Alice in Wonderland (Filmstrip)

    The emperor's new clothes
    Andersen, Hans Christian

    The emperor's new clothes (Filmstrip)   Society for Visual Education, 1960.

    The emperor's new clothes (Motion picture)   Progress Film, Munich. 1959.

Three little pigs
> The three little pigs.

Three little pigs (Filmstrip)

2. Position in relation to longer entries. When there are longer entries beginning with the same word, arrange the entries for the non-book material before the longer entries, disregarding the parenthetical designation of physical medium in relation to the other entries.

Examples:

Hamlet, John

> The hamlet

Faulkner, William

> Hamlet

Shakespeare, William, 1564–1616
> > Editions of this work will be found under the author's name.

> Hamlet (Motion picture)

Baylor Theater's Hamlet (Motion picture)

> Hamlet and Brownswiggle

Reynolds, Barbara Leonard

Alaska (Filmstrip)
Alaska (Motion picture)
ALASKA
ALASKA—ECONOMIC CONDITIONS

3. Subarrangement under same title. Subarrange entries that are identical through the designation first alphabetically by name of producer, then chronologically by imprint date, then by any other distinguishing feature.

Examples:

The challenge (Motion picture)   Audio production, 1959.

Challenge (Motion Picture)   Florida State Alcoholic Rehabilitation Program . . .   1958.

The challenge (Motion picture)   National Foundation, 1959.
The challenge (Motion picture)   U. S. Marine Corps, 1957.   Made by Jam Handy Organization.

Time (Filmstrip)   Eye Gate House, 1961.
> 44 fr., color, 35 mm. and disc: 2 s, 7 in., 33⅓ rpm, 7 min.   microgroove.   (French first year)

Time (Filmstrip)   Eye Gate House, 1961.
> 44 fr., color, 35 mm. and disc: 2 s, 7 in., 33⅓ rpm, 9 min.   microgroove.   (German first year)

E. Phonorecords—Music without uniform titles and non-musical works

Note. Phonorecords for music without uniform titles and phonorecords for non-musical works are identified in the entry by a statement of the physical medium ([Phonodisc], [Phonotape], etc.), inserted after the title.

1. **General rule.** When there is no other entry for the same title file the entry for the phonorecord in its alphabetical place. If there is another entry, file the entry for the phonorecord after the entry for the book, disregarding subtitles on both. When there are two or more phonorecord entries with the same title, subarrange alphabetically by the name of the record publisher, then numerically by the record number.

Examples:

Great operatic scenes. [Phonodisc]

>The great organizers
Dale, Ernest

Great poems of the English language. [Phonodisc]

>Great Presidential decisions
Morris, Richard Brandon

Great Protestant hymns. [Phonodisc]

Whitman, Walt
>Leaves of grass.   [all editions of the book]
>Leaves of grass. [Phonodisc]
>Memories of Lincoln.
>The song of myself (abridged)   [Phonodisc]
>Songs of democracy.
>Walt Whitman speaks for himself; a reading by Arnold Moss. [Phono-
disc]
>The wisdom of Walt Whitman.

2. Uniform titles

Note. If uniform titles have been used for book materials under an author, uniform titles should also be used as appropriate for phonorecord entries under that author, even though these will not be used on Library of Congress cards.

Arrange entries for phonorecords after all entries for the same uniform title without designation. Arrange phonorecord entries that are identical through the uniform title and designation of physical medium alphabetically by transcribed titles. When there are two or more entries with the same title, subarrange them alphabetically by the name of the record publisher, then numerically by the record number.

230

Example:

Shakespeare, William, 1564–1616
  Hamlet.
    For a musical composition based on this work see:
    Thomas, Ambroise
      Hamlet.

Shakespeare, William, 1564–1616
  [Hamlet]
    The tragedy of Hamlet, Prince of Denmark.   Edited by Edward
  Hubler.   [1963]   [last book edition]

    Shakespeare, William, 1564–1616
      Hamlet.
Baylor Theater's Hamlet (Motion Picture)   Baylor Theater of Baylor University, 1958.

    SHAKESPEARE, WILLIAM, 1564–1616
      HAMLET.
Grebanier, Bernard D   N
    The heart of Hamlet; the play Shakespeare wrote.

Shakespeare, William, 1564–1616
  Hamlet. [Phonodisc] Living Shakespeare SH 5A–6A. [1961]

  Hamlet. [Phonodisc. Adapted by John Gielgud. Music composed
and conducted by Harold Levey] RCA Victor LM 6007. [1953]

  Hamlet. [Phonodisc] RCA Victor LM 6404. [1957]

  [Hamlet] Phonodisc.
  John Barrymore in Hamlet.   [With commentary by Mr. Barrymore.
Phonodisc] Audio Rarities LPA 2201. [1954]

Shakespeare, William, 1564–1616
  [Hamlet. German]
  Hamlet, Prinz von Dänemark, von H. Voss.   Wien [1825]

  [Hamlet. Selections] Phonodisc.
  Famous scenes from Sir John Gielgud's production of William Shakespeare's Hamlet. [Phonodisc] Columbia OL 8020. [1964]

  [Hamlet. Selections] Phonodisc.
  Hamlet; 6 excerpts. [Phonodisc] Incidental music by Roger Adams.
Columbia Entré RL 3107. [1955]

  John Barrymore in Hamlet
  see his Hamlet. Phonodisc

  [Sonnets]
  The riddle of Shakespeare's sonnets; the text of the sonnets, with in-
terpretive essays by Edward Hubler [and others] . . . [1962]

SHAKESPEARE, WILLIAM, 1564–1616
SONNETS.
Baldwin, Thomas Whitfield
On the literary genetics of Shakspere's poems & sonnets.

Shakespeare, William, 1564–1616
The sonnets. ₍Phonodisc. New York₎ Crown Publishers ₍1961₎
Lit. B.

₍Sonnets. German₎
Shakespeare sonnette, umdichtung von Stefan George. 1909.

Shakespeare, William, 1564–1616
Sonnets. Selections. Phonodisc.
Anthony Quayle reading Elizabethan sonnets and lyrics. ₍Phonodisc₎
Spoken arts 729. ₍1956₎

Shakespeare, William, 1564–1616
₍Sonnets. Spanish₎
Sonetos. Ilustraciones de S. Marco. ₍1933₎

F. Radio and television programs. Entries for the names of radio and television programs are filed according to the rules for motion pictures and filmstrips (see 37D above).

Example:

Americans at work
Paradis, Adrian A

Americans at work (Radio program)

APPENDIX

Initial articles to be disregarded in filing

The following table lists definite and indefinite articles in various languages *in the nominative case only* (all genders and both numbers) which should be disregarded according to the rule for Articles (Rule 4). Under each language they are listed in the following order: Singular—masculine, feminine, neuter; Plural—same; an elided form follows its corresponding word or group of words; each article is listed only once under each language. The words in parentheses are variant or dialect forms. An alphabetical index to all articles in the table follows the table.

* before an indefinite article indicates that the same form is also used for the cardinal numeral "one," therefore care must be taken to distinguish the meaning (see Rule 4A3).

Language	Definite article	Indefinite article
Afrikaans	Die	'n
Albanian	See footnote 1	*Nji (Një)
Arabic	al-, el-[2]	none
Bohemian, *see* Czech		
Bulgarian	See footnote 1	none
Croatian, *see* Serbo-Croatian		
Czech (Bohemian)	No articles	
Danish	Den, Det, De (Di)	*En, *Et
Dutch	De, Het, 't, 's[3]	*Een, Eene, 'n

---

1. Albanian, Bulgarian and Rumanian have definite articles but they are added as suffixes to the word they make definite.

2. The Arabic articles "al-" or "el-" (or the assimilated forms "ad-, ag-, ak-, an-, ar-, as-, at-, az-," if used) are also disregarded as initial words of names, if written in lower case.

3. Disregard the Dutch " 's" when initial letter, even though it is a contraction of "des," the genitive singular (masculine and neuter) of the definite article.

Language	Definite article	Indefinite article
English	The	A, An
Esperanto	La	none
Estonian	No articles	
Finnish	No articles	
French	Le, La, L', Les	*Un, *Une
German	Der,[4] Die, Das	*Ein, *Eine[5]
Greek, Classical (Romanized)	Ho, Hē, To, Tō,[6] Hoi, Hai, Ta	none
Greek, Modern (Romanized)	Ho, Hē, To, Hoi, Hai, Ta	*Henas (Heis), *Mia, *Hena (Hen)
Hawaiian	Ka, Ke, Na, "O emphatic"[7]	He
Hebrew (Romanized)	Ha- (Ho-), He-	none
Hungarian	A, Az	*Egy
Icelandic (Modern)	Hinn, Hin, Hið, Hinir, Hinar	none
Italian	Il, La, Lo, I, Gli, Gl', Le, L'	*Un, *Uno, *Una, *Un'
Latin	No articles	
Latvian, *see* Lettish		
Lettish	No articles	
Lithuanian	No articles	
Norwegian (Riksmål)	Den, Det, De	*En, *Et
Norwegian (Nynorsk) (formerly called Landsmål)	Den, Det, Dei	*Ein, *Ei, *Eit
Polish	No articles	
Portuguese	O, A,[8] Os, As[8]	*Um, *Uma[9]
Rumanian	See footnote 1	*Un, *Una, *O
Russian	No articles	
Serbo-Croatian	No articles	
Slovak	No articles	
Slovenian	No articles	

---

4. Disregard only when in the nominative case.

5. The numerals "Ein" and "Eine" are sometimes spaced (E i n; E i n e) to distinguish them from the indefinite article.

6. Tō is the dual case of the definite article in Classical Greek. There is no dual case in Modern Greek.

7. In Hawaiian the "O emphatic," used to point out the subject emphatically, seems to be a kind of article and should be disregarded in filing. It is used only with the nominative case, chiefly before proper names and pronouns. It must be carefully distinguished from the preposition "O," in particular, but "O" also serves the Hawaiian language as a noun (with several meanings), a verb (with several meanings), an adverb, and a conjunction.

8. The words "à" and "às" with accents in Portuguese are not articles and must be regarded in filing.

9. The plural forms "Ums" and "Umas" have the meaning of "some" and are regarded in filing.

Language	Definite article	Indefinite article
Spanish	El, La, Lo,[10] Los, Las	*Un, *Una[11]
Swedish	Den, Det, De	*En, *Ett
Turkish (New)	none	*Bir
Ukrainian	No articles	
Welsh	Y, Yr	none
Yiddish (Romanized)	Der, Di, Die, Dos (Das)	A, An, *Eyn,[12] *Eyne[12]

ALPHABETICAL INDEX TO ARTICLES IN ABOVE TABLE

A	English, Hungarian, Portuguese, Yiddish
al-	Arabic
An	English, Yiddish
As	Portuguese
Az	Hungarian
Bir	Turkish
Das	German, Yiddish
De	Danish, Dutch, Norwegian (Riksmål), Swedish-
Dei	Norwegian (Nynorsk)
Den	Danish, Norwegian, Swedish
Der	German, Yiddish
Det	Danish, Norwegian, Swedish
Di	Danish, Yiddish
Die	Afrikaans, German, Yiddish
Dos	Yiddish
Een, Eene	Dutch
Egy	Hungarian
Ei	Norwegian (Nynorsk)
Ein	German, Norwegian (Nynorsk)
Eine	German
Eit	Norwegian (Nynorsk)
El	Spanish
el-	Arabic
En	Danish, Norwegian (Riksmål), Swedish
Et	Danish, Norwegian (Riksmål)

10. The use of the word "Lo" in Spanish as an article is very restricted. It should be disregarded in filing only when combined with an adjective which is used substantively with the force of an abstract noun, e. g.,

> Lo bueno = the good
> Lo mismo = the same

11. The plural forms "Unos" and "Unas" have the meaning of "some" and are regarded in filing.

12. The numerals "Eyn" and "Eyne" are occasionally used in Yiddish in the sense of the indefinite article.

Ett	Swedish
Eyn, Eyne	Yiddish
Gl', Gli	Italian
ha-	Hebrew
Hai	Greek
He	Hawaiian
Hē	Greek
he-	Hebrew
Heis	Greek, Modern
Hen, Hena, Henas	Greek, Modern
Het	Dutch
Hið	Icelandic
Hin, Hinar, Hinir, Hinn	Icelandic
Ho	Greek
ho-	Hebrew
Hoi	Greek
I	Italian
Il	Italian
Ka	Hawaiian
Ke	Hawaiian
L'	French, Italian
La	Esperanto, French, Italian, Spanish
Las	Spanish
Le	French, Italian
Les	French
Lo	Italian, Spanish
Los	Spanish
Mia	Greek, Modern
'n	Afrikaans, Dutch
Na	Hawaiian
Një, Nji	Albanian
O	Hawaiian, Portuguese, Rumanian
Os	Portuguese
's	Dutch
't	Dutch
Ta	Greek
The	English
To	Greek
Tō	Greek, Classical
Um, Uma	Portuguese
Un	French, Italian, Rumanian, Spanish
Un'	Italian
Una	Italian, Rumanian, Spanish
Une	French
Uno	Italian
Y, Yr	Welsh

Glossary

In general, the definitions given here are those in the Glossary in *Anglo-American Cataloging Rules* (p. 343–47). They are supplemented by a few from *A. L. A. Cataloging Rules for Author and Title Entries* (Chicago, American Library Association, 1949, p. 229–35) and *A. L. A. Glossary of Library Terms* (Chicago, American Library Association, 1943). Certain choices and modifications have been made in order to show the specific usage of the terms in the filing rules. These were necessary because of the scope and nature of these rules.

Added entry. 1. An entry, other than a subject entry and additional to the main entry, under which a bibliographical entity is represented in the catalog. 2. The catalog record that begins such an entry.

Analytical entry. An entry for a work or part of a work that is contained in a collection, series, issue of a serial, or other bibliographical unit for which another, comprehensive entry has been made. Analytical entries may be either separate, self-contained entries or added entries that are part of the cataloging of the larger work.

Author entry. 1. An entry of a work in a catalog under its author's name as heading, whether this be a main or an added heading. 2. The author heading chosen for this entry.

Author heading. The form under which an author entry is made,

Author-title added entry. An added entry consisting of the author and title of a work.

Author-title reference. A cross reference consisting of an author and title in the part referred from.

Author-title subject entry. A subject entry consisting of the author and title of a work.

Compound surname. For definitions *see* Rules 21 and 13. (This usage is somewhat broader than the cataloging definition in *Anglo-American Cataloging Rules*, which limits the combination to proper *names*.)

Conventional title. Term formerly used for the uniform title of a musical work. *See* Uniform title.

Corner mark. Information added to the upper right hand corner of a catalog card to indicate title, language, editor, translator, etc., when there are many entries under the same heading, for the purpose of securing an organized filing arrangement.

237

Corporate entry. 1. An entry under the name of a society, institution, government department, bureau, or other organized body. 2. The heading chosen for this entry.

Cross reference. *See* Reference.

Entry. 1. A record of a bibliographical entity in a catalog or list. 2. A heading under which a record of a bibliographical entity is represented in a catalog or list; also, in the case of a work entered under title, the title.

Entry word. The word by which the entry is arranged in the catalog, usually the first word (other than an article) of the heading. (cf. Heading)

Facsimile. An edition the chief purpose of which is to provide exact replicas of the copy reproduced; usually made either by a photomechanical process or by type-facsimile.

Filing title. *See* Uniform title.

Heading. A name, word, or phrase placed at the head of a catalog record to provide a point of access in the catalog. Headings function as entries in the cataloging of particular bibliographical entities. (*see* Entry 2).

Main entry. 1. The complete catalog record of a bibliographical entity, presented in the form by which the entity is to be uniformly identified and cited. 2. The heading under which such a record is represented in the catalog, or, if there is no heading, the title.

Main heading. The first part of a heading that is subject to modification by a subheading.

Phonorecord. Any object on which sound has been recorded.

Proper names. Personal and geographical names.

Reference. A direction from one heading or entry to another.

Romanized title. A title converted to a Roman-alphabet form from either a non-Roman alphabet or a nonalphabetic language.[1] Originally the note "Title transliterated" was used for these two kinds of conversion.[2] A division was made in 1957, the term "Title romanized" being introduced for works in nonalphabetic languages.[3] According to the 1967 *Anglo-American Cataloging Rules*, "Title romanized" will be used for both kinds of conversion.

Secondary entry. 1. An entry, additional to the main entry, under which a bibliographical entity is represented in a catalog (includes both added entries and subject entries). 2. The catalog record that begins such an entry.
 See also Added entry.

Standard title. *See* Uniform title.

Subdivision. 1. A second, or later, part of a subject heading. 2. Comprehensive term for subdivisions of subject headings and subheadings of author headings.

Subheading. A second part of an author heading, following the main heading.

---

1. *Anglo-American Cataloging Rules*, Glossary, p. 346, and Rule 150.
2. U. S. Library of Congress. Descriptive Cataloging Division. *Rules for Descriptive Cataloging in the Library of Congress*. Washington, 1949. Rule 3:23.
3. U. S. Library of Congress. Processing Dept. *Cataloging Service*. Washington, D. C. Bulletin 42, July 1957, p. 11.

Title. The name of a work, exclusive of any alternative title, subtitle, or other associated descriptive matter on the title page.

Title added entry. A title used as an added entry.

Title entry. The record of a work in a catalog under the title.
    See also Title added entry, Title main entry.

Title main entry. A title used as a main entry.

Title proper. *See* Title.

Title romanized [**or transliterated**]. *See* Romanized title.

Transliterated title. *See* Romanized title.

Uniform title. The particular title by which a work that has appeared under varying titles is to be identified for cataloging purposes Formerly called variously "conventional title" (especially for musical works), "filing title," and "standard title."

Bibliography

FILING AND FILING PROBLEMS

"A L A filing rules." *Library Journal* 79:501–02, March 15, 1954.

The Special Committee on Filing Rules of the A L A Division of Cataloging and Classification invites comments on a possible revision of the A L A filing rules. Includes list of questions being considered.

Akers, Susan Grey. *Simple library cataloging.* 4th ed. Chicago, American Library Association, 1954.

"Arrangement of cards in a catalog": p. 162–79.

Essentially a synopsis of the 1942 A L A rules, Appendix V.

A new edition is in preparation (1967), containing a synopsis of the A L A rules 2d ed. abridged.

Allen, Donald Corbin. "A reaffirmation of the basic principles of filing." *Journal of Cataloging and Classification* 8:85–89, Sept. 1952.

The head of the Filing Section of the Library of Congress discusses some of the filing methods used by that library and suggests revision of entry rules when necessary to permit drafting of consistent filing rules that will not be too complex for the average reader to use.

American Library Association. Catalog Section. Committee on Standardization of Alphabeting Practice. "Report." American Library Association. Catalog Section. *Proceedings* [Yearbook no. 1]:30–34. 1929.

Regarding the arrangement of names beginning with Mc and St. in city and telephone directories.

American Library Association. Co-operation Committee. "Report: Alphabeting." *Library Journal* 14:273–75, May–June 1889.

The committee that was charged to study alphabeting rules as a result of Mr. Edmands' paper at the previous conference (see *Edmands, John* below) reports its recommendations.

Chaplin, Arthur Hugh. "Principles of alphabetical arrangement." British Society for International Bibliography. *Proceedings* 8:13–19; Discussion 19–22, Feb. 26, 1946.

An ingenious attempt to describe the principles of alphabetical arrangement. Based on the principle of the separation of words and of the different elements in a bibliographical entry, but with no classification of elements as in Cutter's rules.

Childs, James Bennett. "Rules for alphabetical filing by words in the dictionary catalog of a library, together with 'Manchester,' a specimen of such filing suitable for use in arranging a dictionary catalog." Urbana, Ill., 1921–[22] 13 p.
> Autographed from typewritten copy.

Clapp, Clifford B. "Arrangement of cards under place names in a dictionary catalog." *Library Journal* 38:73–77, Feb. 1913.

Clarke, Norman F. "Alphabeting: an historical analytical search for principle." (Ph. D. dissertation, University of Michigan, in process 1967)

Cranshaw, James. "A word or two." *Library Assistant* 29:259–63, Nov. 1936.
> Problems of filing compound words.

Cunningham, A. D. "The dictionary catalogue." *New Zealand Libraries* 1:85–87, June 1938.
> Filing of analytics, collections of works by or about a single author, geographical entries, and other problem cases.

Dean, Helen Elizabeth. "Numerals vs. words." *Library Journal* 58:559–60, June 15, 1933.
> Details of a plan for writing out numerals in titles, thus indicating the alphabetic arrangement.

Dickie, W. M. "Alphabetization." *Library Association Record* 43:81–85, May; 101–05, June 1941.
> Discussion of some filing problems. Prefers letter-by-letter filing for some situations.

Edmands, John. "Rules for alfabeting." *Library Journal* 12:326–31, 431–35, Sept.–Oct. 1887.
> A plea for consideration of the alphabeting problem. Gives numerous instances of how Poole and Cutter, the two authorities of the day, differed with each other (and with themselves) in alphabeting.

Harlow, Bruce. "Catalog filing." *Library Journal* 66:471–72, June 1, 1941.
> Recommends one straight alphabetical arrangement by interfiling name added entries as authors and by ignoring punctuation, etc., "simply filing all subheads of a subject in one alphabet." Tried successfully at Missouri School of Mines Library, Rolla.

Hastings, Charles Harris. "Proposed manual on the arrangement of cards in alphabetical catalogs." American Library Association. *Bulletin* 9:270–73, July 1915.
> Proposed Library of Congress filing manual. Problems in alphabeting place names, subdivisions under subjects, added entries, editions, books of the Bible, and the umlaut listed.

Haykin, David Judson. *Subject headings: a practical guide.* Washington, U. S. Govt. Print. Off., 1951.
> "Filing problems": p. 81–88.

Hitchler, Theresa. *Cataloging for small libraries.* 3d enl. ed. New York, Stechert, 1926.
> "Arrangement": p. 262–69.

Illinois. University. Undergraduate Division, Chicago. Library. "Flow charts of the American Library Association's Filing Rules, plus a preliminary statement of rules and procedures for composing machine sortable filing copy." [Chicago] 1963. 39 p.

———— "An investigation into the application of data processing to library filing rules." A joint endeavor by the University of Illinois Library, Chicago Undergraduate Division, and the Burroughs Corporation. ₁Chicago₁ 1962. 28 p.

———— "Proposed rules for filing book catalog entries" ₁by computer₁ ₁Chicago, 1964₁ 12 p.

"Interfiling in the Widener catalogues." *Harvard Library Bulletin* 6:271–73, Spring 1952.

    Though the A L A rules recommend straight alphabetical filing only for small libraries, Harvard has demonstrated its value for the large library.

Jackson, Sidney Louis. "Date treatment of broad subject headings in thirty major libraries; a report with comments." *Journal of Cataloging and Classification* 9:21–24, March 1953.

    Advocates some form of chronological arrangement of cards under subjects with many cards.

Jewett, Charles Coffin. *On the construction of catalogues of libraries, and their publication by means of separate, stereotyped titles. With rules and examples.* 2d ed. Washington, Smithsonian Institution, 1853.

    "Arrangement": p. 59–62.

"Just file it!" *Headlight on books at Penn State* 11, no. 1, Dec. 1941.

    Describes filing rule simplification carried out at Pennsylvania State College over a number of years, mostly in eliminating classified subarrangements.

Kaula, Prithvi Nath. "Alphabetization." *Library Herald* 1:186–90, Jan. 1959.

    Review of three methods of alphabeting: letter-by-letter, word-by-word, and gestalt (different value for word, sentence, and paragraph spaces).

Kieffer, Paula. "The Baltimore County Public Library book catalog." *Library Resources & Technical Services* 10:133–41, Spring 1966.

    "Filing": p. 135–37.

    Concessions that had to be made to the machine.

Kleist, Herbert. "Inverse time order and subject filing." *College and Research Libraries* 6:228–31, June 1945.

    Discusses some of the filing methods used by John Crerar Library. Lists many advantages, and some disadvantages, of inverse chronological filing under subjects.

Kroeger, Alice Bertha. "Arrangement of entries in catalogs." *Library Journal* 30:146–47, March 1905; *Public Libraries* 10:18–19, Jan. 1905.

    Results of a survey of 24 librarians show that most follow Cutter's Rules. Cites some changes between the 3d and 4th editions of Cutter.

Latshaw, Ruth N. "A comparative study of some rules for the alphabetical arrangement of entries in library catalogs." Urbana, Ill., 1928.

    Thesis (M. A.)—University of Illinois.

Linderfelt, Klas August. *Eclectic card catalog rules: author and title entries, based on Dziatzko's "Instruction" compared with the rules of the British Museum, Cutter, Dewey, Perkins and other authorities . . .* Boston, C. A. Cutter, 1890.

    "Alphabetical arrangement of titles": p. 46–75.

Lumaree, Phoebe. "Deviation in filing practices from the rules in the standard filing codes for dictionary card catalogs." New York, 1943. 67 p.

    Thesis (M. S.)–Columbia University.

In general, there were many deviations in libraries from their own filing rules, for user convenience, and in the direction of simplification.

Maddox, Eugenia. "Filing in the card catalog." *Wilson Library Bulletin* 26:265–66, Nov. 1951.

University of Tulsa Library simplified its filing, using primarily A L A's alphabetical alternatives, in order to save clerical and user time.

Maloy, Miriam C. "Try this on your catalog." *Library Journal* 65:180, March 1, 1940.

Recommends interfiling main and added entries. Believes the trend is toward elimination of classified arrangements.

Mann, Margaret. *Introduction to cataloging and the classification of books*. 2d ed. Chicago, American Library Association, 1943.

"Arrangement of the dictionary catalog": p. 171–80.

Moakley, Gertrude. "A workable classed-order filing code." *Journal of Cataloging and Classification* 10:144–46, July 1954.

Describes the New York Public Library Circulation Department's new filing code.

Moyer, Vera L. "A catalog in transition." *Library Journal* 66:686–87, Sept. 1, 1941.

Describes Pennsylvania State College's change to straight alphabetical filing.

Nugent, William R. "The mechanization of the filing rules for the dictionary catalogs of the Library of Congress." *Library Resources & Technical Services* 11:145–66, Spring 1967.

Concludes that it would be quite feasible, though difficult, to develop a program for a majority of the rules, but suggests some changes in the rules in the direction of greater consistency and simplicity.

Osborn, Andrew Delbridge and Susan M. Haskins. "Catalog maintenance." *Library Trends* 2:279–89, Oct. 1953.

Includes discussion of simplified filing, and relation of entries to filing, as practiced at Harvard.

Perreault, Jean M. "The computer and catalog filing rules." *Library Resources & Technical Services* 9:325–31, Summer 1965.

Piercy, Esther J. *Commonsense cataloging: a manual for the organization of books and other materials in school and small public libraries*. New York, H. W. Wilson Co., 1965.

"Rules for alphabetical filing in a small dictionary catalog": p. 161–66.

These rules contain a few innovations and departures from established practice for the sake of logic and consistency.

Pierson, Robert M. "Entries for works based upon periodicals." *Library Resources & Technical Services* 6:255–56, Summer 1962.

Filing a periodical as author *after* the title entry for the periodical violates the basic principles set forth in A L A Filing Rule 24 and L C Filing Rule Intro-III.

Popecki, Joseph Thomas. "A filing system for the machine age." *Library Resources & Technical Services* 9:333–37, Summer 1965.

A simplified system designed for conventional use that is very similar to the type of programs that machines demand.

Comments by Gertrude Moakley in *ibid.* 10:405–06, Summer 1966.

Preston, Genie Johanna. "Problems involved in an alphabetical arrangement of a library catalog." Urbana, Ill., 1936. 143 p.

Thesis (M. A.)—University of Illinois.

Gives examples of complex features of present filing codes and tells which should be eliminated. Includes a simplified set of dictionary catalog filing rules.

Abstracted in American Library Association. Catalog Section. *Catalogers' and classifiers' yearbook* 6:115–17. 1937.

Ranganathan, Shiyali Ramamrita and G. L. Gulati. "Alphabetisation in documentation"; *In* Ranganathan, Shiyali Ramamrita, ed. *Public library provision and documentation problems. Papers for discussion at the ninth All-India Library Conference, Indore, 11–14 May 1951.* Delhi, Indian Library Association, 1951. p. 141–50.

Recommends as few conventions as possible and mechanization of alphabetical arrangement.

Scheerer, George. "Card catalog arrangement." *Library Resources & Technical Services* 3:140–45, Spring 1959.

Stresses the relationship between entries and filing, recommending that entries should be such that congruity could be maintained in straight alphabetical filing.

Seely, Pauline Augusta. "A L A filing rules." *Library Resources & Technical Services* 8:15–25, Winter 1964.

Discusses the work of the Subcommittee on the A L A Rules for Filing Catalog Cards, the effect of the new cataloging code on filing, and some particular filing problems, especially place arrangement.

———— "A L A filing rules—new edition." *Library Resources & Technical Services* 11:377–79, Summer 1967.

A summary report of the work of the Subcommittee.

Sharp, Henry Alexander. *Cataloguing: a textbook for use in libraries.* 4th ed. London, Grafton, 1948.

"The arrangement of catalogues": p. 116–23.

Shufro, Herbert E. "Filing the corporate entry for the catalog user." *Special Libraries* 33:53–55, Feb. 1942.

Recommends a single author file, arranged alphabetically by title, of *all* publications of an agency, including its subdivisions.

Smith, Louise. "Filing under names of places." *Library Journal* 64:978–80, Dec. 15, 1939.

Suggests a simplified method of place name arrangement, interfiling all entries in one alphabet and disregarding punctuation.

Steele, H. G. "A note on alphabetical order." *Library World* 15:247–48, Feb. 1913.

Proposes systemization of filing rules according to word-by-word order and includes a simple set of rules.

Vatican. Biblioteca vaticana. *Rules for the catalog of printed books.* Translated from the 2d Italian edition, by Thomas J. Shanahan, Victor A. Schaefer [and] Constantin T. Vesselowsky, edited by Wyllis E. Wright. Chicago, American Library Association, 1948.

"Filing": p. 318–49.

Warner, Gilmore. "Living, fresh, and new." *Journal of Cataloging and Classification* 10:138–44, July 1954.

    Advocates inverse chronological arrangement under subjects rather than alphabetical, since most readers want newer works.

Weber, David C. "The crisis in the voluminous authors." *Harvard Library Bulletin* 7:113–19, Winter 1953.

    Discusses various methods of arranging long files of voluminous authors' works.

Weinstein, Edward A. and Virginia George. "Notes toward a code for computer-produced printed book catalogs." *Library Resources & Technical Services* 9:319–24, Summer 1965.

    "Filing rules and machine sorting": p. 321–23.

Williams, Edwin Everitt. "Alphabetical dilemmas of Widener's catalogues." *Harvard Library Bulletin* 6:322–35, Autumn 1952.

    Summary of problems from working papers on revision of filing rules at Harvard.

Wilson (H. W.) Company. *Style book: a compilation of rules governing the style used in setting the bibliographical publications of the H. W. Wilson Company.* Rev. New York, 1936.

    "Alphabeting": p. 35–47.

    Follows the Pittsburgh filing rules, 3d edition, with certain exceptions and additions.

FILING CODES—GENERAL

American Library Association. *A. L. A. rules for filing catalog cards,* prepared by a special committee, Sophie K. Hiss, chairman. Chicago, 1942. 109 p.

Barnstead, Winifred G. *Filing rules for dictionary catalogues.* 2d ed. [n. p.] Ball, 1934. 18 p.

    "Issued as a supplement to the *Ontario Library Review.*"

    "Recommended by the Minister of Education for use in the public libraries of Ontario."

    Based on Cutter's *Rules for a dictionary catalog.*

British Standards Institution. *British Standard Alphabetical arrangement.* London, 1951. 12 p. B. S. 1749: 1951.

Cutter, Charles Ammi. *Rules for a dictionary catalog.* 4th ed., rewritten. Washington, Govt. Print. Off., 1904. (U. S. Bureau of Education. Special report on public libraries—pt. II)

    "Arrangement": p.111–21.

Hines, Theodore C. and Jessica L. Harris. *Computer filing of index, bibliographic, and catalog entries.* Newark, N. J., Bro-Dart Foundation [1966] 126 p.

Indian Standards Institution, Delhi. *Indian Standard practice for alphabetical arrangement.* Delhi, 1952. 5 p. I S:382—1952.

Moakley, Gertrude. *Basic filing rules for medium-sized libraries: a compend filing code for catalogs of 120 to 2000 trays.* Foreword by Rudolf Flesch. New York, William-Frederick Press, 1957. 60 p.

Rev. and enl. edition of *Introduction to a proposed code for medium-sized public libraries* (New York, 1954).

This code grew out of the work done in the New York Public Library Circulation Department in developing A L A rules 29, 31b and 35 into a complete and consistent code. The basic principle is to file to the first punctuation mark in most cases.

—— *Introduction to a proposed filing code for medium-sized public libraries (120 to 2000 trays)* New York, 1954.

Preliminary version of her *Basic filing rules for medium-sized libraries.*

Tomlinson, Laurence Elliott and Laud R. Pitt. *Filing rules of the Library of Congress: a tentative interpretation.* [2d ed. rev.] Waco, Tex. [Printed by Baylor University Press] 1942. 37 p.

First edition of the above:

Tomlinson, Laurence Elliott. *Library of Congress rules for filing cards in a card catalog: a tentative interpretation.* [Waco? Tex.] 1941. 39 p.

Both editions were published without the approval of the Library of Congress. The Library of Congress does not accept responsibility for this interpretation of its filing practices.

Comments concerning this responsibility were published as follows:

Mumford, Lawrence Quincy. "Without L. C. approval." *Library Journal* 66:742, Sept. 15, 1941; *Wilson Library Bulletin* 16:111, Oct. 1941.

Tomlinson, Laurence Elliott. "Answering Mr. Mumford." *Wilson Library Bulletin* 16:205–06, Nov. 1941.

Mumford, Lawrence Quincy. "Further statement." *Wilson Library Bulletin* 16:350, Jan. 1942.

Review of 1st edition: by Esther A. Smith. *Library Quarterly* 12:125–26, Jan. 1942.

Toronto. University. Ontario College of Education. Library School. *Basic filing rules for use in the course in library records* [by Margaret E. Cockshutt. Toronto] University of Toronto Press [1961] 27 p.

U. S. Library of Congress. Processing Dept. *Filing rules for the dictionary catalogs of the Library of Congress.* Washington, 1956. 187 p.

Although these rules were compiled specifically for the Library of Congress they are included in the "General" group because of their national significance. In general, these are the rules used in the widely distributed printed catalogs of the Library of Congress.

Wellisch, H. *Filing rules, with examples in Hebrew and Roman characters.* Jerusalem, Centre for Public Libraries, 1966. 43 p.

Rules are in Hebrew.

FILING CODES—SPECIFIC LIBRARIES

Many libraries have compiled their own filing rules, either complete, unique codes or local adaptations of the 1942 *A. L. A. Rules for Filing Catalog Cards.* Some 59 of these specific library filing rules, mostly unpublished, were acquired by the

Subcommittee on the A L A Rules for Filing Catalog Cards. Various types of libraries were represented in the collection as follows: college and university—25; public and county—22; schools—5; state—4; special—3.

After completion of the Subcommittee's work this collection of filing rules, except for those that were on loan, will be deposited in the library of the American Library Association, where they will be available to others wishing to make a study of filing rules.

Index

References without designation are to rule numbers; those preceded by p. indicate pages; Ex. denotes reference to an example; references to notes, footnotes, etc. are so designated.